Taylor's Guide to Garden Design

Houghton Mifflin Company Boston

Based on Taylor's Encyclopedia of
Gardening, Fourth Edition, copyright © 1961
by Norman Taylor, revised and edited by
Gordon P. DeWolf, Jr.

Library of Congress
Cataloging-in-Publication Data
Taylor's guide to garden design.
(Taylor's guides to gardening)
Based on: Taylor's encyclopedia of gardening.
4th ed. 1961.
Includes index.
1. Gardens—Design. 2. Landscape
gardening. 3. Gardens—Design—
Pictorial works. 4. Landscape gardening—
Pictorial works. I. Taylor's encyclopedia
of gardening. II. Title: Guide to garden
design. III. Series.
SB473.T37 1988   712'.6   87-26167
ISBN 0-395-46784-5

Prepared and produced by Chanticleer Press,
Inc., New York
Cover photograph: Iris Garden at Ladew
Topiary Gardens, Monkton, Maryland,
by Derek Fell
Designed by Massimo Vignelli
Color reproductions made in Italy
Printed and bound in Japan

First Edition.

DNP   10   9   8   7   6   5   4   3   2   1

A Chanticleer Press Edition

Contents

Contributors

Rosalind Creasy, author of the essay on landscapes to harvest and a contributing photographer, is an expert in "edible landscaping" and author of *The Complete Book of Edible Landscaping* and *Earthly Delights*.

Barbara Damrosch, general consultant, author of the essays on designing your property and landscaping with flowers, and a contributing photographer, is a landscape designer and author of *Theme Gardens*.

Gordon P. DeWolf, Jr., Ph.D., coordinator of the Horticultural Program at Massachusetts Bay Community College in Wellesley Hills, Massachusetts, revised and edited the fifth edition of *Taylor's Encyclopedia of Gardening,* upon which this guide is based. Dr. DeWolf previously served as Horticulturist at the Arnold Arboretum at Harvard University.

Stacey Freed, author of the essay on using garden structures, is a free-lance writer who has been an editor for *Landscape Architecture* and *Garden Design* magazines.

Judy Glattstein, author of the essay on naturalistic gardening, has written for *Garden Design* and *Horticulture* magazines, and frequently contributes to *The New York Times* garden pages. She is an instructor at the New York and Brooklyn botanical gardens.

Joseph Hudak, a Boston-area landscape architect and the author of *Gardening with Perennials, Trees for Every Purpose,* and *Shrubs in the Landscape,* wrote on landscaping with trees and shrubs.

Victoria Jahn, author of the essay on gardening in small spaces, is Manager of Plant Information at the Brooklyn Botanic Garden.

Panayoti and Gwen Kelaidis, authors of the essays on rock and shade gardens, are, respectively, Curator of the Rock Alpine Garden at Denver Botanic Gardens and a landscape designer.

Edward Lam, illustrator of the plans in Landscaping Your Property, has contributed drawings to other volumes in this series.

Elvin McDonald, author of the essay on Japanese-style gardens and a contributing photographer, is Director of Special Projects at the Brooklyn Botanic Garden and a widely published garden writer/photographer.

Barbara McEwan, author of the essays on gardens for wildlife and garden basics, is a writer and a former nursery owner from Goode, Virginia.

William Mulligan, author of the essay on winterscapes, is a garden writer and former editor of *Popular Gardening Outdoors*.

William D. Rieley, contributor of the essay on traditional gardens, is a landscape architect in Charlottesville, Virginia. His office specializes in historic preservation and park design.

Dolores R. Santoliquido rendered the plans accompanying the garden essays. Her work has appeared in numerous books, including the Audubon Society Field Guides, the Audubon Society Nature Guides, and other volumes in the Taylor's Guide series.

Alan Singer, illustrator for this and seven other Taylor's Guides, writes about art and teaches at the New York Botanical Garden. His work has also appeared in *Horticulture*.

Steven Still, consultant on the plant charts and a contributing photographer, is a professor at Ohio State University in Columbus, author of *Herbaceous Ornamental Plants*, and editor of the plant descriptions of perennials and shrubs in the Taylor's Guides.

George Taloumis, author of the essay on gardens by the sea and a contributing photographer, is a veteran gardening columnist for the *Boston Globe* and *Flower and Garden*.

Allan Taylor, contributor of the essay on gardening in dry sites, is a Research Associate at the Denver Botanic Gardens who specializes in growing desert and other drought-resistant plants.

Charles Thomas, author of the water gardens essay and a contributing photographer, is a garden writer and president of Lilypons Water Gardens in Lilypons, Maryland.

Preface

Think of the gardens you have most admired—your grandmother's lush lawn bordered with bright azaleas and tall oaks, a neighbor's front walk flanked with soft-toned perennials, an inviting terrace garden filled with different plants each season. The thriving flowers, trees, and shrubs in these gardens are a tribute to the skill of their owners, but their combined impact comes from more than just careful nurturing. It is the unique choice and placement of harmonious colors, heights, shapes, and textures within a particular space that makes each garden successful. The best gardens are not mere collections of plants—they are designed.

Planning your own memorable garden is challenging and fun, a chance to express yourself through your surroundings. Armed with some practical knowledge and an awareness of the many landscaping possibilities, you can create a plan perfectly suited to your house, your tastes, and your life-style.

Your plan might take advantage of the site, emphasizing its particular assets, such as an ocean view or a rooftop panorama. Or it could work to enhance what you think of as a problem area, transforming a stony site into a rock garden bright with alpine perennials; a moist spot into a bog garden of rustling reeds and cat-tails; or a shady area into a colorful oasis. Rise to the challenge presented by a small space with innovative uses of plants and structures that seem to enlarge it.

Perhaps you would like to design in a particular style, either creating an ordered, formal effect or imitating nature's subtle beauty. Your composition could be as intricate as a medieval-style knot garden, with low clipped hedges and varied plants interwoven in symmetrical patterns, or as simple as a woodland or meadow garden that seems untouched by human hands. You might introduce tranquility by designing a Japanese-style landscape, or choose an historical style that complements the lines of a traditional house.

Consider using plants of a particular type as the basis of a design. The backbone of your garden might be its trees and shrubs, selected to give structure and beauty all year long. If you love flowers, plan beds of annuals, perennials, bulbs, or roses to brighten your lawn from spring through fall. Choose some plants for their winter aspects—bright berries or intriguing silhouettes. Or learn what plants to use in dry areas, existing or created, and enjoy a garden of unique form.

Landscape designs should be functional as well as ornamental. One way to make your garden productive is by combining fruits, herbs, vegetables, and ornamental plants in an attractive design.

Whether you are starting with a bulldozed lot or adapting an established garden to your taste, this guide will give you the practical information you need and show you dozens of examples of well-designed gardens to inspire your creativity.

How to Use This

Designing your property is like decorating your home—it involves personal choices guided by inspiration and practical knowledge. This guide meets both needs, with over 90 color photographs of successful gardens to serve as inspiration and practical essays by experts to tell you how to put your new ideas to work. Rather than restrict you to following a few garden plans, it provides a wide range of tools with which to build a design according to your particular tastes and needs.

Nine volumes in the *Taylor's Guide* series present large selections of flowers, ground covers, shrubs, trees, and other plants, with detailed descriptions and how-to-grow information. This volume takes you a step further, showing you how to combine those and other plants effectively.

How the Guide is Organized
On the following pages you will find three types of material: introductory essays on mapping out and caring for your landscape, color plates illustrating variations on 14 garden themes, and essays by experts on adapting these themes to your site.

Introductory Essays
The essays that open the volume offer the general information you need to shape your whole landscape. The first, Landscaping Your Property, takes you through every step of creating a comprehensive plan for your space—from drawing a base map, through grading the site and planting trees, to laying out areas for work, play, or ornament. An essay on garden structures explains how to incorporate patios, walkways, raised beds, and trellises and offers step-by-step instructions on building simple examples. The essays Garden Basics and Buying Plants guide beginners in selecting, planting, and caring for the plants in a new design.

The Color Plates
Over 90 beautifully landscaped gardens are illustrated in the color plates. They are arranged by theme: Landscapes to Harvest; Landscaping with Flowers; Using Trees & Shrubs; Rock Gardens; Time-Honored Styles; Gardens in the Suburbs; City Gardens; Water Gardens; Shade Gardens; Japanese-Style Gardens; Winterscapes; Gardens by the Sea; Gardening in Dry Sites; and A Naturalistic Effect. Within each group you will see variations on the theme.

Each color section opens with a short essay that offers a quick overview, defining the philosophy behind the style—for example, growing food plants in an ornamental setting, or adding color with well-designed flower beds. The essay gives concrete information about the best sites, plants, and structures to use to achieve the desired effect. A more detailed discussion follows in the garden essay section of the book.

Guide

Opening the color section is a Visual Key, which presents the 14 garden styles at a glance. It shows two examples of each type and gives a short description of its important principles and features.

Captions
Each color plate is accompanied by a caption that identifies the garden by location and name. It also offers specific information about the site—level or sloped; sunny or shady—and lists the most important plants and structural elements shown. The column headed Seasons tells you when the garden was photographed and in what seasons it is at its best. It also gives the age of the garden in terms of how soon after planting it became effective.

Under the column entitled Design Concepts, you will find the keys to the success of each garden. Here are indications of the principles used by the designers to make site, plants, and structures work together harmoniously. Such phrases as "Geometric plan" or "Use of foliage textures" help draw your attention to how those concepts figure in the design. They will teach you a new way of looking at a landscape and help you get ideas for your own space.

Garden Essays
Following the color plates are 14 informative essays by experts in landscape design and horticulture. They explain how to adapt the themes illustrated to your site. Each provides detailed information on which plants to use, how to combine them effectively, what ornamental features might be incorporated, and how to care for your new garden. Many essays include garden plans, and there are illustrations showing how to perform specific tasks.

Plant Selection Charts
Following each essay is a chart listing "Plant Choices"—some of the most attractive and appropriate plants to try in a garden of the style discussed. Each plant is listed by scientific and common name. There is information about its hardiness—either a range of USDA zones or an indication of whether it is a warm-season or cool-season annual; relative height; dominant color or colors; the season or seasons in which it is most effective; whether it is evergreen; and whether it tolerates shade. Often a whole genus of plants is suggested, because any member of the genus that grows in your area would be appropriate.

To direct you to specific cultural information about each plant in the chart, there is a reference to volumes in the *Taylor's Guide* series: A for the Annuals volume, B for Bulbs, G for Ground Covers, Vines & Grasses, H for Houseplants, P for Perennials, R for Roses, S for Shrubs, T for Trees, and V for Vegetables & Herbs. D directs you to a page in this volume on which planting information can be found. Use these charts to get started, and refer to the essays and photographs for additional possibilities.

Landscaping

Barbara Damrosch

The landscape surrounding your home serves as its visual setting—the front yard frames the house as seen from the street or driveway, and the back and side yards offer attractive views from the windows, patio, or walkways. Plants and structures in each area should express your taste, just as furnishings inside the house do. But a well-designed landscape is more than ornamental; it is a functional extension of the house itself. Your indoor space is divided into rooms that serve different purposes, and your outdoor space should be arranged to accommodate various activities, with movement through it directed in a way that makes sense.

To achieve a well-designed landscape, you need to understand some basic design principles. Creating an overall plan for your property will not be difficult if you keep these concepts in mind—many are just common sense. Then, once the practical framework is in place, you can go on to develop certain areas of your property in imaginative ways, designing special gardens that will be a pleasure to create and admire. The essays that follow the color plates will give you specific design ideas for 14 different types of gardens. But first, before you turn to these specifics, it is important to get a sense of the whole picture.

A Comprehensive Plan

Even homes with tidy, well-kept surroundings often suffer from a lack of planning. Their owners design one small area as a need or problem arises, or they go on a shopping binge in a nursery and bring home a load of plants to "find a place for." Often the result is a spotty landscape design—a little of this, a little of that, and nothing to tie it together visually. Much time and money are wasted on plantings of the wrong scale or in the wrong place that later must be torn out.

To avoid such costly mistakes, devise a plan for the use of your entire lot, even if you think it may change later on. If you can afford it, you may wish to hire a landscape architect or landscape designer to devise a detailed scheme. Many people take pleasure and pride in working things out on their own. Consider the compromise of paying for an hour or two of professional consultation to get you started. Whichever route you take, first spend some time walking or driving around to look at other homes in your area, noting which landscaping features you most admire. Your object is not to make a carbon copy of someone else's design but to note which plants thrive in your area and to discover some pleasing visual effects you had not thought of.

Drawing a Plan

No matter how vividly you can picture your ideal design, it is always worthwhile to put the plan on paper. In order to sketch possibilities, you'll need a base map—a record of how your property looks now. If you have an architect's plan of your lot, trace it to

Your Property

save some work. Otherwise, create your own. Your sketch does not have to look professional—just clear and accurately scaled.

All you need is some graph paper, a pencil, a ruler, and a tape measure. Choose graph paper that is divided into squares of a convenient size, such as a quarter inch, in order to work in scale. For example, on quarter-inch paper you might use each square to represent one square foot. Decide how large a piece of paper you will need to represent the area in scale, taping sheets of graph paper together if necessary. Use thumbtacks to attach the paper to a wooden board that you can carry around the area and set down here and there as you measure. Or use small sheets fastened to a clipboard and measure one area at a time, fitting them together when you have finished. Pages 14 and 15 show two sample base maps—one of a house of traditional, formal design and the other of a modern, informal house.

Invest in a 100-foot measuring tape to make your task easier. If no one is around to hold the end, anchor it by sticking a screwdriver through the metal loop and into the ground. First measure the house and any other buildings such as sheds or garages, including all their walls and angles. Draw in the boundaries according to scale. Include marks to indicate the locations of doors and windows, and note how far above the ground the windows are; this will help you avoid planting shrubs that will grow to cover them.

Show the placement of such fixtures as hose outlets, electric meters, and the pipe leading to the oil tank. You may want to camouflage these with plantings, but they must be accessible. Measure existing features such as the driveway, walks, terraces, pools, trees, flower beds, and planting areas. Even if you are going to eliminate some of them later, it is useful to have a written record of their exact positions. Note the direction of north and as much as you can about the location of sunny and shaded areas, wet or dry spots, rocky areas, and wind direction.

When you have everything measured and recorded, the fun begins—deciding what to add to or subtract from the landscape. As you learn about various possibilities, use tracing paper to superimpose sketches of them on the master plan. Spend a long time thinking about what you want. Sit indoors to muse and sketch, then take your favorite plan outside and try to imagine it in place. If you have difficulty visualizing the plan from this schematic, bird's-eye view, draw some elevations to show what the plantings and other features will look like at eye level. You might even take photographs of the house from various angles, blow them up, and draw proposed features directly on them with a grease pencil, or sketch on tracing paper laid over them.

Landscaping Styles

As you develop your plan, give some thought to its overall style. The architecture of your home, the kind of life you lead, and the

Landscaping Your Property

The sample base map on the left shows a traditional-style house; the one on the right is a contemporary layout. Each square on the grid represents an area 4-by-4 feet wide.

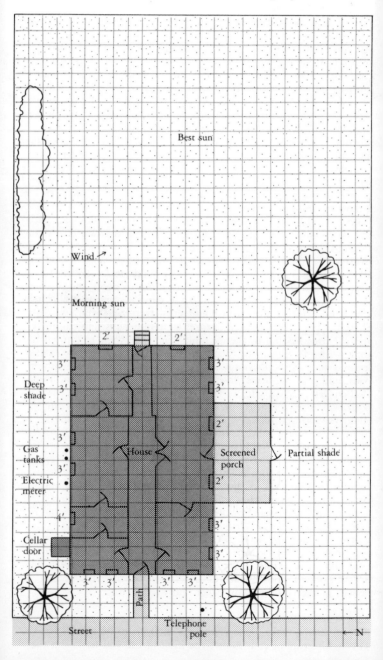

Best sun

Wind

Morning sun

Deep shade

Gas tanks

Electric meter

Cellar door

2'   2'

3''   3'

3'   3'

3'   2'

3'

3'   2'

4'

3'

House   Screened porch   Partial shade

3'   3'

3'   3'   3'   3'

Path

Street   Telephone pole

← N

To make a base map, use graph paper to draw the existing features in scale. Include trees and large plantings, and identify them if possible. Indicate doors and windows, noting how high windows are from ground level. Mark the placement of electric meters, oilfills, and hose outlets. Show the north point, wind direction, areas of sun and shade, and any problem spots.

Use tracing paper to superimpose sketches of design options on your base map.

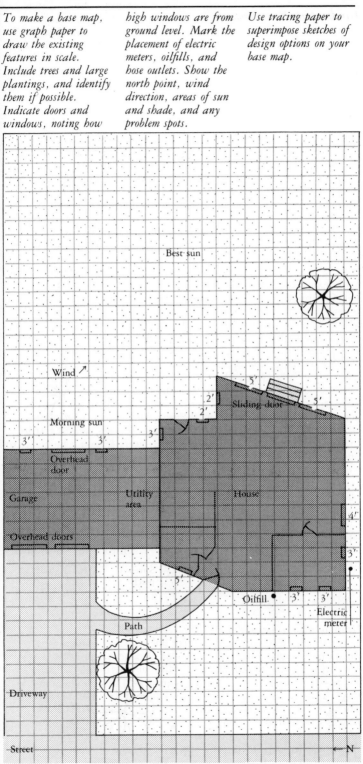

Landscaping Your Property

landscape features you choose should all work together as part of the picture. For example, if your home is of traditional design, its setting should be somewhat formal. If it has a symmetrical floor plan with a central hallway and rooms that are sharply delineated from one another, the landscape plan should echo these features. This does not mean boxy and geometrical; lines in a garden are soft because they are formed by the leaves and outlines of plants. But the effect of regularity will lead both the feet and the eyes in very definite directions, perhaps along an axis that is an extension of the house's center hall.

A more modern house might incorporate curves, odd angles, and an open floor plan. There may be a large "great room" combining living, dining, and cooking areas and leading into the backyard. Of course, you could give the landscape around such a house a formal look, but the casual, asymmetrical floor plan seems to call for more open surroundings and freedom of movement and vision from one area to another. Certain spots will be designated for gardening, cooking, playing, and other activities, but they are not as clearly separated as in a formal plan.

There are always exceptions to these formal-versus-informal categorizations, so be flexible. Often the size of your lot will help determine what style would work best. For instance, if you have a traditional row house on a narrow city lot, using a central axis in the garden would make it look even narrower. It would be better to break up the vista with pathways and plant groupings. The eye would be led not straight to the back but diverted to features in between. Visitors strolling through the space would move around plantings that led to the left, then to the right, discovering new features along the way.

Conversely, your lot might be very large, with areas of wild landscape to manage and define. Your task in this case is to determine which sections to leave wild, which to tame, and which to treat as a sort of controlled wilderness enhanced by selective cutting and planting. There may be views that you want to open up or frame with trees so that the eye is drawn to a distant point outside of the garden.

Implementing Your Plan

You will probably not want to carry out your whole plan immediately. Divide it into a series of manageable projects that you can complete one by one as time and money permit.

There is a natural logic about the sequence of basic tasks. First do major grading and cover bare areas with lawn or ground covers. Then remove unwanted trees and shrubs, and plant trees and hedges that will take a long time to grow. Landscape the most important, visible section of the property, usually the front entrance, then turn to shaping space for general outdoor recreation. Finally, tackle areas where you want special gardens.

Shaping Your Site

After the construction of a new house, the need for landscaping is all too obvious. Bulldozers and other heavy equipment have created a moonscape devoid of vegetation, with heavily compacted soil, and sometimes no topsoil. Often there are no trees close to the house, no hedges to create a sense of privacy. The advantage is that you can create a paradise from scratch, but the task may seem overwhelming. Where do you start?

Begin by molding the ground, or grading. If you are having the house built, order any extra grading while the heavy equipment is still there. Much of the cost of excavation lies in just bringing the machines to your property. Make sure that any driveway or parking areas are shaped and positioned the way you desire. There may be drainage problems still to be corrected, or you may want to create a flat spot for a terrace or lawn, or a raised area for a rock garden. If there are large boulders lying around, have them carted away or moved to an area where they can serve as ornaments.

There may be construction projects such as a deck or pool that you'd like to carry out but have to postpone, either because the house has taken up your building budget or because you are not yet sure how you want to go about designing them. Plan for these areas anyway, indicating them on your map so that you do not plant expensive trees on future building sites.

If your house has already been landscaped, and you are considering special features, it is still a good idea to look at the major ones with a critical eye. Is the parking area large enough and conveniently placed? Is there a poorly drained spot where nothing will grow? Do you need to terrace a slope in order to garden successfully? Even if you are reluctant to bring in bulldozers and backhoes and mess things up, it will still be better to get major construction over with sooner rather than later.

Lawns and Other Ground Covers

Once your site is graded properly, the next priority is to cover the bare earth. Lawn grass, either sown or put in as sod, is the quickest and most popular ground cover. Its lush appearance and durability make it ideal for both ornamental, formal gardens and yards used by active families.

There are many attractive alternatives to the traditional lawn. You can put down gravel or thick mulches, or pave areas with stone, brick, and other hard materials that will keep vegetation from growing. Or you can choose from among a wide variety of ground covers that are easier to maintain than a lawn and especially useful on slopes that are too steep to mow.

Some people are exploring the idea of wildflower meadows to replace lawns. While neighbors might complain if you turned your whole front yard into a wild meadow, they probably wouldn't object to such a naturalized area in the back or side yard. A small

Landscaping Your Property

meadow is pretty to look at and interesting because it will attract butterflies and other wildlife that wouldn't visit a lawn. If your lawn area is very rocky, consider turning it into a naturalized "alpine meadow," with spring bulbs, native wildflowers, and ground covers.

Take Time to Know Your Property

Once you have dealt with major grading and covered the ground, take a breather. You may want to live with your property for as much as six months or a year before you do much major planting. It's too soon to know quite how you will use your land—which entrances will be most popular with you, your children, your pets, and your guests; where you will spend the most time; what neighboring areas will become annoying and need to be screened from view; what new design ideas may occur to you. You may discover a number of microclimates where growing conditions vary. It takes time to know which areas of the yard are sunniest, shadiest, warmest, coldest, or windiest. You will be better able to decide what to plant where after you've gained this knowledge.

Placing Trees

When you do get ready to tackle planting, start with trees—the largest, most permanent plants. Trees serve many different purposes in the landscape. Deciduous types provide shade in summer and let sunlight through in winter, while evergreens offer privacy and year-round protection against wind. Trees are also visual assets, lending grandeur and solidity to your house, increasing its value, and providing beauty that changes with the seasons. Combining different types of trees provides contrast, but placing them is not always easy. Planting trees too close to the house or to each other is probably the most common mistake people make in landscaping their homes.

Take time to educate yourself by talking to local gardeners or nurserymen and reading about trees you admire. Learn about their growth habits and visualize what they would look like at various stages in the space you can provide. Take a cue from some established plantings in your area. Do you like the way white birch trunks stand out against dark hemlocks? Would you like a red-leaved tree such as a Japanese maple or copper beech? Do you want a lot of spring color from flowering crabapples, cherries, and magnolias, or fall color from sugar maples, oaks, and aspens? Decide on several choice trees now; the sooner you get these specimens in the ground, the sooner they will realize their potential.

Draw the trees on your base map, using a compass to make a circle representing the ultimate spread of each tree—not its size at planting time. This will alert you to any spacing problems before it's too late.

If your site is already wooded, choosing trees may be more a process of elimination than addition. Some people are reluctant to cut down trees, especially if they have small lots. They think of the trees, quite rightly, as valuable and difficult to replace. But sometimes desirable trees are too close to the house, crowded together, or cramped by undesirable trees so that none are able to thrive or grow into attractive shapes. It is a good idea to have an experienced, licensed tree surgeon assess the trees on your property, help you decide which ones to eliminate, and do any pruning, cabling, or other repair work that may be necessary.

Entryway and Foundation Plantings
The next step in building your landscape is to design the main entrance to the house. Even if you use the back door 90 percent of the time, you want to give major emphasis to the "official" entrance. Adorning it with plants and other features not only makes it more graceful and inviting, but also helps to define it. Think of the entrance as an explanation of how to get into the house. You have probably had the experience of driving up to a home for the first time and being puzzled as to where the main door is. This should not happen. A path leading from the street or the parking area should say, "This is how you get in." Once you are there, the plantings should say, "welcome."
The best way to achieve this effect is with plants that are interesting in themselves, not just "clothing" for the bottom part of your house. In colonial times, lilacs were often used to frame entrances because of their beautiful, fragrant bloom and their height. Since then the "foundation planting" has evolved. All too often this consists of a rather boring succession of clipped evergreen trees and shrubs marching across the front of a house. Many people do not even think to question whether they need this kind of planting or not. Every house on the street has one, so they assume that is what you are supposed to do.
A foundation planting does serve several purposes: It can hide an ugly foundation and give a sense of solidity to the house—anchor it to the ground, so to speak. But you can achieve these effects without resorting to a clichéd design. Although many people use evergreens because they give the same effect all year long, you should consider planting some deciduous shrubs as well, either alone or mixed with evergreens. Even in winter they soften the transition from house to ground, lending the interest of varying twig patterns, winter berries, or colored bark.
Choose and place your plants so that at maturity they will be exactly the right height and width for their sites. Some judicious pruning here and there may often be a good idea, especially with plants that tend to be sparse or leggy. But don't assume that it is a homeowner's duty to shear foundation plantings all season long to keep them from encroaching on windows and pathways. Unless

Landscaping Your Property

tidy, muffin-like shapes are particularly dear to you, let your shrubs and trees take their natural forms.

Use some imagination in arranging as well as selecting foundation plantings. You are not restricted to a straight row running parallel to the house. Introduce some sweeping curves and interesting plant groupings. Place some groupings at a distance from the house in island beds, with a path that meanders through them. Such an entrance can still be well-defined and logical, but it will make approaching the house more interesting.

Backyards

America's backyards are like living folk art. They are full of bicycles and swing sets, laundry lines and tool sheds, dog- and birdhouses, swimming pools and decks, barbecues and boats. Your front yard is the face you present to the world, but your backyard is a private refuge, the part of your property that most clearly expresses your personality and interests. You may make concessions to conventionality in the front of the house, but you probably feel no such constraints behind it. You do need an overall plan, however, to avoid chaos and to take advantage of your space.

Areas for Relaxing and Entertaining

The top priority in designing your backyard is to create an area to relax in, a place where you can put out a lawn chair and sit, where the children can get some fresh air, where the pets can run around. Often just a lawn is sufficient—large or small, depending on your needs and the size of your lot. But many people want a relaxation area that they can entertain in, that is a little more formal, more "designed" than a grass lawn. They'd like a terrace, a deck, or an enclosed patio that provides a flat surface on which to set outdoor furniture and a barbecue, a surface that dries out faster in wet weather than grass does and absorbs the heat of the sun when it is cold.

Play Areas

Backyard play areas are less formal than relaxation areas, but it can still be helpful to divide them up according to type of activity. Older members of the family may like to tend the garden; teenagers might prefer sunbathing; and the children need a sandbox and a fenced, protected place to play. Take such different interests into account, and balance them with the space available.

Even a small yard can be divided to accommodate many activities, by using fences, hedges, changes in elevation, or just shrubs or trees that screen an area from view. You don't have to physically impede movement from one area to another. Just suggest outdoor "rooms" symbolically—with an archway along a path, a break in a hedge, or a pair of shrubs on either side of a path to say, "Here is where one area ends and another begins."

Swimming Pools

Plan the area around a swimming pool so that various activities can take place there at once. Flat surfaces for sunning, eating, and entertaining will make the pool more than just a swimming hole. Use plantings to set the pool area off in a way that defines it, screening it from the neighbors or the rest of the property, and giving it the feeling of a private family retreat where everyone can congregate.

Work Areas

Utility or work areas are still another part of the backyard landscape. You may want to split and store firewood, wash your car, make compost, grow vegetables, or hang out the laundry. You need a spot where you can do such things efficiently, with the appropriate water and power sources at hand. And you might prefer to keep the process hidden from more formal areas. Evaluate your needs, and set aside appropriate space in your plan. Don't assume that you can fit these activities into ornamental areas later.

Using Plants in the Backyard

Some of your back- and side yard plantings may stand alone as purely ornamental features: a perennial border, a rose garden, shrub groupings, a specimen tree. Others will enhance or define the areas for relaxation, play, or work: flowers that decorate a poolside deck; vines that hang from an arbor to shade a terrace or clothe a fence; fragrant flowering shrubs that brighten, perfume, and shade a private glen and at the same time hide it from sight.

Plantings are often used just to give a pleasant view when you look out the windows, or when you survey the lawn from the terrace. They can create perspective in a short backyard or break up a long, narrow one. Where you place ornamental plants in the backyard is a matter of where they will grow best and how they will look from strategic viewpoints. Also consider whether they will interfere with work or play, and whether activities might injure them.

Four Sample Plans

The plans on pages 24 through 27 show how the two properties illustrated earlier in base maps could be developed. There is both an ambitious and a simplified plan for each property. Although the simpler plans involve less time and money to create and maintain, all four plans are equally successful in serving the needs of the owners and making the best use of their space.

Designs for a Traditional Landscape

The landscape surrounding the traditional house is divided into several areas, which are for the most part ornamental. In the ambitious plan, a rose garden to the south provides something beautiful to look at from the screened-in porch. Fairly tall trees on either side enclose this area, so that visitors feel as if they are in a small, private world. A tall hedge runs the entire length of the property on this side.

The rear of the lot slopes gradually downhill and has been terraced with stonework into three distinct areas. The hallway at the rear of the house has French doors that open onto a flagstone terrace with herb and flower gardens on three sides. Beyond that is a formal lawn surrounded by an herbaceous border, which is in turn backed by a low wall of cut stone. Stone steps lead down from the terrace to the lawn level, and a stone walk bisects the lawn, dividing to go around a rectangular pool that has the same general proportions as the lawn.

At the far end of the lawn, stone steps exactly like the first set lead down to a small orchard planted with eight dwarf or semi-dwarf fruit trees, mown grass, and drifts of spring-flowering bulbs. The path continues through the orchard and ends in a gazebo, behind which is a tall wooden fence. A tall evergreen hedge separates the lawn and orchard from the far corner of the property, where there are utility areas—a shed and vegetable garden.

Notice that the central axis of the back area is exactly in line with that of the front area. The front and back walkways are also of the same material. Why is this important? Because from the middle of the house, in the central hall, there is a view out both the back and front doors, and the aligned axes and unified materials create harmony. The terrace is built of the same material as the paths.

The rose garden also has a central axis that leads from the door to the seat, but a flagstone path follows a winding route from the rose garden to the formal lawn. This little area, shaded by trees and planted with ground covers, has a more informal feeling; it counterbalances the regular geometry of the rest of the property.

The area to the left of the house is screened by a long border of tall shrubs, some deciduous and flowering, some evergreen. Many are fragrant and can be seen and smelled through the windows on that side of the house as well as in the rear yard.

In the less ambitious, lower-maintenance version of this plan, there are no herb and flower beds in the terrace area. Container plants that can be grown more simply accent the terrace. The flower beds bordering the central lawn contain two kinds of low-maintenance plants: peonies and daylilies. Outside the screened porch is a blanket of ground cover interplanted with spring bulbs. At the back of the lot are two ornamental fruit trees that should not have to be sprayed for pests. The long shrub border contains only lilacs. All these areas have the same feeling as those in the other plan, and they interact in the same way, but they require less upkeep.

Plans for a Contemporary-Style Landscape

The house shown on pages 26 and 27 has open areas and informal lines. Here, the owners are an active family with children, so they want a landscape in which form follows function. In the ambitious plan, there is a free-form swimming pool in the southeast corner, totally surrounded by wooden decking. The deck and pool are on the same level as the door. Into it are set three planting areas containing herbs, trees, shrubs, a rock garden, and perennials and ornamental grasses. Some of the shrubs and perennials flower, but the main interest is their foliage. There is a view of this scene through a long wall of windows and a sliding glass door.

Leading from the kitchen area to the pool is a brick path flanked by strips of lawn. Since the lawn is lower than the pool and deck, some brick steps are needed. To the left is a work area—an "outdoor room" that serves as an extension of the indoor utility area in the garage. Beyond that is an attractive vegetable garden with raised beds and paths between them that are mulched with shredded bark. No attempt has been made to hide the garden because the family considers it a work of art.

Behind the vegetable garden is an outdoor "children's room" that can be seen from the pool. The area is set slightly apart from the rest of the yard to give the children a private world that they can "landscape" as they wish—by building structures, digging in the ground, and setting up equipment for sports and games.

In the simplified plan, the deck does not extend around the pool, and the pool, lawn, and children's play area are all on the same level. Steps lead from the deck down to the lawn. The only plantings are trees and shrubs, carefully chosen for ornamental effect, and some containers on the deck for annuals and herbs. There is no vegetable garden, but the work area remains; some low shrubs divide it from the children's area to maintain the feeling of separateness. A simple stone path connects the back door and the gate that leads to the pool area.

Universal Principles

Although your own house and landscape may look very different from the two shown here, the same reasoning processes apply to creating an overall plan. There are also certain aesthetic principles common to all successful designs.

Repetition

There should always be some repetition of materials to give the site a feeling of unity. The repeated use of flagstone in the traditional garden is deliberate. It might be combined with a few other materials, such as brick, with great success, but four or five different construction materials would give a fragmented look. In the contemporary plan, wood is used repeatedly for the same reason. And the three large rocks that have been built into the edge of the swimming pool, one of them for diving, are echoed by the large rocks in the corner rock garden.

Repetitions are effective in the choice of plants, too. For instance,

Landscaping Your Property

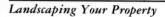

These plans show two landscape designs for the traditional-style house mapped out on page 14. The one on the left is more ambitious, but both complement the lines of the house.

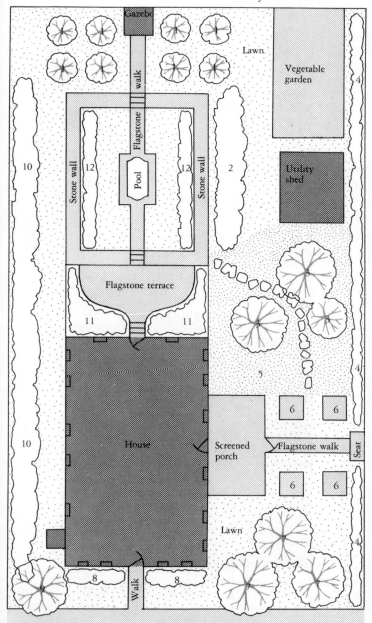

Gazebo

Lawn

Vegetable garden

4

Flagstone walk

Stone wall

10

12

Pool

12

Stone wall

2

Utility shed

Flagstone terrace

11

11

3

4

5

4

6

6

10

House

Screened porch

Flagstone walk

Seat

6

6

Lawn

4

6

8

8

Walk

6

Ambitious Plan

← N

Key:
1. Dwarf fruit trees underplanted with bulbs
2. Tall evergreen hedge
3. Deciduous trees
4. Tall hedge
5. Ground cover and spring bulbs
6. Roses
7. Shade trees
8. Low shrubs
9. Tall evergreen tree
10. Shrub border
11. Herbs and flowers
12. Herbaceous border
13. Flowering crabapples
14. Peonies
15. Daylilies
16. Container plants
17. Lilac hedge

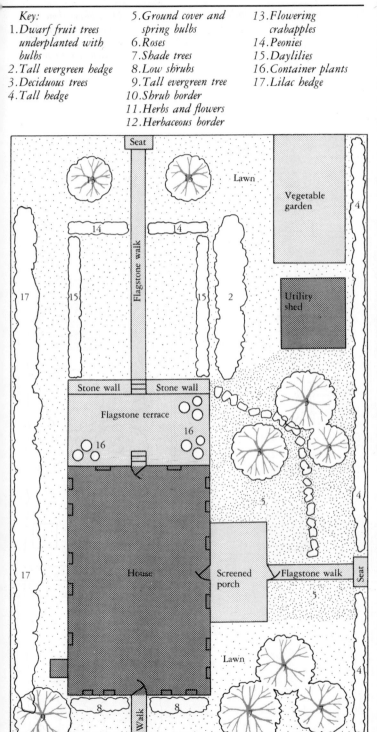

Low-maintenance Plan   ← N

Landscaping Your Property

These plans show two landscape designs for the contemporary-style house shown on page 15.

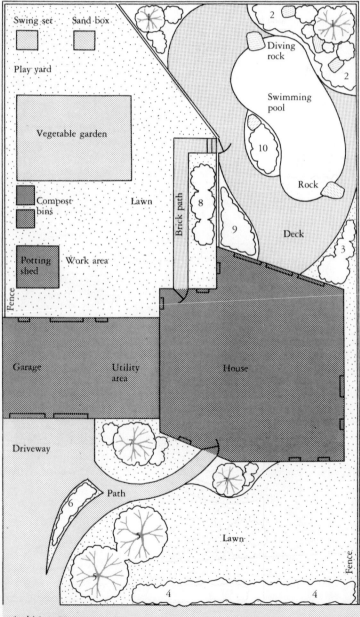

Swing set   Sand box

Play yard

Vegetable garden

Compost bins

Potting shed   Work area   Lawn

Brick path

8

9   Deck

3

2   Diving rock

1

2

Swimming pool

10   Rock

Fence

Garage   Utility area   House

Driveway

6   Path

5

5   Lawn

4   4

Fence

Ambitious Plan   ← N

The one on the left is more ambitious, but both suit the informal lines of the house and serve the needs of a family.

Key:
1. Ornamental trees and shrubs
2. Rock garden planted with perennials
3. Evergreen shrubs
4. Evergreen hedge
5. Deciduous flowering trees
6. Low shrubs
7. Birch trees; broadleaf and evergreen shrubs
8. Tall flowering shrubs
9. Herb garden
10. Ornamental grasses
11. Container plants
12. Shade tree

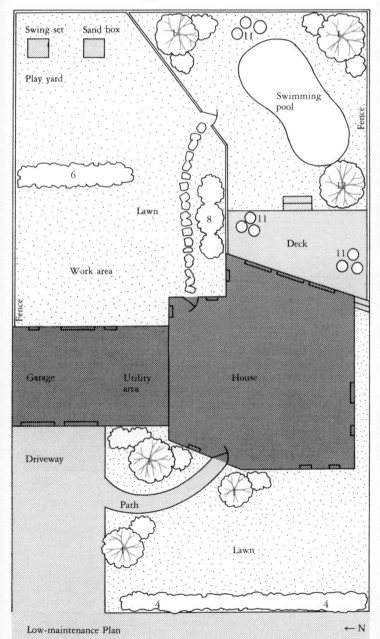

Low-maintenance Plan   ← N

Landscaping Your Property

you might use one type of evergreen, such as hemlock, in different areas, varying the size and shape of each tree: some tall, unsheared specimens in one area and a Sargent's weeping hemlock in another. Or repeat a ground cover, such as myrtle, in many different areas.

Balance
You must also think of your landscape as a series of carefully composed, balanced pictures. This is relatively easy to do in a formal plan like that for the traditional landscape, where there is so much symmetry. The front door, for example, is flanked by two rows of shrubs of equal length. There are large trees at both front corners of the house; the group at the right dominates a larger stretch of front lawn than the single tree to the left.
The entry planting for the contemporary house is balanced as you walk along the path: a group of trees to the right, then a group of trees to the left, then another group to the right. Here again, the size of the plants and groupings has been matched to the amount of ground that they dominate.
In trying to balance your compositions, don't think only in terms of size, but also of weight or impact. Let's say you have a very large plant on one side of a garden picture—a huge sheared yew, for example. You could balance it on the other side with several evergreens of different sizes that give an equal sense of mass. You can give one part of a composition weight by planting a very dense or dark-colored shrub, or lighten it by planting one with a loose, open branching pattern.
Use impact, too, to balance a composition. Suppose you want to give weight to one side of a composition, but there is only a small plot of ground and windows that shouldn't be blocked. Try planting a dark evergreen vine directly on the house, or on a trellis, and then place an evergreen with bright foliage in front of it, such as a variegated euonymus or a gold-needled false cypress. The striking effect will draw your eye in a way that will make up for the small size of the planting.

Perspective
Try playing tricks with perspective to improve your compositions. For example, in the pool area of the plan for the contemporary house, the southeast corner on the far side could be planted with tall, massive background plants to give the area a private, sheltered feeling. But if you felt hemmed-in by the size of the lot and wanted a feeling of larger space, you'd place the more massive shrubs near the windows from which you view the pool and the smaller ones in the far corner, to make the corner seem to recede.

Choosing Plants
Consider all of a plant's attributes when deciding whether it is right for a particular spot—not only its size. What is its shape—

upright, low and spreading, tall and spreading, weeping, conical, or round? What color are its leaves, flowers, fruits, seed pods, and bark? What textures are apparent—fuzzy flowers, glossy leaves, shaggy bark? You'll have fun combining all these features, repeating some for unity, contrasting others for interest. You'll discover combinations that complement one another, such as the light, upward-tilting twigs of dogwood in front of the dark, massive drooping branches of hemlock or Norway spruce, or a fall garden of rich purple asters mixed with yellow and mahogany-colored heleniums.

Evaluating Your Plan

After you have finished drawing your "final" landscape plan, review it carefully to see if it works as a whole. One thing to be on guard against is overplanting. In your enthusiasm to fill your space, you may overwhelm it. Remember that your plants will be healthier and more attractive if they are not jammed into tight spaces.

Also check to make sure you have directed traffic in a logical and interesting way. Notice how, in the traditional plan, the visitor is led directly to the front door but is discouraged from crossing the lawn by the trees and shrubs in front of the rose garden and by the absence of a path in that area. A stepping-stone path leads through the trees on the other side of the rose garden, and continues to the formal lawn, not to the utility shed, which is almost hidden by greenery. You can walk with ease from the orchard to the vegetable garden, however.

If you have given your design "good bones"—that is, a balanced, unified framework in which the major construction features, trees, shrub plantings, lawns, and ground covers are all placed together harmoniously, you will then be able to concentrate on the "fine tuning"—creating theme gardens or special planting areas.

Making Changes

Over the years, your landscape should evolve. You may have children or watch the children leave. You might develop new interests or pastimes or discover new types of plants you want to grow, such as perennials, dryland plants, or wildflowers. Reading the rest of this volume will give you many new ideas—planting for winter interest, for example, or turning a shady area into a woodland garden. As new plans occur to you, you'll need to create new areas, resulting in revisions in your master plan.

If your overall plan has been solidly based on the way you use your property, you will find that new elements will be easy and fun to incorporate. To some extent, landscaping your home is a way of showing it off—putting on your best face for the public. But remember that your yard is also your own personal world, as much a small paradise as you choose to make it.

Patios, Paths,

Stacy Freed

All gardens, no matter what their style or site, are enhanced by structures. Patios, decks, pathways, fences, walls, and raised beds can connect the house to the landscape or be used to shape specific areas, directing movement through them. Within this structural framework, you can arrange plantings according to your needs and taste.

One of the first steps in planning a garden is to decide what kind of structures it should have. There are three considerations: the characteristics of your site; how you plan to use various areas; and what garden style you desire.

Evaluating Your Site
First assess your site: With what conditions are you working? The size and situation of your outdoor living area is determined by a variety of factors, including local zoning ordinances and the original builder's taste. However, by choosing the right structures you can improve your site, making it seem more spacious or private, highlighting beautiful areas and redesigning problem ones.

Exploring the Options
Next, think about how you want to use your space. Perhaps you need an area to entertain in, or simply a place to relax. You can construct areas that serve primarily as spots from which to admire your beautifully formed landscape, or that interact with the house and its environment. Knowing what activities will be going on in various areas will help you decide on the right materials. Keep in mind that your landscape is a reflection of your lifestyle and should be planned to satisfy your needs and dreams.

Setting the Tone
Finally, choose a style. The one you decide on may be influenced by your site. For example, you may plan a seaside garden to take advantage of an ocean view or create a Mediterranean-style garden in a dry area. You may wish to apply a specialized theme—a naturalistic or perhaps a Japanese-style garden. You might also designate portions of your space for specific accents, such as a small water garden in one area or a rock garden in another. Whatever your choices, make sure the structures suit the styles or themes to give the garden unity. If you're not starting from scratch, make changes or additions with care to avoid an eclectic look.

Limit your structures in style and material. If your garden is to be formal, planned along straight lines, it may be complemented by rectangular pools, pea-gravel walkways, or classically ornamented gazebos. Introducing curves gives a softer, more modern look. Make the structures extend the tone of your home into your outdoor space. For example, if your living room is done in a light, airy, California style, continue that feeling in the garden with wooden decks and furnishings and native plantings.

Fences & Beds

Before you start building, take time to think about all the possible types of structures and materials. Here are some ideas and practical advice on how to select the right structures for your garden.

Patios and Decks

Many homes benefit from the addition of attractive, functional patios and decks. These are visually important design elements, hard surfaces serving as transitions from the house to garden spaces. They create contrasts of texture, material, and color with the surrounding plantings. Patios and decks are also economical ways to expand your living space. They may be enclosed for year-round use, or left completely open to the elements. Although they can be placed anywhere, patios and decks are excellent problem-solvers for areas with poor soil or in spots that get little use and need enhancement.

Evaluating the Patio or Deck Site

To locate the best site for a patio or deck, study your yard at different times of the day and during different seasons. Where does the sun remain the longest? You don't want a finished product that is lovely to look at but situated in an area so hot and sunny that no one will use it. Note shady areas, drainage patterns, and views. Refer to your base map (see page 13) to take into account lot dimensions and orientations, house floor plan, locations of underground utility lines or meters, utility outlets, and existing trees or outdoor structures.

Think about the patio or deck not only as it relates to the house but also as it leads into the landscape. Is there a nice view from halfway down a slope? Perhaps terraced decks would be best. Is there an open, level lawn perfect for badminton or volleyball? A nearby patio would allow friends or family to watch the game, and later have refreshments.

Determining the Shape

The shape of your house and yard can suggest the best design for your patio or deck. For an interesting patio, try to echo the roofline of the house using poured concrete. If a patio or deck is to be attached to the house, try to angle it to complement the shape and views of the adjacent indoor room. Or integrate plantings and paving in a grid pattern, with square paving blocks punctuated by inlaid beds. You can soften a small, square lot with a wide sweeping curve, or use a short diagonal to break up a boxy feeling. Shape may also be affected by existing plants.

Be sure to make your walkways and steps wide enough for two people and, especially in a small space, consider the size and shape of your furniture—a table and chairs take up a lot of room. To use deck space more efficiently, consider building attached benches or low, L-shaped walls for seating. Plan for easy maintenance and maneuverability. If the area is enclosed by low walls, design places where debris may be swept off easily, perhaps leaving an opening under the benches. If you place plants in raised beds or pots, more areas will be clear for sitting or strolling.

Choosing a Deck or Patio

Wooden decks give a house a modern look and are perfect for sloped sites, where you can create steps or terraces, or for wooded areas, where you need to circumvent trees. On flat sites they can create different levels without disturbing plantings. But bear in mind that unlike planning a patio, building a deck is major construction: Although you can do it yourself, consult a professional first to help determine overall design, as well as the size, span, and spacing of the deck parts.

Patios are generally easier to construct than decks. Most patios need only a flat foundation set into the graded land. The two most practical options are brick and concrete patios, although other materials, such as flagstone, are also possible.

Building a Brick Patio

One of the easiest materials to work with, paving bricks are made especially for patios and come in at least 40 different shapes and sizes. There is a wide variety of textures and colors, ranging from green to yellow to dark brown. Bricks are usually a standard size— 7½ to 8 inches long, 3¼ to 3½ inches wide, and 2¼ inches thick—but you can buy thinner bricks and lay them in concrete as you would tiles. These thin pavers also come in square and hexagonal shapes.

Although a 20- by 20-foot patio would require more than 2,000 bricks, brick is relatively inexpensive compared to other materials. To cover one square foot, you need four and a half paver bricks with four- by eight-inch faces, four and a half standard bricks with half-inch mortar joints, or five standard bricks without mortar.

A brick patio is fairly simple to construct, as the units are small, easy to handle, and uniform in size. First mark out the area with stakes and string, and dig up about six or seven inches of soil, saving the good topsoil for planting in other parts of the yard. Tamp down the soil to make the area as flat and even as possible. Lay a form, or frame, of two-by-fours around the perimeter. Spread several inches of gravel, then a sheet of plastic punched with holes every few inches. Next spread a two-inch layer of sand, and wet it to keep it down. Level the sand within the form with a screed—a strip of plaster or wood that you can run along the top of the form as a gauge.

Next, lay bricks in a pattern such as herringbone, basket weave, ladder weave, or straight band (see illustrations on page 378). Thinner bricks look better set vertically on edge. With a hammer and small block of wood, tap bricks into place. Then pour clean,

To build a simple brick patio, first mark out the area with stakes and string. Dig up about six inches of soil, then tamp down exposed soil as flat as possible.

Next, lay a frame of two-by-fours around the perimeter. Put several inches of gravel on top of the soil, followed by a sheet of plastic that has been punctured every few inches for drainage.

Spread on a two-inch layer of sand and wet it to keep it down. Level with a screed and lay brick according to your chosen pattern. Finally, sweep sand into the joints until they are filled.

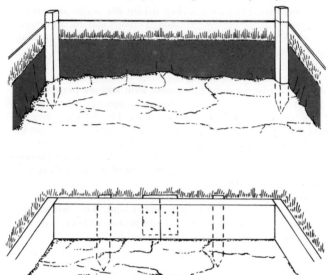

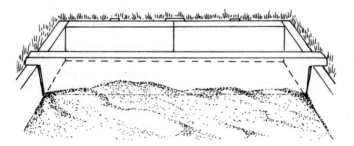

Patios, Paths, Fences & Beds

dry sand over the bricks and sweep it into the joints until they are filled.

Constructing with Concrete

Patios made with concrete are more complicated to construct than brick ones, and they require a variety of specialized tools. The rewards are many, because forms can be installed in varying shapes and sizes to create a patio of interesting contrasts.

First dig and level the soil as for a brick patio. You can save on the amount of concrete by first putting down large chunks of broken stone covered in sand. Next, lay out the form and pour the concrete. Spread it with a rake and shovel, using special equipment such as a concrete tamper, or jitterbug, to level and compact. Use a bull float, a device that looks like a metallic squeegee, to flatten and smooth the concrete. An edging tool will round the edges, separating the concrete from the form. Use another float to smooth the surface, and a jointer to make control joints. These can all be purchased at a masonry supply store.

You can also use concrete in the form of paving blocks, which are generally less costly than bricks. They are available in many shapes, sizes, and colors, and are very durable. Lay them as you would bricks or tiles. Keep in mind that their texture is rougher than that of a poured concrete patio, which may hamper some activities requiring a smooth surface, such as moving things on wheels.

Paths and Steps

Decks and patios provide established meeting places from which you can appreciate and admire the landscape. But paths and steps are the subtle directors of the garden, showing visitors where to go and getting them there. Their direction can evolve naturally from the way your lawn is used, or it can be imposed. Similarly, you can design paths to echo surrounding patterns or to meander and set a mood. Remember that indirect routes from spot to spot can highlight ponds or borders but that too many paths will become confusing. Make sure they take you somewhere—to a fixture, a view, a bench, or the house.

Steps, whether made of brick, stone, wood, tile, or concrete, can add warm accents to any garden. In an informal space, try using railroad-tie risers for the vertical portion of concrete steps to create an attractive, functional design. Steps of railroad ties or rot-resistant lumber look especially nice in seaside yards. Tree stumps of various heights make intriguing banisters, and boards raised off the ground with pipe supports can give the visual effect of floating platforms.

Directing Traffic

To determine where to place steps and paths, begin by taking notes on who goes where—the kids rush to the shed for their toys, you go from house to driveway for the car, guests walk from the front

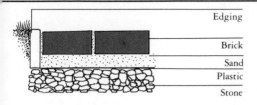

Edging

Brick

Sand

Plastic

Stone

gate to the front door. Obviously, you'll need paths or steps to get you to those spots. Then think of how you want visitors to move through your space. How quickly do you want them to go from one spot to another? Perhaps you have a large clump of azaleas, behind which a small dining nook is hidden. Weave your path around the shrubs for a surprise effect. Follow the course of the land and, where it curves, create a serpentine path. Sloping areas may need to be terraced, but keep in mind that moving earth takes large amounts of time and money. Steps, terraced decks, or waterfalls may be better ways to dress slopes.

Paving

You can cover the pathways and gathering areas of your garden with a variety of materials, from informal loose bark or woodchips spread over soil to more permanent installations of wood, brick, or concrete. Least expensive are organic products such as woodchips, sawdust, bark chunks, and shredded bark, which also make good mulches when spread around plants. For more formal spaces, inorganic materials such as gravel, rock, or crushed stone are perfect. Other materials include ceramic tile, slate, adobe, flagstone, and wood.

The type and design of paving that will best suit your garden depends on its style. The Japanese use gravel, fine stones, and moss to create artistic texture variations. These can be dramatic—white stone paths inlaid with black slate stepping-stones. Or they may be soft—gray pea gravel and crushed stone of muted hues placed near delicate green moss. You can use brick in many patterns; for example, circular designs create a widening effect. Remember that with rectangular stone and concrete as much interest comes from the joints as from the color and texture. Also take into account that dark-colored paving will absorb heat while light colors will reflect it. Plan ahead and think about what's best for you.

If you decide to use loose materials such as crushed stone or woodchips, keep them from scattering by digging up several inches of soil, adding gravel for drainage, and lining the edges of the area with brick or rot-resistant boards set edgewise. Cover the soil beneath your material with black sheet plastic or roofing felt to keep weeds from growing through. Punch holes in the sheet every foot or so to allow for water drainage.

Using Edgings

Pathways, patios, and planting beds are good ways to organize your space, and the best way to visually tie them together is by edging them. Edgings can help define space and proportion as well as contain soil and make mowing easier. While plants grow, change, and die, an edging's permanence supports and unifies your design. For pathways and patios coming up against a lawn, it's a good idea to include a mowing strip—a hard, flat surface level with the

Patios, Paths, Fences & Beds

Edgings both outline and unify the garden, anchoring it within a sturdy framework. There are many styles, ranging from soil-containing railroad ties to a border of irregular flagstone.

Vertical bricks

Angled bricks

Railroad ties

Two-by-six boards

Flagstones

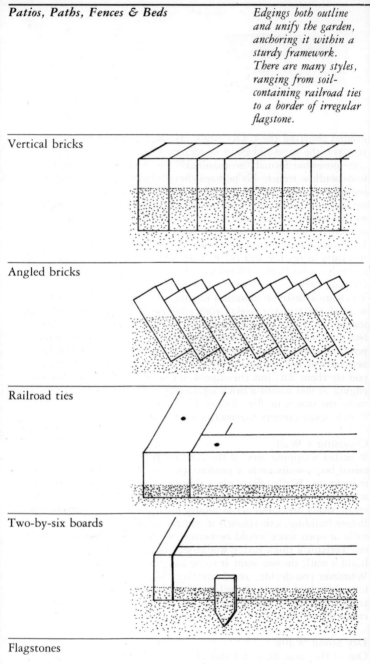

ground abutting the lawn's edge, one mower wheel wide. This will save you the time and effort of tedious hand trimming later.

The somewhat formal "no materials" edge—just a one- or two-inch-wide shallow trench—is perhaps the easiest edging, especially for separating concrete from lawn areas. You can make a more decorative edging with bricks angled and sunk halfway into the soil so that only the triangular tops are above ground. For more durability, set them in a mortar base.

Flagstone, railroad ties, and brick edgings lend interesting contrast to plants in texture and color. They seem to anchor the garden with a sturdy, solid frame. Plants such as dwarf box, which needs clipping only once or twice a year, can also be used as edging.

To create a basic no materials edging, use string and wooden stakes to mark the straight line of your edge; a garden hose or heavy rope will do nicely for curved edges. Use a square spade to cut about four inches into the soil. For a flat brick edge, make cuts wider and pour some loose sand into the trench. Tamp bricks down either vertically or flat, using the string as a guide. You'll use less brick if you lay them flat, but the edge won't be as stable. Lay a flagstone edging as you would a brick edge, adjusting the amount of sand to make the stones lie flat. Railroad ties can be laid in a sand-filled trench; spike corners together to keep them steady.

Choosing a Wall

Whether wrapping around the garden's perimeter or terracing off raised beds, walls unify a garden. They enclose a landscape, making it intimate. Walls offer a place to nurture young plants, storing warmth even after the sun goes down. They can also be used to create shady areas and act as windbreaks.

Before building, ask yourself if you really want a wall or whether a solid or open fence would be better. Will mere boundary markers do? Perhaps a thick hedge would serve your purposes. If you do build a wall, do you want it to be forbidding or inviting? Whatever you decide, avoid anything flimsy or unstable, and don't forget to check for local building codes that may affect height or contain restrictions on materials. Walls are usually made of stone, concrete, or brick.

Dry Stone Walls

One of the most beautiful and unusual options for the country or suburban garden is a dry stone wall—a wall held together by packed soil rather than mortar—because it can double as a sort of vertical, sheltered rock garden. Dry walls weather the elements better than mortared walls, which can split if water seeps in, freezes, and thaws. Building such a wall is something of an art, involving careful selection and arrangement of rocks with the right shapes. If you are interested, consult a contractor or do some further research.

Concrete Walls

In a small city garden concrete walls will ensure privacy and muffle sound. Decorative, prefabricated concrete blocks with open grillwork, or hollow-core concrete blocks turned sideways allow air to circulate. The blocks may be textured or sculpted and can be painted, stuccoed, or covered with climbing vines. Poured or broken concrete may also be used, smoothed or left rough for interesting contrasts.

Building a High Brick Wall

A very versatile building material, brick can be used to construct low, solid retaining walls or higher walls for privacy. Screening walls should be at least six feet high, but a solid wall of that size can be monotonous, even if the pattern is broken by vines or bricks of interesting texture. Be advised that building a safe, solid brick wall over two feet in height calls for a professional.

To add interest, you can build brick walls in a zig-zag pattern to resemble the edges of pinking shears, or set them ragged, stepped in and out. There are also various patterns to create in open brickwork, with the spaces between bricks forming squares, rectangles, or crosses.

In your attempt to relieve the monotony of a solid wall, avoid going to the other extreme of using too many materials in one expanse. This will cause confusion, detracting from the garden itself. For the best effect, make the color, pattern, and texture of a wall compatible with its surroundings. For example, if you live in a brick townhouse, try a patterned brick wall broken by concrete piers.

Building a Low Brick Wall

You can erect a low brick retaining or decorative wall with little difficulty. First, sight the boundaries with stakes and string. Avoid areas near large trees, as their roots may damage the wall's foundation. Also be careful not to encroach on adjacent properties. Once you've staked out the lines, dig a foundation ditch twice the width of the wall, planting vertical rods for reinforcement. Any wall over two feet high should be about eight to twelve inches thick. Poured concrete is necessary for the foundation's footing, except if the wall is less than twelve inches high. Such low walls can be laid in mortar on a poured concrete base, or on six to eight inches of sand. Concrete footings for higher walls should be twice the wall's width and extend below the frost line.

Start building by placing one layer of bricks along the foundation as a test. Check to see that it is flat and level, and that the pieces are properly aligned. Then remove the bricks and spray them and the foundation with water. Replace the bricks, set them with good, smooth mortar, and check again that they are level. Build from the corners first and step down to the center.

Use small amounts of mortar with each layer, placing it between small ends of bricks as well as on their surfaces. Tap each brick level and scrape off excess mortar. When the wall is completed, hose it down and keep it moist until the mortar is cured.

Using Fences

If you have a large area to enclose, a fence is a good idea. It will function in the same way as a wall—screening off unsightly areas, reducing wind and noise, forming warm, sunny pockets, and acting as a foil for flowers, shrubs, and vines—but more economically. Fences can also be used to distort perspective, making an area look larger or smaller. For example, a fence of stepped wooden slats that are higher near the house and lower farther away will make the space appear longer.

You can choose among many types of fencing material, ranging from chain link, wire mesh, and cast- or wrought-iron, to bamboo and various kinds of wood. Chain link is not the most attractive option, but if it's already in place you can camouflage it with a thick, fast-growing vine such as Virginia creeper or Boston ivy. Again, think about your motives—do you want something inviting or forbidding? Low wrought- or cast-iron fences are costly, but their open bars allow air and light through, and they are pleasing to passersby. They can also be attractively styled with quadrefoils and corkscrew patterns, elegant references to another time.

Styles in Wooden Fences

Wood is an excellent fence material, whether you use it to build a low picket fence or a six-foot, or taller, solid fence for privacy. You can buy wooden fencing in prefabricated sections, but it may be less costly to design and build to your own needs.

First decide on one of the many styles. The familiar colonial-type picket fence is usually under five feet high and can create various effects, depending on the height and spacing of the posts. Use rail fences to form low, horizontal boundary markers. For a greater sense of enclosure and privacy, try grape-stake fences or the more formal redwood or cedar-slat fences as tall dividers. Post-and-board fences, such as the basket weave, in which thin boards are bent around vertical or horizontal spacers; board-and-board designs; and fences with horizontally or vertically angled slats are among the easiest to construct.

Installing Posts and Rails

Constructing a stable and aligned framework of posts and rails is the most important step in building any fence. Once this is done properly, the rest is easy. Most people use vertical four-by-fours as posts and connect them near the top and bottom with horizontal boards, or rails. These tie the fence together and support the weight of any siding you choose.

Patios, Paths, Fences & Beds

Five popular wooden fence styles are shown below. Picket and post-and-rail are most often used to mark a boundary, the taller grape stake and basket weave to screen a view.

Picket

Post-and-rail

Grape stake

Basket weave

Post-and-board

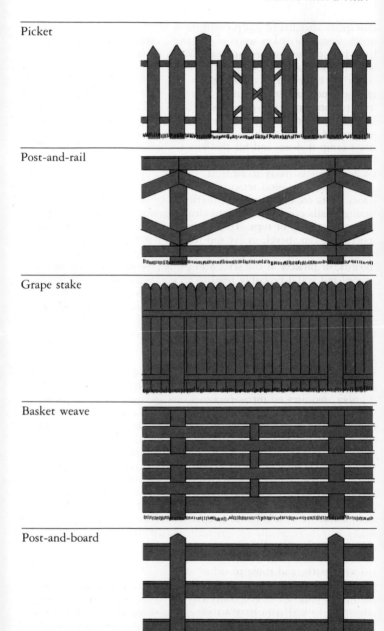

Use posts that have been pressure-treated with preservative or are made from the darker wood of the tree's core, known as heartwood. It is best to use a rot-resistant species such as cedar. For stability, sink posts into the ground so that at least one-third of their total length is buried. You can set them without concrete where soil is well-drained and stable, and if there's no fear of heavy frost. Place two to three inches of gravel or a flat stone in the bottom of each hole for proper drainage. Then lower the post in and check that it is level. Add two to three more inches of gravel around the post, then tamp it down and fill the hole with soil, creating a small mound around the post base.

Where there is likely to be frost, bury the posts very deep—at least to the frost line—and set corner posts in concrete.

Once posts are evenly placed, mark rail positions with tape or string. Rails can be nailed into cleats between posts or lapped across post sides or tops. To prevent moisture from soaking into post tops, cap, bevel, or lay top rails across them.

With this framework in place, you are ready to nail on slats, boards, or pickets in the style you choose. Once your fence is completed you'll probably need to treat it with water repellent before staining, bleaching, or priming. Be sure to read the manufacturer's directions before applying anything to the wood surface.

Building a Board-and-Board Fence

In a board-and-board style fence, boards are nailed alternately on opposite sides of a simple, horizontal wooden frame, providing both security and ventilation. Such a fence is built with relatively little lumber, requires no intricate joints, and is attractive from both sides. Before building, consult with your neighbors on acceptable fence materials and check local building regulations. Get a permit if necessary.

Plot your course by staking end and corner posts and tying string around the perimeter. Drive stakes along the twine about four to eight feet apart, closer together for heavier woods that need more support. If you have a large tree in the fence line, stop the fence on either side of the trunk—do not use the trunk as a post. Slashing into a tree with nails leaves it open to infection.

Structures for Small Spaces

Most American homeowners have only one-third to one acre of land to work with, and those in urban areas have considerably less. Small spaces pose a challenge to the gardener, calling for restraint and good judgment. Too many elements will give your space a cluttered look. If you have a rooftop or walled garden, raised beds and containers may be your best design bet. Raised beds are easy to maintain and adaptable to any type of surface and can be permanent or temporary. Containers are versatile design elements, adding dimension and visual interest to small areas, and can be arranged and rearranged fairly quickly.

Remember that everything in a small space vies for the eye's attention, so you need to create focus areas. Think in terms of proportion. If you have one lovely, large terra-cotta vase, allow it its glory and subordinate other ornaments to its color and scale. To many people, terra-cotta pots—even the smallest, plainest ones—represent purity in function and design.

Building Raised Beds

Raised planting beds are not difficult to create and have a number of advantages over flat beds. Raised beds drain better, are small enough that you can reach across to work in them without compacting the soil, and warm up faster in the spring than ground-level beds. They can be constructed on nearly any surface, and you can fill them with special soil mixes to accommodate almost any plant.

The simplest raised beds consist of four to eight inches of soil with no sides at all. Such beds may be shaped into low walls, or berms, one to three feet high, with sitting space around the perimeter. Berms create strong patterns and walkways and raise plants closer to eye level, where they can also be easily tended. Add intriguing contours by curving them to break up the boxy feeling of a small courtyard or backyard.

You may prefer to contain a raised bed within a frame of wood or rocks. One simple style involves using two-by-eight or two-by-ten boards of rot-resistant or pretreated lumber. Set them on edge about one or two inches into the ground. Nail them together at the corners and hold them in place with one-by-four or two-by-four stakes. Railroad ties can also be used, perhaps arranged in tiers to heighten the bed. Lay the ties around the bed's perimeter, connecting inside corners with galvanized angle irons. Or drill holes through them and spike them with an iron pipe.

You may want to use brick or stone for your raised bed perimeter. Do this on your own only if it's to be one or two feet high. For higher beds you must call in a professional. Whatever materials you decide to use, check local codes for restrictions and make sure that the surface you've chosen is structurally sound enough to hold your work. Some raised beds may be too heavy for rooftops, for example.

Ornamental Features

The list of decorative garden elements is nearly endless. Most obvious are the larger features, but smaller structures such as trellises, arbors, gazebos, furniture, and statuary add important accents. Their appropriateness is often easier to assess after the heavier groundwork is in place. Many times it's not until you get a clear sense of the total composition by planning larger structures that you can blend in smaller accents.

Freestanding trellises and arbors can be used as transition features from one area of the garden to the next. Covered with wisteria, climbing hydrangea, or grapevines, they become attractive focal points. Even in winter their stark skeletal tracery is dramatic against the snow. They can also be used as frames for distant views.

Trellises

A trellis is easy to design and build yourself. It is useful to screen unsightly views and can break up the monotony of a brick wall effectively while supporting climbing plants. Two-by-fours or two-by-sixes make the sturdiest frames; match the sturdiness to the type of vine. Build the frame on the ground and then set up the completed piece.

Construct a frame with two-by-four posts, using lapjoints and screws to connect them. Put an upright post every eight to ten feet, and leave two feet of post at the bottom to go into the ground. Use 1⅛-inch cross-pieces in patterns such as a criss-crossing lattice, basket weave, or varied geometric shapes.

Consider using round dowels for an unusual effect. Always use either treated wood or a rot-resistant species. Paint your trellis and place it against a wall, or allow it to stand alone, supporting it with braces after sinking the posts.

Using Statuary

While the latticework or plant-covered arch of an arbor can serve as a focal point or dramatically frame a vista, you can arrange statues and planters to achieve the same effects.

Think about what you want someone to focus on when he steps onto your patio or deck. Is there an existing view you wish to highlight, or do you need to create a point of interest? If you set two statues or planters at opposite sides of the top step leading out to the garden, what do they frame? A sundial or birdbath perhaps, or an old wagon wheel propped against a wall, or a more distant mountain view. Just as paths lead visitors' feet to discover the complexity of your garden, strategically placed statuary can lead roving eyes to its individual accents.

A Flexible Framework

It would be ideal if you could imagine the overall plan for your garden from the very start. But you may well find that it is easier to design incrementally, missing some opportunities and creating new ones. Structures can help organize your space while forming a framework to support and tie together various areas and plantings. Many, despite their apparent solidity, can be rearranged if your needs or desires change. This is the beauty of forming a garden. It's an opportunity to grow with your landscape, making it your own.

Garden Basics

Barbara McEwan

Every gardener, novice or expert, dreams of the perfectly designed garden—well-proportioned, interesting year-round, and bountiful in its harvest. The essays in this volume will provide you with many good ideas, accompanied by plans that show you how to integrate plants and structures into existing environments and plans that impose their own mood on the setting. But remember, even the best designed landscape will not be effective if the plants are not healthy and well tended, and this requires advance planning as well as continued care.

Evaluating Your Property

Whether you are starting your garden from a bulldozed lot or changing the landscaping of an established yard, your gardening success will be much greater if you understand and work with your existing conditions. Extensive chats with neighbors and your local nurseryman will yield invaluable information. They will be able to tell you what does, and does not, grow in your particular area, and you can learn from their mistakes. With proper planning, you can create a congenial environment for those plants you wish to grow.

Hardiness Zones

One of the first things to determine before planning any garden is which plants will survive in your climate. The ability of plants to survive harsh conditions is known as their hardiness. Although hardiness is affected by other conditions like soil and water, temperature is the most important factor.

The Department of Agriculture has devised a map dividing the U.S. and Canada into ten zones based on average minimum temperatures. (See page 46.) These zones are numbered from north to south. Most planting guides assign plants zone numbers to indicate the region or regions in which they can be expected to survive. For example, if the plant you want in your garden is labeled as hardy to zone 6, it can be expected to thrive in gardens in zones 6 and southward. If you plant it in more northerly zones— say zone 4 or 5—it will probably die in a severe winter.

The map is based on lowest temperatures, but extreme heat is as dangerous to some plants as cold. Certain northern plants will not live long on the warm coastal plain of the eastern United States. To alert you to this danger, some information on hardiness involves a range of zones—for example, "zones 5 to 9." This tells you not only how far north a plant may be grown, but also how far south. Be careful to choose plants that are hardy in your zone.

Before making final choices of woody or perennial plants based on zone information, call your county Cooperative Extension Service to learn the lowest temperatures for your area. This information may contradict the map, as within each zone conditions can fluctuate because of variations in elevation. Protected or exposed pockets on your own property may be more favorable to some plants than other areas. Rely on the county agent's word as the most accurate for your locale. Also ask for the dates of the last spring and first fall frosts in your area—crucial guides to planting annuals and harvesting vegetables. Seed packets and planting instructions usually specify when to plant in relation to these dates.

Soil Types

All soils consist of particles of weathered rock mixed with organic matter. The heavier the soil, the smaller and tighter its components, so that small roots, water, and air have difficulty penetrating. The size of the inorganic particles determines a soil's type. If they are very small, the resulting heavy soil is called clay. Very large particles create coarse, sandy soils through which water drains quickly. A well-balanced loam contains medium-sized particles mixed with abundant organic matter.

To find out what type of soil you have, dig a hole a foot deep wherever you propose to have a garden and work the moist soil around in your hand. A sandy soil will run through your fingers, a clay soil will clump, and a loam soil, the best, will crumble easily. If your soil doesn't crumble, you must add organic matter before planting.

The importance of organic matter in garden soil cannot be overstated. It holds water and nutrients while allowing air to get to plant roots. You can add it in the form of peat moss, humus, rotted leaves, or composted garden wastes. Avoid using very fine material however, because it will decompose too rapidly.

If there is sufficient organic material in your soil, earthworms will thrive. Their castings are much richer in minerals than the soil they ingest, so they help create topsoil and increase fertility. They are also nature's rototillers, burrowing to six feet and thereby aerating and loosening the soil for easy root penetration. Many other animals, mostly microscopic, feed on organic matter and help build healthy soil.

Assessing Your Soil

Before planting, determine the properties of your soil and amend it if necessary. First, check the soil's pH level—its degree of acidity or alkalinity. Levels are measured on a scale of 0 to 14, with 7 being neutral, lower numbers indicating an increasingly acid soil, and higher ones increasingly alkaline. A neutral soil is preferred by most plants. Non-neutral soils are less likely to release nutrients, so correcting the pH may effectively solve some nutrient problems. Acid soils are common in the East; alkaline soils are often found in the West. Excessively acid soils can be treated by incorporating lime into them.

To grow acid-loving plants such as some evergreens or blueberries in alkaline or neutral soils, treat them with aluminum sulphate, a heavy mulch of pine needles or oak leaves, specifically designated

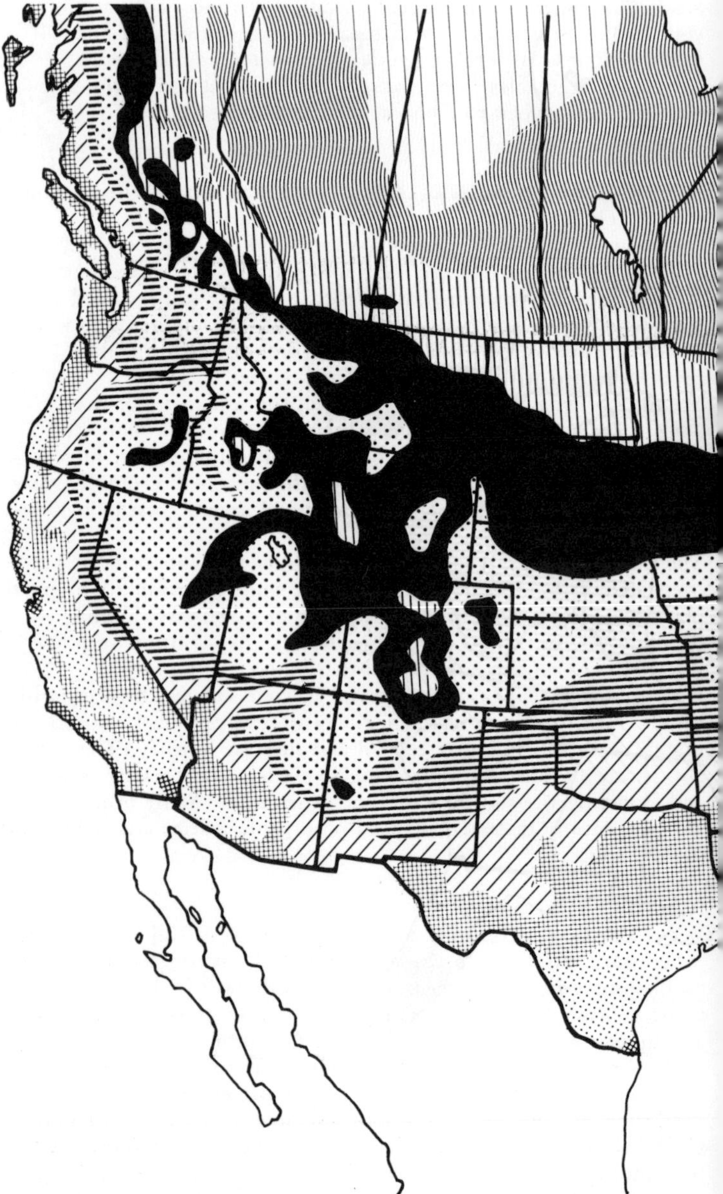

This map was compiled by the United States Department of Agriculture as a broad guideline to temperature extremes in your area.

The key below gives you the average minimum temperatures of the ten zones.

Determine if your area corresponds to its zone allocation by comparing your coldest temperatures with those given in the key.

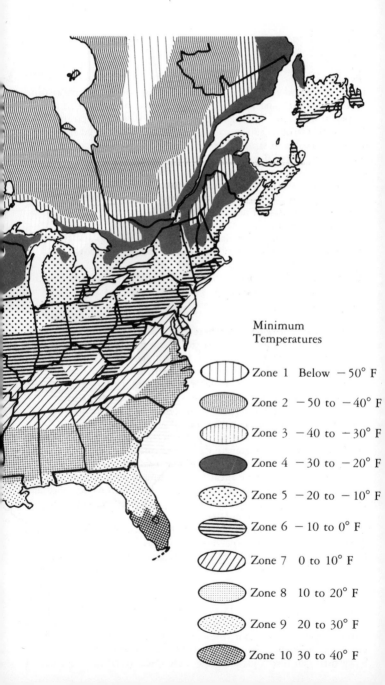

Minimum Temperatures

Zone 1 Below −50° F

Zone 2 −50 to −40° F

Zone 3 −40 to −30° F

Zone 4 −30 to −20° F

Zone 5 −20 to −10° F

Zone 6 −10 to 0° F

Zone 7 0 to 10° F

Zone 8 10 to 20° F

Zone 9 20 to 30° F

Zone 10 30 to 40° F

fertilizers, or a combination of these. Organic matter will help neutralize both acid and alkaline soils.

Nutrients

Three major soil nutrients—nitrogen, phosphorus, and potassium—are essential for good plant growth and must be present in the proper proportions. Nitrogen is closely allied with green leaf color. Too much nitrogen causes excessive foliage and delayed flowering; too little results in stunted growth, retarded development of leaves and flowers, fewer flowers, and premature leaf drop.

Phosphorus is necessary for vigorous root development. Important in promoting sturdy stems and hastening maturity, it encourages flower and fruit production and enhances vegetable yields. Too little phosphorus generally causes leaves to become a dull bluish green with tints of purple.

Potassium (potash) is also needed for general good plant growth. Deficiencies cause stunted plants, poorly developed roots, and spotted or disfigured leaves.

Plants also need so-called trace elements, most commonly calcium, magnesium, boron, manganese, sulphur, iron, and zinc. These are available through commercial fertilizers.

Organic and Inorganic Fertilizers

Imbalances or deficiencies in nutrients can be corrected by the proper use of fertilizer. There are two kinds of fertilizers: organic, or naturally occuring, and inorganic, or man-made. Although organic nutrients become available to roots more slowly than those from inorganic sources, they are less apt to burn plants or leach from the soil. Organic fertilizers also help build soil, keeping its pH neutral and encouraging beneficial animal life.

By judiciously mixing several organic fertilizers such as cottonseed meal, bone meal, and granite dust, you can easily create a formula to meet your particular needs. The first two are good organic sources of nitrogen; bone meal and phosphate rock supply soil with phosphorus. Supplement potassium-poor soil with wood ashes and granite dust. Manure is an effective organic fertilizer containing low levels of all three major nutrients.

Chemical, or inorganic, fertilizers generally work faster than organic nutrients. They provide specified amounts of each major element, with the percentages indicated numerically. For example, a package marked 5-10-5 contains 5 percent nitrogen, 10 percent phosphorus, and 5 percent potassium. The remaining 80 percent is made up of inert materials.

Chemical fertilizers come in two forms: granular types, which are spread on the ground, and liquid forms, which are mixed with the water supply. Be sure not to exceed the recommended amounts given on the container—too much fertilizer can burn your plants. Since nitrogen forces growth, use a chemical fertilizer high in nitrogen in spring to help plants form new shoots. Concentrations of phosphorus help harden plants for winter, so make sure fertilizer applied after midsummer is low in nitrogen and high in phosphorus.

Rain, Sun, and Shade

Part of your site evaluation will be to note the amounts of rainfall and sunshine in various areas. If you have dry conditions, you should choose plants that are adapted to arid environments. In wet areas try to improve drainage, or plant moisture-tolerant varieties.

Assess the light available at the site at different times of the day and in various seasons. How many hours of sun does it receive? Is it mainly morning or afternoon sun? Is it direct or filtered by trees? Watch the proposed site for a few days, considering the movement of shadows and how you might provide more or less shade by adding plants or pruning existing ones. Except for sun-loving vegetables, a multitude of plants enjoy both sun and shade.

Taking into account the soil type, climate, and other physical qualities of your site limits your choices, but in a sensible way. You'll find that there are many plants that will thrive in your conditions, and you'll be reasonably assured of success. This preliminary research—along with reading and seeking out tips from other gardeners in your area—is well worth the extra time it takes.

When to Plant

After the nursery catalogues arrive in midwinter, ablaze with colorful flowers, the typical gardener waits impatiently for clement weather to begin planting. For annuals this is sensible, as frost would kill most of them, but trees, shrubs, and perennials are another matter. Many need time to establish their root systems before expending energy on new leaves. For many, fall is the right planting time, when the soil is still warm even if air temperatures are not, allowing the roots to thoroughly readjust before spring's demands. Of course, all plants should begin winter well watered and mulched.

In very cold climates, plant trees in early spring because planting in fall might cause any roots that are not well secured to heave out of the ground during late winter, when the soil alternatingly freezes and thaws. The same logic applies to most newly planted shrubs and perennials in cold climates. In the South, where summer heat is often more lethal than winter cold, fall planting is usually better.

Planting times for annuals and perennials vary with their bloom times. Perennial flowers and herbs that have not been dug out of local fields in early spring should be hardened-off, or gradually acclimated to the outdoors out of direct sun and wind, for a week

Garden Basics

to ten days. Plant them when your trees begin to leaf out. Many perennials, vegetables, and herbs can be started indoors from seed and transplanted outside when the weather settles. Seed packets provide full instructions. Plant bulbs in spring or fall, depending on the species.

Preparing to Plant

Ideally, you should prepare beds a year before planting. To break up the ground initially, hire someone to do the job, buy or rent a tilling machine, or dig your bed by hand with a spade. First cut down the existing vegetation, taking care to remove perennial weed roots completely or they will resprout. Then dig across the width of your plot, turning soil over to the depth of your spade's blade—about 18 to 20 inches. Unless your soil is crumbly to that depth, amend it with compost, leaves, or peat moss as you refill. Place a sprinkler on the bed for a few hours to settle the soil; then rake the ground.

Another method is to cover the stubble of existing vegetation with black plastic or other material to deprive it of light, killing both the above-ground portion and the roots. Do this in fall in preparation for digging in spring.

For the first year or two after making a new bed, amend the soil in each new hole or trench you dig. Most plants will do reasonably well provided you add enough organic matter in the immediate root zone. Try to avoid stepping on the soil and compacting it, perhaps by using raised beds with walkways, or stepping stones.

Raised Beds and Containers

In excessively sandy or clay soils, consider using raised beds with sides of stones or of pressure treated, rot-resistant boards held in place by stakes or timbers. Filled with good quality loam, such beds solve many gardening headaches—providing better soil than you may have in your garden, minimizing drainage problems, and allowing for an earlier planting season. Beds should be no more than four feet wide so you can reach across them to care for the plants.

Consider planting in containers as another way to control soil conditions. Use them in a variety of ways: as hanging baskets, as window boxes, or as planters placed in strategic spots on a porch, deck, or walkway. Cover drainage holes with a layer of pebbles and fill pots with garden soil modified with peat moss or vermiculite so it will not dry out easily. After several years, plants may become root-bound and need repotting or root-pruning. Water container plants thoroughly and often, watching the root zone for dryness in summer and freezing in winter.

Planting Trees and Shrubs

The first plants to plan for in your landscape, trees and shrubs must be carefully placed so that they have room to mature without overwhelming other plantings or structures. In size alone, they will dominate your composition—healthy ones will become focal points, failing ones hazardous eyesores.

Before ordering trees and shrubs, evaluate your soil and add any necessary organic matter such as peat moss or compost. Be aware, though, that soil amendments are ineffectual for large-growing tree species, and that you can only expect success with trees that tolerate your existing soil conditions.

Keep in mind that water travels horizontally as well as vertically, and a hole dug in clay will act like a bucket, drowning your tree or shrub. You can avoid this by digging an extra wide, extra deep hole with straight, rough-surfaced sides. Putting a layer of coarse stone a foot deep at the bottom will improve drainage.

Balled and Burlapped Plants

Some trees and shrubs are sold in a form called balled and burlapped. The plants are dug out of their growing medium so that a ball of soil surrounds the roots. This root ball is then wrapped in burlap or other material and tied for transporting. Stress on the plant is minimized because its roots remain covered with the original soil. A disadvantage is that the soil ball is extremely heavy—you may need one or more helpers to move a large plant. Set balled and burlapped plants into the ground in the late fall or early spring when they are dormant.

Plant balled and burlapped trees and shrubs in holes of generous breadth and depth—roots need ample room to expand during the first weeks of growth. Follow the grower's directions for planting, placing the shrub or tree in the hole burlap and all, positioning its crown at soil level, slightly higher in heavy soils. Partially back-fill the hole, cut the ropes tying the root ball, and pull the burlap away from the top, working it down along the sides.

If the rope and covering materials are not real burlap and hemp but some form of plastic or polymer, leave as little of them around the root ball as possible. They will not decompose and can eventually strangle the roots. Natural materials will rot, but do not leave burlap exposed above the soil, as it will act as a wick, drawing water away from the roots. Pruning is seldom necessary if stock is dormant and bought from a reputable nursery. Timed-release fertilizers are the only kind to put inside a hole, and there is some dispute whether even these are necessary.

Bare-Rooted Plants

More care must be taken with bare-root stock, which should also be planted only when dormant—in late fall or very early spring. This method of transplanting is the most traumatic, so plants need special care for a longer period of time than those sold in other forms. Dig ample holes before delivery is expected, returning the

Garden Basics   Place a balled and burlapped plant in the hole with burlap still attached.   Partially fill the hole, cut ropes, and push burlap down into the hole. If wrapping is not biodegradable, remove it before planting.

Handle bare-rooted plants with care, and keep the roots wet until planting.

Prune branches to compensate for root damage. Stake to prevent toppling by winds.

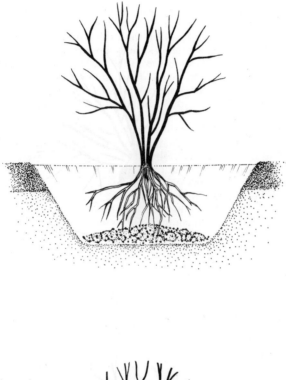

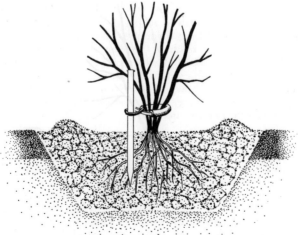

soil to the hole and covering it with a plastic bag. Be prepared to modify the hole's dimensions at planting time.

Never let bare roots dry out. Fill a wash tub with water, then prune off any damaged or proportionately long roots. Plunge the plant's roots into the tub so that even the finest ones are covered, and let them soak for a few hours. Take the tub to the hole, and lift the plant out carefully to see how it fits. You may need to modify the size of the hole. Return the plant to the tub until you're ready to plant.

A helper holding the tree or shrub makes the job of planting much easier. Insert the plant into the hole with its crown at soil level or a bit higher in heavy soils, as fresh soil often settles too deeply after planting. Gradually fill around the roots with crumbly soil, making sure to leave no air pockets, which would dry out the roots. Work your fingers around, pushing soil into every nook and cranny. When the hole is half full, lightly tamp the soil and pour in a half pail of water. Add the remaining soil, creating a ring of mounded soil around the plant to funnel water to its roots. Do not fertilize. Be sure to follow any specific instructions offered by your nurseryman or the mail-order nursery.

The bare-root stock you ordered may have been pruned by the nursery to compensate for roots lost in digging it out of the growing bed. If not, you need to prune after planting by removing a third to half of each branch; the length will depend on how you want to shape the plant. A common mistake is to prune too little, to the detriment of the plant. If you have planted in fall, wait until early spring to do this pruning.

Bare-rooted plants, especially large ones, need staking after planting because they have no root ball to anchor them. In general, you can tell that a plant needs staking if you see empty space around its stem at the soil line—the result of the plant whipping about in the wind. Drive a wooden stake into the ground close to the stem and on the side of the prevailing winds. Fasten the main stem securely to the stake with raffia or heavy twine. Using soft twine wire enclosed inside a piece of hose, tie trees at two spots. All trees should be staked for two to three years.

Container-Grown Plants

Many smaller plants—shrubs, perennials, and bulbs—are sold in the same metal or plastic containers in which they were grown by the nursery. They are easy to carry, so move them around to see how different arrangements would look before digging in. To plant, dig a hole with a trowel or spade, and carefully tap the container to release the root ball—or cut the container away. Cut back any long, circling roots and place the root ball in the hole, filling any air spaces with garden soil. Always place the crown at the same level as the surrounding ground. Water well, unless the ground is already damp, directing a slow stream to the root zone.

*Container-grown plants
may be pot-bound.
Check for girdling roots
and cut them off close
to the crown. Pry long
roots out of the root
ball and direct them
into the new soil.*

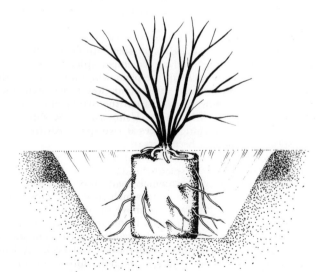

Garden Basics

Planting Seeds

Seed packets give detailed information on when to plant and how far apart and deep to make your hole or rows. These figures vary by species and even by season. For example, instructions may tell you to plant seeds deeper as temperatures get warmer, or to start some seeds indoors. For an earlier display, germinate annual flowers such as marigolds indoors under fluorescent lights or on a window sill. This way you will have seedlings to plant as soon as the weather warms. Perennial seeds can also be started inside. Closely monitor the dampness of the soil until they reach transplant size.

Propagation

If you are trying to fill a bare lot, you will want to purchase well-established trees and shrubs for your garden. Propagation—producing new plants from those you have—is best left to the expert with special equipment. There are a few exceptions, such as willows and forsythia, which are easily rooted in moist soil by planting a twelve- to eighteen-inch stem cutting directly in the ground. Some shrubs, such as azaleas, can be rooted by layering—taking a lower branch of an established plant and pinning the center of it under a shallow layer of soil.

Annual vegetables, flowers, and herbs are propagated from seeds, and most perennial flowers and herbs are increased in one of three ways—by seed, cuttings, or division. If you are interested in propagating your own plants, do some research into the best methods.

Transplanting

Every gardener is eventually faced with rearranging his or her handiwork by transplanting. Although it is not difficult, transplanting does require a certain amount of skill. The most important consideration is water—transplants should never dry out, either while you are moving them or after they are planted.

It is best to transplant in early fall, after the summer heat is past and autumn rains are beginning, or in early spring. Generally speaking, spring planting is better in areas of cold winters; fall planting is preferable farther south. In the warmest areas of the South and West, you may transplant throughout the winter if no freezes occur. Never transplant a tree or shrub more than once during a twelve-month period.

Basic Maintenance

All the best planning and careful planting can be negated without the proper follow-up. A few simple maintenance tasks can make all the difference in achieving an attractive, healthy garden.

Mulching

One of the most important things you can do for any plant once it is in the ground is to provide a mulch—four inches deep for woody species, less for non-woody ones. Mulch discourages competition from weeds, maintains soil moisture except under the driest conditions, and insulates against excessive heat and cold. Mulch breaks down slowly over time, releasing nutrients necessary to good soil structure and minimizing nutrient leaching. It will also help discourage insect and disease outbreaks.

For mulching vegetables, use straw or spoiled hay. Some people tear bales apart and fluff the pieces into loose masses, or you can section the bale into mats four to six inches wide. Pulled weeds, pea pods, and other plant refuse otherwise bound for the compost pile are easily tucked under these mats and will quickly decompose. Meanwhile the mats have the added bonus of giving your garden a tidy appearance.

Protect vegetable gardens in winter with a mulch several inches deep to prevent wind and water erosion and unnecessary soil leaching, and to add humus. Some perennial flowers should also be covered during winter. Use evergreen boughs or old Christmas trees. Chopped fallen leaves, dried grass clippings, and compost can also be used as mulch.

To lend a more formal tone to flower beds, use a one-half- to two-inch-thick layer of bark mulch, chopped tree leaves, or the hulls of cocoa beans, rice, buckwheat, or cottonseed. Mulch ornamental trees and shrubs with pine or redwood bark nuggets, but take care to keep mulch away from the trunks, where it could cause rotting or foster diseases. Woody shrubs with shallow root systems, such as azaleas and hollies, need extra mulch.

Check garden centers for other sources of mulching materials. There are many decorative possibilities to complement your garden's style, but be sure they are also practical and effective.

Watering

If you've chosen plants suited to your conditions, normal rainfall should be sufficient to keep them watered, but it may be necessary to supplement this during dry spells. Water can do more harm than good to a garden unless it uniformly penetrates the soil at least an inch, preferably two. Get water to the root zone of larger plants by soaking them individually. Overhead oscillating or pulse lawn sprinklers waste a great deal of water because of evaporation. A drip irrigation system, available in kits from major mail-order catalogues, can be more useful. Some are designed for row crops, others for individual plants, and they can be installed permanently or for seasonal use.

Pruning

There are many reasons to prune trees and shrubs: for better shape, to induce new growth, to counteract the shock of transplanting, to keep a plant in scale, or to remove weak or competing limbs. And

Garden Basics

To transplant, make a continuous cut 10–12 inches from the stem and 10–12 inches deep. Make sure all roots are severed.

Using a spade as a lever, lift the plant carefully out of the soil. Carry or drag it on a tarpaulin to the new hole.

*Place at the same
depth as the plant
grew in the original
hole.*

*Prune off about
one-third of the top
growth to compensate
for severed roots and to
encourage new growth.*

Garden Basics

Remove competing leaders as they develop.

A spacer board improves an acutely angled branch.

Weights also improve the angles of upright limbs. For most trees, 45° above horizontal is ideal.

After 3 years of heading back, these are the last temporary branches to remain.

Props increase the angle of a sagging limb.

Early training and proper pruning will add greatly to a tree's beauty and longevity. Upon planting, remove only broken, crossing, or competing branches.

Year by year, head back the lowest branches and remove weak and poorly placed ones to form a spirally tiered pattern.

there are several techniques to use, depending on your purpose and the type of plant. Pruning is commonly done during the dormant season, but most spring-flowering trees and shrubs should be pruned just after blooming. Although pruning is not difficult, it must be done correctly or serious damage can result. Take time to find out exactly how and when to prune the particular plants you've chosen, and hire knowledgeable experts to prune mature trees. Pinching, or pruning the tip of a plant or its shoots, is done to perennials during the growing season to control height or to make a plant bushier. You may also need to pinch off dead blooms so that more or bigger flowers will appear. Try to control weeds by hand or hoe to avoid using herbicides that can find their way into our water supply.

Fall Cleanup
In the autumn, before the first killing frost, clean flower beds of all dead foliage to reduce disease and eliminate areas where insects can overwinter. Don't cut back ornamental grasses though; they will be beautiful for most of the winter. Add leaves and clippings to the compost pile and continue mowing and watering the lawn as long as it shows growth. Before the ground freezes, thoroughly water woody evergreens. Evergreens, especially those newly planted and in windy sites, will also benefit from an anti-desiccant spray.

Preventive Maintenance
Much garden maintenance can be avoided by careful planning. Where possible, use disease- and pest-resistant varieties. Providing optimal growing conditions, including a good mulch, will also discourage health problems. If you do see signs of pests or diseases, check plant guides or the nursery for information on the best way to control them. Burn or bag and discard any plant parts that are diseased or bear insect eggs or feeding larvae.

Keeping Track
There is no substitute for a written record of what you've done in the garden. Keep a journal to list names of seeds or plants and where you bought them, the dates of planting, and the results. Each year these records will become more valuable.
Whatever design style you have settled upon, the time spent in carefully assessing your soil, understanding your microclimates, and properly planting and transplanting will almost guarantee your garden's success. A healthy, well-planned garden will teach you a new gardener's credo—imitate nature and receive the sincerest form of flattery.

Buying Plants

Once you know what style garden you desire, have researched which plants will grow in your area, and have listed good possibilities, you're ready to buy. It may all seem very straightforward from here, but there are still some things you should know. First, you may well be bewildered by the variety of outlets where you can purchase plants. Then, once you decide on where to go, you may find the plant matching the name on your list bears little resemblance to the prototype in your neighbor's yard. In both cases you need to understand the language of gardening before filling your order.

Scientific and Common Names

Every known plant has one scientific name consisting of at least two parts. For example, *Acer saccharum* is what you may know as the sugar maple. *Acer,* the genus name, groups this tree with all other maples. *Saccharum,* the species name, distinguishes it as a particular type—the sugar maple.

This system of nomenclature, developed in the 18th century by the Swedish naturalist Carolus Linnaeus, provides a standard name for each plant that is accepted worldwide. It clears up confusion not only among speakers of different languages but also among gardeners who may use different names in one language for the same plant. Such common names—like "sugar maple"—are more recognizable and evocative than scientific names, and they can often be used without creating confusion. But to communicate clearly when ordering or asking advice about plants, learn and use the correct scientific names.

Varieties

Sometimes the scientific name of a plant consists of more than genus and species names. Species may also be subdivided into varieties. These are naturally occurring variants of a species, usually with an origin in a different geographical region than the typical species plant. For example, *Allium cyathophorum* var. *farreri* grows wild in Kansu Province of China, while the typical *Allium cyathophorum* is found in central Asia. Some references omit the abbreviation "var.," to create a three-part name: *Allium cyathophorum farreri.*

Cultivars

Bred with the intention of enhancing or minimizing certain inherited traits—color, fragrance, hardiness, size, or habit of growth—the selected plants or groups of plants developed under cultivation are known as cultivars. They are commonly but incorrectly called varieties. The name of a cultivar is added to the end of the scientific name, set off by single quotation marks. For example, *Acer palmatum* 'Dissectum' is a cultivar of the Japanese maple, *Acer palmatum.* It was developed for its deeply cut, fern-like leaves. Cultivars are preserved through vegetative propagation and, in some cases, may be an inbred line of plants that now invariably reproduce from seed.

Hybrids

Seed companies and nurseries are obliged to come up with new selections every year to excite the imaginations of gardeners. The emphasis is on desirable qualities—disease resistance, dwarfness, and new types of fruits and vegetables that freeze or can better than older ones. One way to accomplish this is through hybrids. The offspring of two plants of different species, hybrids are more vigorous than either parent.

This does not mean older types are bad or the new selections better; they may merely be a different color. But sometimes a truly new and useful plant—such as the hybrid poplar tree—comes onto the market. Mail-order nursery catalogues are good textbooks, but remember to choose plants based on your particular conditions.

Sources of Plants

At local garden centers or nurseries you can see a selection of plants and choose a specific one for its height, habit, flowers, or other characteristics. At nurseries the plants have been out of the ground only briefly so that transplant shock is minimal: They are usually larger than those you would receive from a mail-order nursery. The varieties offered will be those hardy to and proven successful in your area. Best of all, the personnel know the plants and your area and can give you detailed cultural information.

Make sure the plants you choose look vigorous and healthy, with no dead stems. They should have green leaves free of brown patches, which indicate dead or dying tissue. Insufficient water is the greatest enemy of nursery stock; do not accept plants with severely wilted or dry foliage.

Local nurseries and garden centers do not always stock rare or unusual plants. There are many specialty mail-order houses for specific plants and for plants that will do well in difficult climates. A top-notch nursery will send your plants at the correct planting time for your area. While you can buy a wide variety of vegetable and flower seeds off the rack locally, take the time to read catalogues to learn what is available and make comparisons.

Customer Satisfaction

If you receive a damaged plant, write to the supplier, specifically describing the problem and indicating whether you want a refund or a replacement. All reputable plant outlets will also replace plants or seeds if they do not produce. But keep in mind that you have the responsibility of choosing wisely and providing good growing conditions. Your report to the nursery helps the manager to provide more accurate information in the future.

Designing a garden is a pleasure that begins long before your spade touches the ground. At least half the fun is in picturing all sorts of possibilities before settling on the ideal scheme. The plates that follow will help by offering ideas and inspiration. They illustrate variations on 14 different themes: Landscapes to Harvest; Landscaping with Flowers; Using Trees & Shrubs; Rock Gardens; Time-Honored Styles; Gardens in the Suburbs; City Gardens; Water Gardens; Shade Gardens; Japanese-Style Gardens; Winterscapes; Gardens by the Sea; Gardening in Dry Sites; and A Naturalistic Effect.

The Captions
To help you appreciate the garden designs, the captions offer specific information about the sites and the design concepts that make them successful. Important decorative elements and the most prominent plants are also identified. The age of the garden is given in terms of how soon after planting it became effective. For example, "Over 2 years old" means that if you were to create a design similar to the one shown, you could expect to wait two years for it to fill out.

The Visual Key
Preceding the color plates there is a Visual Key that presents an overview of the 14 garden themes. Two examples of each type of garden are illustrated, and there is a short explanation of the important features and principles behind each theme.

Visual Key

Landscapes to Harvest	The eight gardens featured here show how vegetables, herbs, and fruits can be grown for beauty as well as bounty.	In each garden, the plants are arranged by colors and textures to make them attractive through a long growing season.
Landscaping with Flowers	This section features flower gardens in eight different sites and styles.	They illustrate how to use flowers in sunny lawns or shady corners, in informal groupings or geometric patterns.
Using Trees & Shrubs	These photographs show eight landscape designs featuring mainly trees and shrubs.	Contrasting shapes and textures are important in these large-scale designs.
Rock Gardens	Inspired by alpine landscapes, these six gardens make use of low, spreading plants with delicate flowers and foliage.	Rocks and evergreen plants form their backbones, making them attractive even in winter.
Time-Honored Styles	The seven gardens in this section were designed in time-honored, formal styles.	The principles at work—symmetry, balance, and order—can be applied on a smaller scale to home gardens.

67

*This chart shows you
examples of the 14
types of gardens in
the color plates.*

Pages 72–89

Pages 90–107

Pages 108–125

Pages 126–139

Pages 140–155

Gardens in the Suburbs	Backyards are the sites of these seven gardens, each of which treats a small area in a different way.	An important element is scale. The goal is to enhance but not crowd the space.
City Gardens	This section illustrates how six city-dwellers have turned rooftops and balconies into private oases of color.	Raised beds help bring plants closer to eye level, and containers allow for rearrangement and easy care.
Water Gardens	The eight gardens shown here incorporate water in their designs.	There are ideas for designing around pools, ponds, or waterfalls or for planting in wet areas of a yard.
Shade Gardens	Shady sites offer the chance to grow a surprising variety of attractive plants, as the six gardens here attest.	They show how to enhance such areas as a wooded backyard, an entryway shaded by a house, or the area under a large tree.
Japanese-Style Gardens	The five gardens here incorporate the ancient Japanese ideals of simplicity, harmony, and quiet beauty in the landscape.	They range from small courtyard gardens to hill-and-pond gardens.

Winterscapes	A garden does not have to look desolate in winter, as these six examples demonstrate.	They include a wide range of plants, all of which are attractive when spring and summer blooms have gone.
Gardens by the Sea	The seven gardens in this section exist at water's edge or slightly inland, but they have sandy soil, sun, and wind in common.	They include plants that thrive in these conditions, such as silver-toned foliage plants, sculptured pines, and colorful flowers.
Gardening in Dry Sites	Plants native to arid regions have dramatic shapes that lend interest to the five gardens shown here.	These designs provide ideas for landscaping dry areas and for combining these distinctive plants with more traditional garden varieties.
A Naturalistic Effect	These seven gardens bring the beauty of the natural landscape into your yard. Based on meadows and woodlands, they are designed to look undesigned.	Once established, a naturalistic landscape needs relatively little maintenance.
	Many of these gardens attract wildlife because they resemble their native habitats.	You can increase the number of visitors to your garden by choosing plants that are favored by the wildlife you want to observe.

Landscapes to

Though fashions in eating wax and wane, the desire for fresh, vibrant produce remains constant. There is nothing better than a dish whose ingredients were picked a few feet from the kitchen, minutes before the meal. Traditionally, produce has been grown in the back or side yard, but recently gardeners have realized that they can combine beauty and fresh gourmet produce within a unified, well-designed "edible landscape."

A Practical Purpose
Using food in an ornamental setting is both practical and aesthetically pleasing. Ornamental design principles apply, but beautiful annual and perennial edible plants are substituted for some of the more traditional flowers, trees, and vines. The goal is a mixture of beauty and utility—rarely are all the plants grown for consumption. Careful planning and judicious planting will result in a yard that is flavorful, practical, and visually pleasing.

Choosing the Right Site
An understanding of your yard's microclimate—the promises and limitations of soil, sunshine, and moisture—added to your own taste, will help you select a site. There are tasty, ornamental edible plants for just about any garden setting. The sunniest spots with the choicest soils are best reserved for annual vegetables; plant the next-best soils with fruit trees. There are culinary herbs suitable for rocky or poor soils, and even a few perennial edibles for wet sites. Only the shadiest areas and muckiest soils are not suitable, and here raised beds of improved soil may be the solution.

The Plants to Use
Theoretically, any edible plant can be used in an ornamental landscape, but of course some are more suitable than others. Plants with unique, distinctive fruits include 'Yellow Pear' tomatoes, with bright yellow skin and flesh; 'Rosa Bianca' eggplant, whose skin is pastel pink; and brilliant yellow 'Gold Rush' summer squash. Some edibles are prized for their dramatic foliage. Giant Japanese red mustard presents a fountain of large, curled, emerald green leaves with purplish red highlights; the ornamental kales come in a rainbow of reds, pinks, cream, and blue-green. Ornamental perennials with dramatic fall color include persimmon, pear, and quince trees. Many plants have boldy shaped foliage or colorful blossoms, and some offer the bonus of pleasing scents.
These and other edible plants can be combined in many creative ways. For instance, border the garden with lettuces and spinach mixed with impatiens or the edible dwarf nasturtiums. All types of pepper plants are striking when combined with dwarf marigolds or planted against a background of tall red salvias. Or, you might use the blue-gray foliage of lavender as a setting for deep purple eggplants.

Harvest

Important Principles

The most important design elements for a successful food garden are strong, firm line and form—as defined by brick pathways or patios, railroad-tie planters, wooden pathway edgings, structures such as trellises or fences, and even evergreen plants and hedges. Growing a variety of foods for your table means working with a greater range of textures, forms, and colors than you might choose for a typical ornamental landscape. The large, stable elements in the design will serve to counterbalance this variety.

The seasonal nature of the garden presents an additional challenge. You must think about blooming and fruiting times and the occasional periods of reduced drama due to necessary transplanting, fallow periods, harvesting, and soil cultivation. During these times the importance of strong line becomes clearly evident.

Colorful annual bedding plants, either edible or ornamental, can help tie the composition together and provide accents to captivate the eye. Plant them in long arching strips alongside vegetable beds, or intersperse them among the plants to be harvested. The eye will be intrigued by the color and skip over temporary holes in your composition.

To maintain a simplified, tight design, use no more than three types of building material and avoid the tendency to clutter the garden with too much pottery, sculpture, trellis work, or lawn furniture. Container plants help perk up any landscape, but beware again of too much color or variety in planters.

Getting Started

Soil development is both the most crucial and time-consuming element of success. Remember, time and effort spent on amending your soil during the first several years will mean healthy, productive plants and lower maintenance in the long run. Expect that the perennials in your garden will take from three to five years to look mature. On the other hand, annual beds filled with herbs, vegetables, and flowers can have a colorful and tasty impact the first summer.

Some Shining Examples

On the following pages you'll see eight gardens to harvest; from a small, terraced backyard to larger areas laid out in geometric patterns to designs featuring raised beds and trellises. Notice the placement of plants according to heights, colors, and shapes. See how they are separated into carefully designed rows or beds bordered by paths of brick, stone, or mulch. Whether the overall effect is formal or casual, there is a well-considered plan that holds all the elements together and raises what might have been just a vegetable patch to the level of an integrated landscape design.

**Los Altos,
California
Creasy Garden**

Site:
Small, square yard
Partial shade
Rich, well-drained soil

Design Concepts:
Multilevel planting
Path leads into design
Symmetrical repetition
of colors
Use of small-leaved
plants
Enclosure by fence

Decorative Elements:	Plantings:	Seasons:
Patterned brick path	Corn	Photographed in
Railroad-tie steps	Squash	summer
Terra-cotta planters	Tomatoes	Productive spring to
Picket fence	Peppers	fall
Wooden trellis	Beans	Over 2 years old
	Herbs	
	Perennial flowers	

**Los Altos,
California
Creasy Garden**

Site:
Small backyard
Partial sun
Rich, well-drained soil

Design Concepts:
Diagonal lines to
enlarge space
Repeated bands of pink
Raised beds as focus

Decorative Elements:
Angled brick patio
Railroad-tie planters
Trellis
Containers
Hanging planters

Plantings:
Japanese red mustard
Green and red lettuces
Chamomile
Peas
Parsley
Ferns
Primroses

Seasons:
Photographed in spring
Productive year-round
Over 10 years old

**Kennett Square,
Pennsylvania
Kitchen Garden,
Longwood**

*Site:
Edge of large, level
lawn
Full sun
Average soil*

*Design Concepts:
Repeated parallel lines
Planting in blocks
Woods as backdrop
Lawn, edging, and
paths for contrast*

Decorative Elements:	Plantings:	Seasons:
Brick edging	Snap beans	Photographed in
Picket fence	Cabbage	summer
Gravel path	Swiss chard	Productive spring to
	Carrots	fall
	Sweet corn	1 year old
	Spinach	
	Marigolds	

Ann Arbor, Michigan Herb Garden, Matthaei Botanical Garden

Site:
Level, open area
Full sun
Average soil

Design Concepts:
Geometric plan
Symmetrical plantings
Heights decreasing toward center
Low hedges as outline
Green and yellow theme

Decorative Elements:	Plantings:	Seasons:
Brick wall	*Chives*	*Photographed in early summer*
Stone mosaic design	*Yarrow*	
	Rue	*Productive spring to fall*
	Sage	
	Boxwood	*Over 2 years old*
	Achillea	

Sonoma, California Sebastiani Garden	Site:	Design Concepts:
	Patio area of large yard	Use of stone throughout
	Full sun	Raised planters
	Rich, well-drained soil	Archway as focus
		Repeated rectangles

Decorative Elements:	Plantings:	Seasons:
Stone walks	Runner beans	Photographed in
Wrought-iron fencing	Bush beans	summer
Terra-cotta planters	Squash	Productive spring to
	Onions	fall
	Herbs	Over 5 years old

**Gloucestershire,
England
Verey Garden**

Site:
Large, level yard
Cool climate
Average soil

Design Concepts:
Repeated squares in
beds and paths
Use of gray foliage
Repetition of plant
types
Low boxwood for
edgings

Decorative Elements:	Plantings:	Seasons:
Patterned block paths	Artichokes	Photographed in late
Wooden trellises	Onions	summer
	Broccoli	Productive spring to
	Cabbage	fall
	Brussels sprouts	Over 10 years old

Far Hills, New Jersey
Toth Garden

Site:
Small backyard
Full sun
Rich, well-drained soil

Design Concepts:
Intensive planting
Wood as unifying theme
Strong vertical lines
Use of dark foliage

Decorative Elements:	Plantings:	Seasons:
Wooden trellises	Tomatoes	Photographed in summer
Raised wooden beds	Pole beans	
Wood-chip paths	Broccoli	Productive spring to fall
	Eggplant	
	Lettuce	1 year old
	Malabar spinach	

**New Vernon,
New Jersey
Kinkaid Garden**

Site:
Stable courtyard
Partial shade
Rich, well-drained soil

Design Concepts:
Rectangular raised beds
Chevron-shaped
plantings
Paths to define beds
Gate as focal point

Decorative Elements:	Plantings:	Seasons:
Wooden edgings	*Leeks*	*Photographed in*
Sawdust path	*Lettuce*	*summer*
Planters	*Parsley*	*Productive spring to*
Painted wooden gate	*Nasturtiums*	*fall*
Vine trellis	*Bush beans*	*1 year old*
	Squash	
	Daylilies	

Landscaping

Nothing brightens your surroundings quite like a flower garden, whether it's a large formal border or a simple row of marigolds. Its beauty can extend inside, in the form of cut flowers; and you can spend hours at the window watching the bees, butterflies, and hummingbirds it attracts. For many gardeners, the greatest reward of a flower garden lies in the planning, a process that is more art than task. In effect, it is painting a picture with flowers.

Gardens for Every Site
There are gardens to plan for almost any site—small or large, formal or casual—and for any soil type or climate. If you have a sunny site, the possibilities are almost limitless; but if your yard is partly shaded, don't despair. You can create a subtle garden in which bright spots of flower color light up the shade, framed by a background of different foliage textures. Look for fairly flat areas that are focal points in the landscape, spots that you gaze at often from windows, the street, or outdoor seating areas. Flower gardens in such sites become jewels of color set among the green of lawns.

Annuals, Perennials, and Bulbs
Most flower gardens are composed of either annual flowers, which live for one season, or perennial flowers, which come up in the same spot each year. Sometimes the two types are combined in one garden. Spring, summer, and fall bulbs play a part as well, either by themselves or mixed with annuals or perennials. Flowering shrubs and trees, though usually too large for the flower garden, often frame the picture with seasonal color. Some gardeners choose to plan just one flower bed; others create separate gardens for different types of plants, or plan beds that will provide blooms at specific times of the year.

Planning for Seasonal Color
The first thing to consider when you sit down to make a flower-shopping list is the period of bloom you desire. Do you want a spring garden of bulbs and early perennials? A summer garden of annuals, perennials, or a combination? Or a fall garden full of chrysanthemums and asters? Perhaps you'd like several gardens, each to grace a different season. A garden can cleverly span a long period, beginning with spring bulbs and perennials, overplanted with annuals for summer, and ending with fall perennials. You might combine perennials that will bloom over a relatively short period—a month or two, perhaps—but make a spectacular show.

Defining Your Style
Flower beds can assume many shapes and sizes: a long, rectangular herbaceous border in the grand English style; a naturalized planting of woodland perennials scattered in drifts under apple trees; a jubilant explosion of annuals along a split-rail fence. Your taste and

with Flowers

the style of your house and existing plantings should suggest what would look best.

The color scheme is the most personal of all the choices to be made. Do you like brilliant splashes of reds, yellows, and oranges? If so, plant a composition of gaillardia, rudbeckia, and coreopsis. Do you prefer misty blues, pinks, and lavenders? Then design a romantic garden filled with delphiniums, scabiosa, and bellflowers, accented with white feverfew and baby's-breath.

There are practical considerations, too. Tall flowers go in the background, short ones in the foreground. Flower shapes that make pleasing contrasts, such as spiky veronica with flat-topped yarrow, add interest. Remember that foliage also has various shapes and colors that can enhance the overall scheme.

The Temptation to Overplan

With all these possibilities to excite your imagination, you'll have to resist the temptation to run amok at the nursery. Flower gardens can take a lot of time to establish and maintain, so first decide how ambitious your plan should be. A small bed of annuals is not hard to replant each year, but large beds can involve hours of work each season. A perennial bed is more permanent but calls for careful preparation and will never be maintenance-free.

For instant effect, annuals are usually best. Beds made with perennials may take longer to become established. Many perennials are rather insignificant the first year, blooming sparsely and not attaining their full heights. Even when they do, you may need to reevaluate the design from time to time. Did something grow too tall? Is there too much purple? Is all the red in one area? Maintaining a garden is not a job with a definite beginning, middle, and end. It is an ongoing endeavor that is never the same from year to year.

That's exactly why it's fun. Whether you plant new beds of annuals each year or ever-evolving borders of bulbs and perennials, there will always be a new variety, a new color combination, or a new site to experiment with, and something new to look at each year.

Designs to Inspire

From a small-scale planting in a shady corner to large island beds on sunny lawns, the designs on the following pages are just a few examples of the myriad ways to landscape with flowers. Color schemes range from cool roses and blues to bright yellows and reds. Planting schemes are simple and elegant or subtly complex. In all of them, notice the combinations of colors, heights, and textures— not only how they are grouped, but also how they are repeated throughout the design to lend balance and carry the eye along. Covering a range of seasons, from early spring to late summer, and of sites, from England to California, these gardens offer a wealth of ideas ready to be put to work in your own landscape.

**Fairfield County,
Connecticut
Muller Garden**

Site:
Large lawn
Gentle slope
Full sun
Average soil

Design Concepts:
Informal island beds to
be viewed from path
Bright, clear colors
White as accent
Woods as backdrop

Decorative Elements:	Plantings:	Seasons:
Flagstone path	Lilies	Photographed in summer
Pillars in entryway	Phlox	Blooms late spring to summer
	Shasta daisies	Over 2 years old
	Irises	
	Delphiniums	
	Balloon flowers	

**Philadelphia,
Pennsylvania
Hallowell Garden**

Site:
Small yard
Sunken area
Partial shade
Alkaline soil for
flowers

Design Concepts:
Small-scale planting
Color in shady corner
Use of foliage textures
Bench as focus and as
viewing point

Decorative Elements:	Plantings:	Seasons:
Bark mulch	Dogwood	Photographed in spring
Stone walls	Rhododendrons	Blooms early to
Flagstone path	Primroses	mid-spring
Stone bench	Ferns	Well-established garden

**Lincolnshire,
England
Gunby Hall**

Site:
Large, level yard
Full sun
Average soil

Design Concepts:
Wide herbaceous
borders
Graduated heights
Purple and white
accents
Use of foliage textures
Plantings soften path

Decorative Elements:	Plantings:	Seasons:
Flagstone path	*Daylilies*	*Photographed in late summer*
Gravel edging	*Helenium*	*Blooms mid- to late summer*
	Goldenrod	*Well-established garden*
	Feverfew	
	Yarrow	
	Sea lavender	

Middlesex, England
Private Garden

Site:
Small, level yard
Full sun
Average soil

Design Concepts:
Formal bedding pattern
Repeated circular
shapes
Colors repeated in vase
Red as outline

Decorative Elements:	*Plantings:*	*Seasons:*
Stone vase	Begonias	Photographed in summer
Patterned brick path	Violas	Blooms all summer
		Over 1 year old

Bakersfield,
California
Private Garden

Site:
Large front yard
Level lawn
Full sun
Average soil

Design Concepts:
Formal beds, showy
impact
Curves contrast with
right angles of house
Wide variety of colors
White for clarity

Decorative Elements:	Plantings:	Seasons:
Concrete edging	Japanese black pine	Photographed in early
Brick wall and pillars	Pansies	spring
	Candytuft	Effective year-round
	Iceland poppies	Over 1 year old

**Shelburne Falls,
Massachusetts
Bakalar Garden**

Site:
*Yard bordering
meadow
Gentle slope
Full sun
Average soil*

Design Concepts:
*Wide herbaceous border
Harmonious use of color
Careful height
gradation
Woods as backdrop*

Decorative Elements:	Plantings:	Seasons:
Natural features	*Hidcote lavender*	*Photographed in*
	Phlox	*summer*
	Bee balm	*Blooms all summer*
	Globe thistle	*Over 3 years old*
	Delphiniums	

New Hope,
Pennsylvania
Jamison Garden

Site:
Large, level lawn
Full sun
Average soil

Design Concepts:
Long island bed
Tall plants in center
Bedding annuals as
edging
Tree for focus, contrast

Decorative Elements:	Plantings:	Seasons:
Natural features	Spider flowers	Photographed in summer
	Cosmos	Blooms all summer
	Pinks	About 3 years old
	Daylilies	
	Wax begonias	
	Dusty miller	

**Stamford,
Connecticut
Levitan Garden**

*Site:
Lawn bordering woods
Gentle slope
Partial shade
Acid soil*

*Design Concepts:
Woodland effect
Intensively planted
Grass paths connect
areas
Pastel colors
Red as accent*

Decorative Elements:	Plantings:	Seasons:
Natural features	Dogwoods	Photographed in spring
	Tulips	Blooms early to late
	Forget-me-nots	spring
	Doronicum	Well-established garden
	Pansies	
	Johnny-jump-ups	
	Azaleas	

Using Trees &

As our largest and most permanent plants, trees and shrubs shape the space in a landscape. You can think of them as defining the boundaries of an outdoor "room," with the canopies of tall trees forming a ceiling, large shrubs serving as walls, and lower shrubs creating a floor. Within this room you might place other trees and shrubs to further partition the space or simply to beautify it with color and sculptural form.

A Vast Variety
There is an immense variety of plants to choose from—evergreens; deciduous types; those grown for showy flowers, glistening fruits, vivid fall color, attractive foliage, or pleasant scent. Their outlines are wonderfully diverse—rounded, conical, columnar, weeping, vase-shaped, and prostrate, to name a few. Each seems to have its own character and impart a certain style to its surroundings.

Consider the Site
The bewildering task of choosing from among so many attractive trees and shrubs is made much easier when you consider the conditions in your growing area. Begin by using only plants that are reliably hardy and pest resistant where you live. Then focus your list to satisfy the particular soil, exposure, and light conditions at your site. You will soon learn that flowering plants do best in sunny areas but that many beautiful shrubs and small trees will tolerate some degree of shade. Before planting, it is a good idea to check shady areas for excess dryness caused by the greedy roots of shade trees. In exposed, windy sites, choose flexible deciduous plants over most evergreens. Assess the moistness of your soil, avoiding wet areas where few plants can thrive. Also avoid barren, rocky locations. If you can't plan around such problem areas, find plants that are specially adapted to adverse conditions.

Plants for a Purpose
Once you have limited your list of desirable trees and shrubs to those that will thrive in your space, pare it down further by defining the purposes you want the plants to serve. You may need them for shade, to block a view or create a windbreak, as ground cover or foundation plantings, or simply to provide showy accents in the landscape. There are trees and shrubs that are especially useful for each of these purposes. For example, tall yews and junipers make good screens to block out unwanted views, noise, or wind. Tall deciduous shade trees such as oak, maple, or sycamore actually help lower your air-conditioning costs while allowing enough sun through in winter to provide solar heat and help melt snow.

The myriad trees and shrubs for ornament include spring-blooming dogwoods and rhododendrons, glistening evergreen hollies with bright berries, sumacs with crimson fall foliage, and stately blue-

Shrubs

tinged spruces. Ornamental trees and shrubs can be used singly, as specimens, or in groups arranged so that their features harmonize and provide interest over a long season.

Elements of Design
No matter how simple or ambitious your garden plan, it should suit the style and size of your house and grounds and blend well with existing plants. Your goal is a harmonious, restful landscape in which colors, textures, and plant outlines work to accent or complement each other. Knowing three basic design principles— repetition, sequence, and balance—will guide your choice and placement of trees and shrubs. Some people prefer formal balance in entryway plantings, especially if their homes are of traditional style. More informal balance can be more interesting to look at because it makes the eye a bit uneasy, causing it to search for other patterns in the landscape.

Starting Out
If you're faced with a new, barren lot, the first thing to do is plant several large trees for shade or screens. Buy ornamental trees in small, less expensive sizes. While you wait for them to mature, fill in with fast-growing shrubs for instant effect. If, like most gardeners, you have a yard already planted with several large shrubs and trees, work to incorporate the existing plants into your plans. It seldom pays to tear everything out, but you can vastly improve a landscape with a few well-considered additions or subtractions.
The best time to buy plants is in spring or early fall. Check them for healthy, sturdy stems and leaves with no signs of discoloration, disease, or pest damage.
When you plant new trees or shrubs, be particularly careful about spacing them. Find out how large and fast each plant grows and place it accordingly. Most of us crave that filled-in look as soon as possible, but it is no fun to spend weekends pruning and clipping because you forgot that a vigorous plant does not necessarily stop growing once it meets your requirements. If your space is especially small, learn about the many dwarf and compact trees and shrubs on the market.

Beauty on a Grand Scale
On the following pages you will see trees and shrubs used to landscape entire backyards, secluded corners, and steep embankments. Some designs make use of formal, sculptured shapes; others rely on natural outlines to create the effect of a wild woodland. Emphasis may be on a showy floral display or a more subtle arrangement of foliage colors and textures. Evergreens are often valuable as backdrops, and some deciduous plants are chosen for their bright fall colors. These gardens show natural beauty on a grand scale, changing with the seasons but lasting a lifetime.

Site:
Secluded, level lawn
Partial shade
Acid and average soils

Design Concepts:
Use of sculptured
shapes
Evergreen backdrop
Contrasting foliage
textures
Rounded edgings mirror
plant shapes
Mulch to unify design

Decorative Elements:	Plantings:	Seasons:
Bark mulch	*Birches*	*Photographed in late*
Topiary pruning	*Pines*	*spring*
	Japanese maples	*Effective year-round*
	Azaleas	*Over 20 years old*
	Viburnums	

Milly la Forêt,
France
Courances

Site:
Level, wooded area
surrounding pond
Partial shade
Moist, acid soil

Design Concepts:
Woodland effect
Varied shapes, textures
Cool green theme
Red as contrast

Decorative Elements:	Plantings:	Seasons:
Natural features	*Japanese maple*	*Photographed in*
	Columnar junipers	*summer*
	Yews	*Effective spring to fall*
	Copper beech	*Over 15 years old*
	Ferns	
	Cotoneaster	

**Wilmington,
Delaware
Pool Garden,
Winterthur**

Site:
Sunken area below
strong embankments
Partial shade
Acid soil

Design Concepts:
Secluded woodland
effect
Lacy foliage softens
geometric design
Steps lead into design
Pool as focus and to
reflect colors
Containers as accents

Decorative Elements:	Plantings:	Seasons:
Large pool	Dogwoods	Photographed in early spring
Sculpture	Azaleas	
Stone walls and steps	Maples	Effective spring and summer
Bluestone paving	English ivy	
Container plants	Hollies	Over 20 years old
	Viburnum	

**Philadelphia,
Pennsylvania
Andalucia Garden**

Site:
Level, open area
Full sun
Acid soil

Design Concepts:
Lawn leads into design
Bench area as focus
Use of sculpted shapes
Varied textures
Pink and white accents

Decorative Elements:	Plantings:	Seasons:
Rustic bench	Dogwood	Photographed in early
Bluestone paving	Broom	spring
	Yucca	Effective year-round
	Junipers	About 10 years old
	Umbrella pine	
	False cypress	

**Stamford,
Connecticut
Levitan Garden**

Site:
Narrow, grassy
passageway
Generally level
Full to partial sun
Acid soil

Design Concepts:
Showy spring display
Planting in graduated
heights
Tall plants as screens
Use of warm colors
Blue, white to soften

Decorative Elements:	Plantings:	Seasons:
Natural features	*Azaleas*	*Photographed in early*
	Lily-flowered tulips	*spring*
	Forget-me-nots	*Blooms in spring*
	Dogwoods	*Well-established garden*
	Rhododendrons	

**Philadelphia,
Pennsylvania
Roland Garden**

*Site:
Raised bed in small
yard
Partial shade
Acid soil*

*Design Concepts:
Circular theme
Graduated heights
Foliage as edging
Pink and white
contrast with
dark greens
Varied textures*

Decorative Elements:	Plantings:	Seasons:
Retaining wall	Dogwoods	Photographed in early
Stone terrace paving	Mist Maiden	spring
	rhododendrons	Blooms in spring
	Azaleas	Effective year-round
	Horizontal junipers	About 15 years old

**Larchmont, New York
Private Garden**

Site:
Embankment at edge of
lot
Partial shade
Acid soil

Design Concepts:
Showy spring display
Use of one plant type
Stone steps as focus
Oak trees as backdrop
Repeated colors
Coral masses for
balance

Decorative Elements:	*Plantings:*	*Seasons:*
Rustic stone steps	*Azaleas*	*Photographed in spring*
	Oaks	*Blooms in spring*
	Ferns	*Effective spring to fall*
	Japanese red maple	*Over 10 years old*

Larchmont, New York
Epstein Garden

Site:
Large woodlot
Gentle slope
Partial shade
Moist, acid soil

Design Concepts:
Emphasis on view from house
Attention to fall color
Repeated plant shapes
Meandering lawn as focus
Oak trees as backdrop

Decorative Elements:	Plantings:	Seasons:
Natural features	*Oaks*	*Photographed in fall*
	Enkianthus	*Effective year-round*
	Summer-sweet	*Over 10 years old*
	Viburnums	
	Azaleas	
	Rhododendron	

Rock Gardens

A garden that uses rocks as its backbone can evoke some of the
most beautiful natural landscapes—brooks splashing through
blooming meadows, flowering alpine peaks—on an intimate scale.
Any site, from a small raised bed in a courtyard to a large sloping
yard, can be transformed by a rock garden that, once established, is
easy to maintain and provides interest all year long.

A Showcase for Miniatures
The rock garden serves as a magnificent set piece for delicate,
diminutive perennials and bulbs, many of which are native to
alpine landscapes. Such plants benefit aesthetically from the height
and framework of well-placed rocks. The rocks also provide the
coolness and good drainage the plants need to thrive. Carefully
chosen foliage plants create low mats or upright mounds from silver
to deep green in color, with delicately textured leaves. Conifers and
dwarf shrubs form the living architecture of the garden, softening
the lines of the rocks and providing backdrops to the flowering
plants.

Year-Round Interest
Part of the appeal of a rock garden is that it looks attractive and
inviting all year. The foliage plants are effective in summer and
winter, and the conifers and dwarf evergreens also help the garden
hold its shape and interest. Against this background of various
greens, there can be something in bloom at almost any time of
year.
The first and most dramatic wave of color comes with the spring
thaw, the time when natural alpine landscapes burst into bloom. In
well-designed rock gardens, bulbs and drabas might be the first to
show, followed by primulas and saxifrages and then a massive
display of pinks. A judicious variety of campanulas and composites
in summer carry their show well into the autumn, when the foliage
plants and evergreens—and the dramatic rocks themselves—take
over.

Keeping to Scale
Since a rock garden is truly a miniature landscape, it is most
successful when it relies on small plants. Compact habit, as well as
finely textured foliage, helps suggest larger plants in the natural
landscape. For example, a carpet of flowering ground covers can
have as much effect as a meadow of tall wildflowers; a compact
shrub will resemble its taller relatives. Not many large perennials
are found in the best rock gardens. Aside from visually
overpowering the smaller neighbors that the garden is meant to
show off, they may threaten their root systems.
Keeping a rock garden in scale does not necessarily mean primping
and pruning its shrubs and mats. Some gardeners choose to do
some trimming to improve the plants' outlines, but as a rule the

right plants, carefully chosen and placed, will not outgrow their settings. They actually look best left to their informal ways.

Planning the Garden
The best site for a rock garden is one that is sunny but not hot, such as a slope facing away from the hottest sun but open to the sky. The plants should not have to compete with large trees or shrubs for soil or light. If you are lucky enough to have natural rock outcrops on your property, simply create your garden around them. If you are bringing in rocks, choose and place them so they resemble local landscapes. It's a good idea to use a scale model of your site—small rocks in a tray of sand will do—to help you visualize how various arrangements might work.

Before digging in, decide what kinds of plantings are best suited to your personal gardening style as well as your site. Do you have the time and interest to develop a large collection of alpine plants that may have special needs? Or would you prefer to grow weed-suppressing ground covers and low-maintenance perennials? A rock garden can be undertaken in stages and gradually expanded; so consider starting small, whatever your preference. Begin with the choice plants that are the essence of a rock garden, filling in with background plants later. Or carpet your new rock work quickly with spreading mat plants and replace them with alpine gems gradually, as you gain confidence.

Some of your planning can be done on paper. It is also wise to seek the advice of neighbors who have successful rock gardens. But the final test will be in the garden itself. Some plants will grow much faster than your research predicts; others may fail altogether. Constant readjustment is a large part of any type of gardening, and it can be a pleasant, creative experience.

Variety and Versatility
The color plates that follow show rock gardens in diverse sizes and sites. There are large open areas with little or no slope—one cut by a meandering brook, another treated as a rock-strewn meadow. A natural stone cliff is planted with dwarf conifers and cascading perennials. Rock walls create terraces in a steep shady bank, and plants are tucked into the tufa stone walls of a bright backyard garden. In all these gardens, rocks provide structure and unified backgrounds; plants are arranged in bright compositions of color; and compact evergreens lend height and texture to the design. Different choices and arrangements of plants, however, make each as unique as its designer.

Looking carefully at these gardens and analyzing their components may inspire you to consider a rock garden for your own property. Whether you use it to landscape a steep bank or add interest to a level lot, you'll be rewarded with an unusual tapestry of color through most of the gardening year.

**Unionville,
Pennsylvania
Glencoe Farm**

*Site:
Open, level area
Full sun
Well-drained loam*

*Design Concepts:
Alpine meadow effect
Brook leads into design
Emphasis on texture
Boulders to unify
design
Large trees as backdrop
Repeated yellows and
purples*

Decorative Elements:	Plantings:	Seasons:
Boulders	Alberta spruce	Photographed in late spring
Gravel paths	Juniper	Blooms spring to early summer
Wooden bridge	Geraniums	Effective year-round
	Helianthemum	Over 3 years old
	Grass pinks	
	Blister cress	
	Irises	

Long Island, New York Private Garden	Site: Steep bank Protected by trees Partial shade Humus-rich soil	Design Concepts: Terraced plantings Rocks to unify design Contrasting foliage Pink and white accents

Decorative Elements:	*Plantings:*	*Seasons:*
Sandstone walls	Lilies	Photographed in
Flagstone path	Ferns	summer
Wrought-iron railing	Creeping phlox	Blooms spring to
Small path lamps	Canada hemlock	summer
	Astilbes	Over 3 years old
	Hostas	
	Boxwood	

**Coastal
Massachusetts
Parrot Garden**

Site:
Steep natural cliff
Partial shade
Amended rocky soil

Design Concepts:
Treatment of steep slope
Repeated colors,
textures
Effect of spilling plants
Plant shapes echo rock
shapes

Decorative Elements:	*Plantings:*	*Seasons:*
Natural features	*Creeping phlox*	*Photographed in spring*
	Alyssums	*Blooms in spring*
	Dwarf white pine	*Effective year-round*
	Compact Hinoki cypress	*Over 3 years old*
	Dwarf Norway spruce	
	Mountain avens	
	Violets	

**Hudson River
Valley, New York
Stonecrop**

*Site:
Large, level site
Minimal shade
Amended rocky soil*

*Design Concepts:
Mountain meadow
effect
Gravel and rocks unify
design and set off
plants
Balanced plant masses
Shrubs as backdrop*

Decorative Elements:
Pea gravel
Stone wall
Large boulders

Plantings:
Lilac
Dwarf spruces
Rock jasmine
Penstemon
Dwarf boxwood
Peonies
Candytuft

Seasons:
Photographed in spring
Effective year-round
Over 2 years old

**Kent, England
Private Garden**

Site:
Walled bank bordering
lawn
Full sun
Porous soil

Design Concepts:
Closely spaced plants
Multilevel plantings
Trees, shrubs as
backdrop
Emphasis on
individual plants
Stone to unify design
Lawn as contrast

Decorative Elements:	Plantings:	Seasons:
Tufa stone walls	Ghent azaleas	Photographed in late
Stone trough	Japanese maple	spring
Flagstone paving	Persian candytuft	Blooms in spring
	Broom	Effective year-round
	Scilla	Over 10 years old
	Primroses	

Kennett Square,
Pennsylvania
Hillside Garden,
Longwood

Site:
Steep bank
Full sun
Average soil

Design Concepts:
Alpine effect
Repeated colors
Contrasting foliage
Path leads into design

Decorative Elements:	Plantings:	Seasons:
Boulders	Cymbalaria	Photographed in spring
Natural features	Basket-of-gold	Blooms spring to
	Candytuft	summer
	Pinks	Effective year-round
	Creeping juniper	Well-established garden
	Spreading English yew	
	Mugo pines	

Time-Honored

Fashions in landscape design change constantly, but certain styles
have stood the test of time. In them, art is fused with nature
according to established principles. Although their styles are
wide-ranging, these gardens are all alike in being carefully
arranged by human hands.

Styles Over the Centuries

Changes in garden styles over the centuries have reflected the
different philosophies of their creators. For example, the famous
French formal gardens of the 17th century, of which the Gardens at
Versailles are the most famous, symbolized the supreme authority of
Louis XIV over his domain. The English landscape style of the
18th century, inspired by poets and landscape painters of the time,
was designed to celebrate the aesthetic and moral power of nature.
Some aspects of both styles reappeared in the early 20th century in
the celebrated gardens of Gertrude Jekyll. Her perennial flower
borders combined the order and structure of formal designs with
the sweeping irregular lines of landscape gardens.

Modern Applications

These and other famous gardens can offer inspiration and instruction
to today's homeowners. In fact, traditional gardens have captured
an increasing interest in recent years, for two reasons. First, more
people have become involved in preserving and restoring older
houses, and they are looking for landscape treatments that will
match them in periods and styles. Second, there is a growing
realization that traditional principles of garden design have stood
the test of time for a reason—they work.

Two Garden Styles

Our heritage in garden design can be divided into two general
families, commonly referred to as "formal" and "informal." These
terms can be misleading, since both styles are dependent on form
and structure for their success. They are simply organized according
to different design principles. In general, formal gardens are laid
out geometrically, while informal designs have more free-flowing
lines.
Formal or geometric gardens delight and refresh through their order
and regularity. Geometric plans are often perfect for the small
garden, intimately associated with the house because they naturally
extend its regular lines. In informal gardens, the influence of the
designer is expressed more subtly.

Plants as Design Elements

In any type of garden, plants are used in three primary ways: for
structure, ornament, and utility. Structure is the most important of
the three in traditional gardens; it transforms a mere collection of
plants into a unified design.

Styles

Large evergreen hedges form the vertical planes of traditional gardens. Such plants as hemlock, arborvitae, Leyland cypress, hollies, and boxwood are especially effective. Densely branched deciduous trees such as hornbeam or hedge maple are also useful if properly trimmed and shaped. A looser kind of vertical plane may be created with a mixture of flowering shrubs.

The ground plane of the garden is usually carpeted with plants, often with a well-manicured grass lawn. Lawns create even, green carpets that are wonderful complements to the other elements of the garden. Where there is no foot traffic, low evergreen ground covers such as periwinkle, pachysandra, and juniper provide a variety of textures.

The canopies of shade trees gracefully fill the overhead space. Some of the best are honey locusts, ashes, and hackberries. Another style of ceiling may be created by vines grown on a pergola.

Time-Honored Principles

Whatever their period or style, all gardens share some fundamental design considerations. One of these is the concept of enclosure. A geometric garden must have the enclosure formed by wall, fences, or hedges to make it distinct from other parts of the property. The boundaries of informal gardens are generally more irregular, but they must exist to some degree.

Balance in a composition comes from our ability to sense an equality of form on both sides of a view. Geometric gardens usually exhibit a virtual mirror image called symmetrical balance. You can create asymmetrical balance in a less formal design by placing unlike elements so that the sum of their effect on the viewer is generally equal.

Another component of traditional gardens is repetition, which unifies and brings harmony to the design. It may be expressed in forms, as in the repetition of columns or trees, or in color, as in a perennial garden of only blue flowers. Other important principles are scale and color. Areas of profuse and varied color are usually confined to separate, clearly delineated beds in traditional gardens.

The vista is a major element of a traditional garden. It is a focused view toward an important scene or object, created by placing plants and other forms so that they form a frame.

The Principles Applied

On the following pages you will see how all these elements work together in successful—often famous—traditional gardens. Geometric plans are evident in many, as are enclosure by hedges or fences, balance of colors and shapes, and vistas leading to focal points created by pools, gazebos, and restored houses. By blending your own tastes with precedents such as these, you can design a home landscape that is a refreshing balance between art and nature.

Philadelphia,
Pennsylvania
Meadowbrook Farm

Site:
Level terrace
Partial shade
Average soil

Design Concepts:
Symmetrical plan
Balance of color, shapes
Enclosure by walls,
plantings
Gazebo as focus

Decorative Elements:
Pool with spiral jet
Cast stone and
wrought-iron gazebo
Stone walls and
edgings
Cast stone statuary,
pots

Plantings:
Clipped yew
Wax begonias
Pickerelweed
Water lilies

Seasons:
Photographed in spring
Most effective spring
and summer
Well-established garden

Hampton, England
Hampton Court
Parterre Garden

Site:
Level area
Full sun
Average soil

Design Concepts:
Geometric pattern
Santolina used as
outline
Use of annuals for
summer color

Decorative Elements:	*Plantings:*	*Seasons:*
Gravel walks	*Gray and green santolina*	*Photographed in summer*
	Snapdragons	*Effective late spring to frost*
	Calendula	*Over 5 years old*
	Verbena	
	Marigolds	
	Begonias	

Athens, Georgia
Knot Garden,
University of
Georgia

Site:
Level lawn
Full sun
Average soil

Design Concepts:
Circular plan
Plant shapes repeated
in regular pattern
Sundial as focus
Enclosure by fence

Decorative Elements:	*Plantings:*	*Seasons:*
Brick walks	Boxwood	Photographed in early
Picket fence	Camellia	spring
Sundial	Daffodils	Most effective in spring
Bench	Tulips	Over 20 years old
	Forget-me-nots	

*Colonial
Williamsburg,
Virginia
Formal Backyard
Garden*

Site:
Level area
Partial shade
Sandy soil

Design Concepts:
Geometric pattern
*Perennial beds bordered
by clipped edgings*
*Corner marked by
outbuilding*
Use of topiary

Decorative Elements:	Plantings:	Seasons:
Oyster-shell walks	English boxwood	Photographed in spring
Brick edging	Common boxwood	Most effective in spring
Picket fence	Yaupon holly	Over 30 years old
Wooden bench	Daffodils	
	Tulips	
	Forget-me-nots	
	Roses	

Colonial
Williamsburg,
Virginia
Boxwood Parterre
Garden

Site:
Open, level area
Partial shade
Sandy soil

Design Concepts:
Symmetrical plan
Rectangular beds
Central axis broken by
circular bed
Topiary as focus

Decorative Elements:	Plantings:	Seasons:
Brick-edged gravel walks	Yaupon holly	Photographed in late summer
Picket fence	English boxwood	Effective year-round
Gate	Aucuba	Well-established garden
	English ivy	
	Dogwood	

Kennett Square,
Pennsylvania
The Sunken
Garden, Longwood

Site:
Gentle slope
Full sun
Average soil

Design Concepts:
Square plan
One-color beds
Colors repeated in
standards
Pool as focus
Enclosure by hedge

Decorative Elements:	Plantings:	Seasons:
Tiled pool with fountain	Standard-trained lantanas	Photographed in summer
Stone edging	Zinnias	Most effective in summer
Steel-edged asphalt walks	Chrysanthemums	Well-established garden
	Arborvitae hedge	

Stratford-upon-Avon, *Site:*   *Design Concepts:*
England   *Level lawn*   *Simple rectangular bed*
Hallscroft Hall   *Full sun*   *Profusion of color and*
                    Average soil   *shapes*
                                        Graduated heights
                                        House as backdrop
                                        Lawn for contrast

Decorative Elements:	Plantings:	Seasons:
Natural features	False dragonhead	Photographed in
	Hollyhock	summer
	Asters	Most effective spring
	Salvia	and summer
	Delphiniums	Well-established garden
	Standard roses	

Gardens in the

Small suburban gardens have an intimacy that larger gardens cannot match. They are extensions of the home, reflecting personal taste and style of living. Whether your garden is very functional— designed around areas for eating, playing, or relaxing—or mainly decorative, it must be carefully planned to take advantage of the space without overpowering it.

A Private Space

Your neighbors' yards may be perfectly lovely, but chances are they do not match yours in style. The best way to make your space distinctive and private is to enclose it with plants or structures that will direct the mind and eye inward. It is also wise to plan around a focal point, such as a patio, lawn, pool, or arbor, that will draw attention to the garden's center and away from distractions outside it.

The Importance of Careful Planning

Since mistakes can easily dominate a small landscape, careful planning is a must. Start by listing all the ways you plan to use the yard. Consider whether and where you might want to entertain, cook and dine, play, store garden tools or trash bins, and keep pets. If you have time to garden only on weeknights, plan to include lighting. If you hate mowing the lawn and don't have room to store a mower, think about installing a patio and surrounding it with ground covers.

In planning any construction, begin with the architectural framework—fences, terracing, walls, steps and paving. Then place trees, shrubs, herbaceous plants, bulbs, and ground covers, in roughly that order.

Thoroughly analyze your site for potential problems. Soil tests are essential for a small garden, which may contain building rubble or dumped subsoil left over from construction. Some areas of the yard may drain poorly. Evaluate how much light reaches various areas, noting especially where nearby buildings, fences, or walls cast deep and constant shade. In very small gardens there may be only an hour of direct sun at midday. It makes sense to choose shade-loving plants for such sites. In general, rather than struggling to eliminate adverse conditions, choose plants that will survive them.

Selecting Plants

Since there are so many types of suburban gardens it is impossible to offer a list of plants specifically recommended for them. There is no special Lilliputian breed suited to all environments—in fact, you are not restricted to small plants. Large trees and shrubs can fill empty spaces and achieve screening height quickly, so they are especially valuable in new, bare lots. Some may need to be removed in ten or fifteen years. Other large plants can be controlled by pruning, shearing, trellising, or root-pruning.

Suburbs

To keep maintenance to a minimum, avoid plants that drop seed into cracks in pavement, send sprawling suckers into brick paths, or heave up sidewalks with shallow roots.

As accents in the small garden, use eye-catching, variegated and large-leaved plants, but add them sparingly. They can overwhelm the garden, resulting in a restless, busy design that lacks unity. Keep the number of different plant types down to about a dozen, but use them lavishly, arranged in masses. Rounded, weeping, and horizontal shapes work best. Assertively upright plants tend to look like exclamation points, leading the eye out of the design.

Structures in the Garden

Although plants are the stars in most gardens, in the small landscape architectural elements such as fences, decks, and paving are just as important. They can help hold the design together, provide privacy, and make the space appear larger.

Many small gardens endure a great deal of foot traffic, so paving is usually a necessity. It might consist of a few irregular stones set in the lawn or a formal brick patio filling nearly the entire space. Sometimes a decorative fence will steal center stage. It can block out visual clutter in neighboring yards—clothes lines, picnic benches, tool sheds, or gardens of conflicting style. A tall hedge or clusters of small trees can also screen views and will unify and enlarge the area.

Another way to fool a viewer into thinking your garden is more spacious is by adding levels—terraces, berms, or a raised deck, for example. A multilevel landscape makes the eye travel a greater distance, and it makes your walk through the garden take a bit longer, too. Two other visual tricks you might try are adding steps and a gate, even if the gate is purely decorative and doesn't lead anywhere. Both of these features imply movement, either up and down or through the space. They make wonderful focal points, too.

Small Gardens in Many Styles

The gardens on the following pages are restricted only in size. Their designers' ingenuity is otherwise boundless, expressed in styles as diverse as their individual tastes. Notice the feeling of enclosure in each, whether created by a decorative fence, hedge, wall, or raised bed. Each garden is arranged around a focal point—a brick courtyard, a small pond, a lush lawn, a formal fountain, or a bluestone patio. Some are oases of cool green tones, while others are cheerful palettes of color. Plants with tiny, delicate leaves and flowers lend a sense of space, and attractive foliage plants grace shady areas with their subtle variety. Look for plant groupings, structures, or layouts that might work in your own suburban garden, making it an original, inviting extension of your home.

New Canaan,
Connecticut
Van Pelt Wilson
Garden

Site:
Small patio
Half-day sun
Average soil

Design Concepts:
Circular plan
Dogwood as focus
Enclosure by fence
Varied textures
Pink accents amid cool
greens

Decorative Elements:
Brick paving
Wooden screen
Low picket fence
Containers
Plant stand

Plantings:
Dogwood
Asparagus fern
Impatiens

Seasons:
Photographed in
summer
Effective spring to fall
Over 2 years old

New Canaan,
Connecticut
Van Pelt Wilson
Garden

Site:
Small backyard
Full sun
Average soil

Design Concepts:
Strong symmetry
Geometric design
Fence as backdrop

Decorative Elements:	Plantings:	Seasons:
Low picket fence	Standard-trained lilacs	Photographed in early fall
Brick paving	Chrysanthemums	
Lamp post	Impatiens	Effective spring and summer
Terra-cotta birds		
Containers		After 1 season
Wood-chip mulch		

Berkeley, California
Blake Garden

Site:
Enclosed yard
Gentle slope
Full sun
Dry soil

Design Concepts:
Informal planting
scheme
Bench and pool as focus
Use of silver foliage
Varied foliage textures
Hedge forms strong
horizontal line

Decorative Elements:	Plantings:	Seasons:
Water lily pool	*Shasta daisies*	*Photographed in early*
Concrete bench	*Blue fescue*	*fall*
Gravel paths	*Lavender*	*Effective spring through*
	Santolina	*fall*
	Yew	*Well-established garden*

**London, England
Private Garden**

Site:
Enclosed courtyard
Partial shade
Acid soil

Design Concepts:
Terraced planting
Variety of colors
Corner boundaries
hidden by lush
planting
Gray walls for
contrast

Decorative Elements:	Plantings:	Seasons:
Brick walls	Rhododendrons	Photographed in late
Wooden fence with	Azaleas	spring
trellis	Maple	Effective year-round
Bluestone paving	Marigolds	Over 3 years old

Site:
Small backyard
Level lawn
Sun and shade
Average soil

Design Concepts:
Emphasis on foliage
Varied textures
Curved edge leads to
tree as focal point
Enclosure by fence

Decorative Elements:
Wood paling fence
Log edging

Plantings:
Birch
Hostas
Weeping Norway
spruce
Juniper
Blue fescue

Seasons:
Photographed in
summer
Effective spring and
summer
Over 2 years old

Charleston, South Carolina Private Garden

Site:
Walled garden
Level lawn
Partial shade
Acid soil

Design Concepts:
Wall for privacy and effective backdrop
Colorful blooms contrast with dark foliage
Pink repeated throughout

Decorative Elements:	*Plantings:*	*Seasons:*
High brick wall	*Azaleas*	*Photographed in*
Fountain	*Ferns*	*mid-spring*
Wall ornament	*Impatiens*	*Effective spring and*
Hanging planters	*Hawthorn*	*summer*
	Shrubs	*Over 4 years old*
	Pansies	

**Sherborn,
Massachusetts
Private Garden**

Site:
Small patio
Level area
Full sun
Average soil

Design Concepts:
Intimate scale
Patio as focus
Varied foliage colors,
textures
Pink as accent

Decorative Elements:	Plantings:	Seasons:
Bluestone patio and paths	Eastern redbuds	Photographed in early summer
	Standard-trained wisteria	Effective spring and summer
	Roses	Over 2 years old
	Lavender cotton	
	Cleome	
	Thyme	

City Gardens

A city garden is a haven, an area of cool serenity only a few steps from the noisy, crowded streets. Nothing quite matches the feeling of delight to be had in escaping from a busy sidewalk into a private courtyard oasis, or opening a stairwell door onto a rooftop filled with colorful plants.

A city garden may be as modest as a decorative planter of cheerful tulips set on a balcony, or as extensive as a backyard garden divided into landscaped "rooms." Many city dwellers who have glimpsed such private enclaves from their office windows don't realize how easy it is to bring a bit of the country into their own urban spaces.

Using Tricks of Perception

Much of the success of a city garden depends on the manipulation of space. There are many simple but often overlooked visual tricks to employ to make an area seem larger or more private. They involve carefully choosing and placing masses of plants, ornaments, and architectural features. Often it is possible to create a sense of both intimate enclosure and expansion in the same design.

The simplest way to unify a small garden is to enclose it, creating a cozy, intimate space. Try grouping trees and shrubs so that they form small areas for sitting or dining. Place a tree near the garden's entrance, where it can frame the view beyond. To focus the eye inward and downward, add visual interest in the form of decorative paving, ground covers with pleasing colors or textures, or even a small pool.

If your space is long and relatively narrow, consider separating it into two or more distinct areas. This will enhance the feeling that you are walking through a larger area. Add levels in the form of terraces, berms, or raised beds.

If your space is shallow, use the principles of perspective to your advantage. Deepen the space by gradually reducing plant heights toward the back of the garden. If a path is part of your scheme, make it narrowest at its farthest point. Place strong, hot colors in the foreground and soft, cool pastels farther away so that they appear to fade into the mist. Use an arbor to connect two distinct areas, creating a tunnel effect that seems to add length.

Choosing and Arranging Plants

A small space does not restrict you to the use of small plants. On the contrary, too much reliance on dwarf plants and low ground covers may cause a dollhouse effect. Sizeable evergreen trees such as false cypress, Japanese hemlock, and Arizona cypress are especially useful as screens and backdrops. Small to medium-sized deciduous trees can offer lovely blossoms and dappled shade. Try crabapples, flowering cherries, or star magnolias.

Vines are especially useful in city gardens for softening walls and fences, anchoring the house to its surroundings, and filling a space quickly with rapid growth. Clematis, jasmine, passion-flower, and

wisteria are ideal candidates to train on a trellis or arbor.
Almost any plant you admire whose needs you can meet is a
possibility for your city garden. There is no definitive list of the
best plants. What is most important is that you limit the number
of different varieties and plant them in masses rather than
sprinkling them throughout the scene.

Gardening in the Sky
City gardens on rooftops, terraces, and balconies are blessed with
glorious, expansive views. These lofty locations can create some
special problems, but they are easily solved by forethought and
extra care.
Take advantage of the view while combatting that giddy, exposed
feeling you can get on high floors by using trees or shrubs as
screens. Leave spaces for lower plants in other places to frame a
particular vista. Fences and trellises also work effectively as
screens.
Although it is possible to build beds of earth directly on rooftops,
there are advantages to planting in containers—including
portability, neatness, and the ability to grow plants with fairly deep
roots. If your roof is covered only with tar paper, reinforce it with a
stronger material. Some attractive choices are glazed tile, brick
pavers, or the new stone-and-resin pavers that look like granite but
are much lighter.

Care of Backyard Gardens
While rooftop and balcony gardens suffer extremes of exposure, city
gardens at ground level are subject to problems caused by poor air
circulation. The enclosure created by nearby buildings is desirable
for privacy, but it increases the incidence of fungal disease on
plants, so you should choose varieties especially resistant to such
diseases. It is also a good idea to hose down the garden regularly to
remove deposits of soot that screen sunlight from leaf surfaces. In
general, choose rugged plants with vigorous, almost weedy, growth
for your backyard landscape.

Urban Oases
The city gardens on the following pages are all on rooftops and
terraces, but each has a distinctive style. The simplest designs
brighten small areas with just a few well-placed flowers and trees;
the more ambitious use paving and ground covers to break up
larger spaces; and one garden offers the delightful surprise of a
perennial border planted along a penthouse wall. Notice how
containers, fences, patterned paving, and garden furniture have
been used as accents or to tie a scheme together. These rare
glimpses into private urban gardens may make you see your old
tar beach in a completely new light.

New York, New York
Private Garden

Site:
Narrow rooftop terrace
Partial sun, wind

Design Concepts:
Trees frame view
Raised bed brings color closer to eye-level
Tulips in bands of color

Decorative Elements: *Plantings:*   *Seasons:*
French doors   *Hawthorn*   *Photographed in spring*
Brick paving   *Crabapple*   *Most effective in spring*
Raised brick planter   *Tulips*   *First season*
Wrought-iron fence

New York, New
York
Kips Bay Boy's
Club Showhouse,
1987

Site:
Terraced rooftop deck
Full sun

Design Concepts:
Multilevel space
Use of small-flowered,
low plants in small
space
Trees as accents
Varied foliage colors

Decorative Elements:	Plantings:	Seasons:
Red cedar deck	Sargent crabapples	Photographed in spring
Flagstone paving	English ivy	Effective spring and
Wooden fence	Variegated euonymus	summer
Brick parapet	Dwarf Alberta spruce	First season
	Bar Harbor juniper	
	Leucothoe	
	Fragrant viburnum	

New York, New York
Angulo Garden

Site:
Rooftop garden
Large, enclosed area
Full sun

Design Concepts:
Private yet open effect
Low groupings break
up space
Trees for shade,
privacy
Dark foliage offsets
colorful blooms

Decorative Elements:
Wooden planters
Quarry tile
Japanese lantern
Victorian wrought-iron
furniture
Concrete wall
Urn as planter

Plantings:
Prostrate junipers
Geraniums
Transvaal daisies

Seasons:
Photographed in
summer
Effective spring and
summer
About 10 years old

**Seattle, Washington
Private Garden**

Site:
Small balcony terrace
Partial shade

Design Concepts:
Potted plants provide
seasonal color
Seating area as focus
Trees act as screen
Yellow-orange theme

Decorative Elements:	Plantings:	Seasons:
Patterned glazed tiles	*Tulips*	*Photographed in spring*
Brick and wood seating area	*Daffodils*	*Effective in spring*
Concrete balustrade	*Dusty miller*	*Over 1 year old*
Plant containers	*False cypresses*	

New York, New York
Private Garden

Site:
Narrow penthouse
terrace
Full sun

Design Concepts:
Perennial border in
unusual setting
Wall as backdrop
Graduated heights
Dramatic use of color
and texture

Decorative Elements:	Plantings:	Seasons:
High white walls	Bergamot	Photographed in
Brick paving	Cosmos	summer
Table, umbrella, and	Dahlias	Effective in summer
chairs	Geraniums	Over 1 year old
Raised planters	Roses	

New York, New York
Burgee Garden

Site:
Narrow penthouse
terrace
Full sun, wind

Design Concepts:
Enclosure by planters
Planters bring design
closer to eye-level
Trees for vertical lines
Cool color scheme
White walls as
backdrop
Chair as focus

Decorative Elements:	Plantings:	Seasons:
Classic concrete balustrade	White birch	Photographed in late spring
Glazed tiles	Trailing junipers	Effective year-round
Unpainted planter boxes	Azaleas	5 years old
Teak deck chair	Rhododendrons	
	Clematis	
	Grandiflora roses	
	Campanula	

Water Gardens

There is something special about a water garden, with its sounds of splashing, trickling, and churning and the shimmering reflections of sunlight, moonlight, and graceful plants. Whether it is created in a small container or a man-made pond, at the edge of a lake or in a boggy area, a well-designed arrangement of aquatic and moisture-loving plants adds a calm, mysterious beauty to the home landscape. Modern advances in pond construction and new, hardier plant hybrids have brought water gardening within the grasp of almost everyone. Once the heavy work of excavation is completed and the plants chosen and placed, there is little maintenance required. Many of the best designs include relatively few plants, most of which can be enjoyed during the first gardening season.

A Sunny Site
Since most water-garden plants need at least six hours of sunlight daily, an open location is best. The ideal site is relatively flat and free of rocks, so it is easy to excavate. It should lie within range of electricity, if your design calls for pumps and lights, and near running water to use in refilling. Stay clear of deciduous shrubs and trees whose leaves would create a maintenance problem, and avoid extremely low-lying areas where groundwater runoff might float a man-made pond off its foundation.

Decide whether your water garden is to be the main focus of the landscape or an accent in one area. Think about the style of your house and grounds and design a water feature that blends in. Geometrically-shaped pools fit well into somewhat formal gardens, whereas freeform ponds and bog gardens blend naturally into more modern landscapes.

A Simple Pond
Creating a pond or a pool is surprisingly easy, involving digging a hole of the desired shape and lining it with a sheet of polyvinyl chloride or laying in a prefabricated fiberglass pond. Installing concrete pools, streams, and special features such as waterfalls and fountains may require the help of a professional, but once the construction is complete, you can enjoy selecting and placing the plants that best complement your new scheme.

Poolside Gardens
Although landscaping around swimming pools does not involve the use of aquatic plants, it does require incorporating water into the design. The goal is to make the pool blend into its surroundings, to soften the jolt of bright blue that can overwhelm an entire scene. Often this is accomplished with carefully selected plants, but the pool itself can be made to look more natural if given a dark lining. Black-lined pools have become increasingly popular for this reason. Because of the bright sun, heat, and wind conditions in most poolside areas, choose sturdy plants and give them special care.

The Plants

One of the biggest pleasures of water gardening is the opportunity to grow some of nature's most beautiful and exotic plants. Their unusual colors and shapes can create any feeling, from completely natural to very formal. The foliage is especially interesting, ranging from light to very dark green—often tinged with blue, sometimes banded with yellow or mottled with purple. Leaves come in almost any shape.

Water lilies are the royalty of the water garden. They are so dramatic that they can easily serve as the main, or only, feature of the garden. There are other floating plants to choose from, including the delicate yellow or white snowflakes and the floating hearts, so-called because of their heart-shaped leaves.

There are plants that grow beneath the water's surface, taking advantage of the extra dimension of depth that makes a water garden different from any other landscape design. These underwater plants add mysterious color and texture to a pond's interior.

Emergent plants are those that root in the shallows and rise to heights from several inches to four feet or more. Cat-tails, reeds and rushes, water irises, and lotuses are some familiar examples to try.

The Design

Each plant in a water garden is so unique and intriguing that too many can crowd a design, confusing the observer about where to look first. A crowded plan also obscures an important design element—the water itself. Patches of unobstructed water are essential to provide background, reflection, a sense of calm space, and a window through which to observe submerged plants and aquatic wildlife.

It is best to rely on a few "stars," such as a dramatic water lily or patches of elegant irises, and surround them with more subtle plants whose shapes and colors will harmonize but not overpower these focal points.

Water Gardens to Inspire You

The color plates that follow will give you an idea of how many forms a water garden can take. Designed around swimming pools, ponds, streams, and waterfalls, these gardens include traditional garden plants as well as aquatics. They vary in style from very formal to naturalistic, but in each, the water feature is the focal point. You'll see a poolside garden that is a riot of colorful perennials and another that's a cool oasis of trees and shrubs. There is a manicured pond designed in Old World style and a free-form pond that evokes the jungle. The plants placed near a natural stream emphasize its quiet beauty, while those flanking a man-made stream create a dramatic, formal effect. Each design provides different clues to how you might transform your own landscape by creating a water garden.

Columbus, Ohio
Private Garden

Site:
Border of swimming
pool
Full to partial sun
Dry soil

Design Concepts:
Path as contrast
Graduated plant
heights
Yellows repeated

Decorative Elements:	Plantings:	Seasons:
Concrete path	Petunias	Photographed in
Wooden fence	Purple loosestrife	summer
Sundial	Astilbes	Effective spring to fall
	Daylilies	Over 2 years old
	Cleome	
	Norway spruce	

**Fairfield County,
Connecticut
Private Garden**

Site:
Swimming pool area
Full to partial sun
Dry soil

Design Concepts:
Pool, lawn, and bed
in parallel strips
Use of silver foliage
Plantings enclose area

Decorative Elements:	Plantings:	Seasons:
Patterned concrete patio	Artemisia	Photographed in
Mesh furniture	Easter lilies	summer
White planter	Russian sage	Effective spring to fall
	Astilbes	Over 2 years old

Dorset, England
Black Down
Garden

Site:
Level area
Borders woods
Full to partial sun
Wet soil

Design Concepts:
Woods as backdrop
Statue for focus
Lily foliage as anchors
Maple, ferns for
softness
Pink and purple
accents

Decorative Elements:	Plantings:	Seasons:
Man-made pond	Water lilies	Photographed in late
Statue	Azaleas	spring
Natural features	Viburnums	Effective year-round
	Cutleaf Japanese maple	Well-established garden
	Irises	
	False acacia	
	Golden club	

Site:
Gentle slope
Partial shade
Moist soil

Design Concepts:
Fence as textured
backdrop
Rocks for natural look
Water lilies as focus
Contrasting leaf shapes

Decorative Elements:	Plantings:	Seasons:
Man-made pond	Ferns	Photographed in spring
Wooden fence	Elephant's-ears	Effective spring to fall
Rock wall	Reeds	Well-established garden
Small waterfall	Water lilies	
	Lotus	
	Umbrella plants	
	Cat-tails	

Stockbridge,
Massachusetts
Berkshire Garden
Center

Site:
Raised banks
Dense shade
Wet soil

Design Concepts:
Foliage backdrop
Bench for focus
Plants spill from banks
Contrasting flower
shapes
Pink as accent

Decorative Elements:	*Plantings:*	*Seasons:*
Man-made pond	*Japanese primroses*	*Photographed in summer*
Wooden bench	*Astilbes*	*Effective spring to summer*
Rocks	*Forget-me-nots*	*Well-established garden*

Monkton, Maryland
Iris Garden, Ladew

Site:
Large, level lawn
Border of man-made
stream
Gently sloping banks
Full sun

Design Concepts:
Woods as backdrop
Parallel beds and
lawns
Symmetry of plantings
Lawn for contrast

Decorative Elements:	Plantings:	Seasons:
Stone bridge	Bearded irises	Photographed in early summer
Wooden bench	Perennials	Effective spring to summer
	Hemlocks	Over 3 years old
	Japanese yew	

**Philadelphia,
Pennsylvania
Roland Garden**

Site:
Woodland setting
Partial shade
Moist soil

Design Concepts:
Evergreen backdrop
Graduated heights
Red and white accents
Contrasting foliage
types

Decorative Elements:	Plantings:	Seasons:
Man-made waterfall	Dogwoods	Photographed in early
Rocks	Azaleas	spring
Natural path	Hemlocks	Effective year-round
	Japanese pieris	Well-established garden
	Ferns	

**Boston,
Massachusetts
Private Garden**

Site:
Large yard
Gentle slope
Wooded backdrop
Full sun
Average soil

Design Concepts:
Multilevel plantings
Pool and waterfall as
focus
Use of evergreens
Repetition of shapes
Emphasis on texture

Decorative Elements:
*Man-made pool and
waterfall
Landscape rocks
Stone steps
Patio blocks*

Plantings:
*Dwarf spruce
Tanyosho pines
Daylilies
Purple Gem
rhododendrons
Marsh marigolds
Dwarf viburnum
Mosses and ferns*

Seasons:
*Photographed in
summer
Effective year-round
1 year old*

Shade Gardens

Shade, like time itself, seems to advance inexorably in the garden, with sunny beds becoming shady and shady beds turning shadier, until many traditional plants no longer flourish. Here, and in the forgotten corners hugging the house, are potential oases—peaceful retreats awaiting your trowel and imagination.

While many gardeners enjoy the coolness that shade provides, few take advantage of the variety of plants that do best where there is least sun. Shade is often the best place to grow rhododendrons and azaleas—the most glorious of garden shrubs. Woodland wildflowers and a host of ground covers flourish in shady environments, where impatiens and begonias offer a long season of rich hues. Properly conceived and planted, the shade garden can be ablaze with color and interest for much of the year.

Varieties of Shade

Shade can be caused by many things, trees being the most obvious. It is important to realize that many plants will flourish under shade trees. Dense shade from Norway maples or conifers poses a challenge to be met with vigorous ground covers. The cool shade cast by buildings and fences is especially congenial to many broadleaf evergreens and plants of borderline hardiness.

Preparing the Site

The greatest problem in growing most plants in shade is often not the darkness but the impoverished soils that are found around aggressive tree roots and alongside unyielding concrete in many urban neighborhoods. Soil preparation is essential: Ferns and choice woodland plants need constantly moist and humus-rich soil. To grow healthy plants in filtered light, you need to frequently top-dress shady beds with compost and topsoil.

Many traditional sun-loving plants will tolerate considerable shade, provided they have sufficient water and nourishment at their roots. There is also a rich palette of plants that require shade to flourish: Broadleaf evergreen trees and shrubs such as barberries and hollies often benefit from some shade in the hottest summer or in winter when sunscald is a problem. Boxwood, mountain laurel, and daphne thrive in these conditions, even tolerating alkaline soils.

Specialties in Shade

Woodland plants and those from cooler, wetter climates naturally do best in a shady environment. These can be used in more formal bedding schemes as well as in the traditional woodland garden. Wild ginger makes a fine ground cover, and bugbane adds a dramatic accent to the shady border. Hostas and lilies are major groups of garden plants that do best in considerable shade. Quite a few garden annuals—beginning with the glamorous and long-season bloom of impatiens—are being bred for shady conditions. The variety of plants available is practically endless.

Contrasting Foliage

The effect of foliage contrast is a principal theme for growing plants in shade. Shade-lovers such as bergenia, hosta, peltiphyllum, and rodgersia are characterized by leaves of tropical size and luxuriance. Combine these with plants of finer texture, different shades of green, or variegated foliage, and you can create a rich and varied canvas.

Some colors are especially effective in the shade: Most pastel tints seem to glow in a shady garden, and whites are particularly striking against a dark background. In the sun, snowy goatsbeard is hardly noticeable, but it is positively pyrotechnic in a shady corner. Select plants for a shade garden first on their merits as foliage plants then with an eye to combining colors.

Creating an Oasis

Who isn't calmed by the thought of a shadowed canyon or a sheltered hollow where there is the cool drip of water on even the hottest summer day? You can create your own secluded retreat—a shade garden in which to seek refuge from the heat, entertain in cool comfort, or enjoy the subtle play of light and shadow. The shady corner is an ideal spot for a bench or a seat on which to relax during a hot day and view the rest of the garden. Such areas are the first in your landscape to get dark and the last to lighten up in the morning. Introduce some decorative lighting features to enhance both the romance and the safety of your garden.

The Goal

The color plates that follow present a variety of shade gardens: plantings along foundations, retreats carved into sun-dappled woodlands, and restful compositions filling small, level spaces. Foliage is used as backdrop and focal point, and shade-loving plants lead the eye from ground to treetops in graduated heights. Tall shade trees shelter understories of shrubs, annuals, perennials, and ground covers, their glimmering flowers and textured foliage providing a long season of interest.

In each of these gardens, the types of shade and soil helped determine the choices of compatible plants. With the same kind of careful and creative planning, you can transform a dark, bare corner into a shimmering, lush paradise. Few gardens will be more soothing to the eye or to the soul.

**Holland, Michigan
Private Garden**

*Site:
Foundation planting
bordered by path
Situational shade
Average soil*

*Design Concepts:
Rounded area for
contrast
Graduated heights
Foliage as backdrop
Green and red theme
Potted plants as accents*

Decorative Elements:	Plantings:	Seasons:
Terra-cotta containers	Plain and variegated	Photographed in early
Wooden edging posts	hostas	summer
Hanging planter	Geraniums	Blooms in midsummer
	Wax begonias	About 2 years old
	Bugleweed	

Columbus, Ohio
Private Garden

Site:
Small, level area
Dappled tree shade
Average soil

Design Concepts:
Woodland effect
Fence as backdrop
Path leads into design
Lawn area as focus
Use of curved lines
Contrasting textures

Decorative Elements:	*Plantings:*	*Seasons:*
Wooden paving blocks	*Hostas*	*Photographed in*
Picket fence	*Variegated bugleweed*	*summer*
	Lungwort	*Effective spring to fall*
	Impatiens	*Over 2 years old*

**Princeton, New
Jersey
Hester Garden**

Site:
Level clearing in
wooded area
High shade
Humus-rich soil

Design Concepts:
Woodland effect
Path leads into design
Gazebo as focus
Contrasting textures
Plantings parallel path
Cool green theme

Decorative Elements:	Plantings:	Seasons:
Wooden gazebo	Rhododendrons	Photographed in spring
Broken flagstone path	Shield ferns	Effective spring to
Wood-chip mulch	Sword ferns	winter
	Bluebells	Over 3 years old
	Beeches	

Richmond, Virginia
Virginia House

Site:
Enclosed, level area
High shade
Enriched, acid soil

Design Concepts:
Geometric design
Paths as outlines
Boxwood as edging
Repeated plantings
Pink and white theme

Decorative Elements:	*Plantings:*	*Seasons:*
Sculpted stone wall	Boxwood	Photographed in early
Brick and stone walks	Dogwoods	spring
Small formal pool	Rhododendrons	Blooms in spring
	Triumph tulips	Well-established garden
	Forget-me-nots	

New Hope,
Pennsylvania
Jamison Garden

Site:
Small area under oak
Tree shade
Humus-rich soil

Design Concepts:
Bright colors contrast
with shade
Graduated heights
Hostas as border
Yellow and orange
theme
Purple as accent

Decorative Elements:	Plantings:	Seasons:
Boulders	Oak	Photographed in early summer
	Variegated hostas	
	Hybrid lilies	Blooms in summer
	Spiderwort	About 3 years old

**New Hope,
Pennsylvania
Benner Garden**

Site:
Wooded area
Gentle slope
Tree shade
Humus-rich soil

Design Concepts:
Woodland effect
Planting in drifts
Cool colors
Orange-pink as accent

Decorative Elements:	Plantings:	Seasons:
Natural features	Foamflowers	Photographed in early spring
	Phlox	Blooms in early spring
	Azaleas	Effective spring to fall
	Primroses	Well-established garden
	Columbines	

Japanese-Style

Japan is a country of lush greenery, rocky waterfalls and streams, and rolling hills and valleys. Much of Japanese religion and philosophy derive from serious contemplation of this natural beauty, which is thought of as not only lovely but meaningful. Nature is a sort of book to be "read" and studied for clues to profound truths. Gardens in Japan serve a similar inspirational purpose. They are understated suggestions of natural scenes that, in addition to being decorative, are meant to encourage contemplation and meditation. Relatively few elements are included, and emphasis is placed on the natural beauty of each rock, plant, or structure as well as on the harmony of the scene as a whole.

Familiar Plants in an Unusual Setting
While the Eastern philosophy of garden design may seem unusual to Westerners, the plants themselves are often familiar because the Japanese climate is similar to that in many areas of the U.S. Mosses, bamboo, hostas, irises, many types of ferns, and azaleas are commonly used, as are the many plants whose English common names indicate their origin, including Japanese maple, Japanese holly, and the "Japanese" forms of white pine, flowering cherry, and wisteria. Evergreens are heavily relied on, often pruned or trained to appear old because maturity is valued by the Japanese.

A Total Design
Landscape and architecture are inseparable in the Japanese tradition of garden design. A garden is an outdoor room, an extension of the structure it surrounds. Japanese ideas and traditions have endless applications for Western homeowners. A Japanese-style garden can be designed for a space of any size, and it can shape the environment to screen out unsightly views and call attention to picturesque areas, make a small space seem larger, or create feelings of tranquility even in a noisy city. In fact, a small city lot is an ideal site for a Japanese garden.

Aesthetic Principles
The refreshing simplicity of a Japanese-style garden is not difficult to achieve, but it does require careful thought about perception and scale. Create the illusion of space by placing large plants or objects in the foreground and decreasing their size toward the back of the garden. Use this exaggeration of perspective in placing rocks and trees, or in creating islands in a pond. Limit the number of different types of plants and construction materials used to avoid a cluttered look. Plan level, open spaces such as expanses of water, gravel, moss, sand, or ground covers. These flat planes, combined with horizontal architectural details such as low roof lines, railings, or footbridges add to the sense of placid space.
Strive for asymmetrical balance by placing the main mass of your design—perhaps a large pine or a rock outcrop—to one side in

Gardens

the garden. Create vantage points throughout the garden from which a visitor can stop and appreciate the line, texture, and nuances of color you have arranged. Consider adding a water feature for its refreshing appearance, sound, and reflective qualities. Finally, include some plants that appear old and weathered or that can be pruned or trained to look that way.

Traditional Styles

There are several different styles of traditional Japanese gardens, and you might want to model your own design after a particular type. In the hill-and-pond garden, one of the oldest styles, the hills and ponds are man-made, shrubs are shaped to echo the undulating forms of mountains and clouds, and trees are pruned to look old and windswept. In the *roji,* or tea garden, there is a stepping-stone path, representing a mountain trail, leading to the ceremonial tea house. A stone lantern and water basin are usually included, and the plants are mostly subdued evergreens.

A stroll garden also features stepping stones, stone lanterns, and often a teahouse or pavilion, but its main feature is an irregularly shaped pond with islands. Visitors are meant to move through the garden around this pond, viewing it from various vantage points. The dry landscape garden, associated with Zen temples, is a small area for meditation consisting only of stones, raked gravel or sand, and moss. A courtyard garden is a variation on this theme, including a few carefully placed plants and perhaps stepping stones and lanterns, as in a tea garden.

Eastern Answers to Western Problems

The tranquility and harmony that are sought after in Japanese gardens can be very valuable to soothe Western problems of stress, pressure, and increasingly crowded living conditions. The Oriental message that less can be more is very comforting.

On the following pages you will see Japanese-style gardens on vast, rolling hills and in small city courtyards. Notice how winding paths, rounded plant shapes, reliance on subtle evergreens, and the inclusion of ornamental features such as stones, bridges, lanterns, and ponds contribute to the overall effect of peacefulness. These gardens work in every season, and their changing aspects serve to increase their value. The small gardens shown here are especially simple in line and content. In one, a stone path is designed to resemble a stream winding through the scene. The stroll garden promises new vistas around every corner, and the hill-and-pond garden demonstrates what water can add to the landscape. Each of these gardens contains effective combinations of plants, rocks, and structures that could be adapted to your own landscape. Even the smallest element borrowed from such time-honored Japanese designs can bring new pleasure to your gardening experience.

Brooklyn, New York	Site:	Design Concepts:
Roji Garden, Brooklyn Botanic Garden	Enclosed courtyard	Contrasting textures
	Long, narrow space	Secluded, peaceful effect
	Partial shade	Path suggests a river
	Average soil	Cool green tones
		Distinctive shapes

Decorative Elements:	Plantings:	Seasons:
Wooden fence with narrow roof	Needled evergreens	Photographed in summer
Bamboo-framed trellis	Broadleaf evergreens	Effective year-round
Disappearing stone path	Mosses	Over 5 years old
Pebble border	Ferns	
Ornamental rocks		

**Boston,
Massachusetts
Private Garden**

*Site:
City courtyard
Small, rectangular
space
Fully enclosed
Partial sun
Well-drained, moist
soil*

*Design Concepts:
Cool, secluded effect
Strong geometric design
Dark foliage contrasts
with white pebbles
Ivied wall as backdrop*

Decorative Elements:	Plantings:	Seasons:
Offset brick path	Japanese maple	Photographed in late
Bamboo fence	Climbing euonymus	spring
Walk-through gate	English ivy	Effective year-round
shelter	Boston ivy	Over 5 years old
Stone lantern	Ferns	
Assorted rocks	Trilliums	
Pebble mulch		

Charlestown,
Pennsylvania
Swiss Pines Garden

Site:
Large, open area
Gentle slope
Full to partial sun
Well-drained soil

Design Concepts:
Stroll garden
Pebbles suggest stream
Round shapes repeated
Contrasting textures
Red as accent

Decorative Elements:	Plantings:	Seasons:
Boulders	Scarlet maple	Photographed in fall
Stone lantern	Japanese holly	Effective year-round
Wooden fence	Mugo pines	Over 10 years old
Small stones	Firs	
Concrete path	Pachysandra	
Birdhouse		

Brooklyn, New York
Japanese Hill-and-Pond Garden, Brooklyn Botanic Garden

Site:
Large, open area
Man-made hills and pond
Sun and shade
Well-drained, moist soil

Design Concepts:
Use of sculptured forms
Pool for focus and contrast
Reliance on foliage plants
Red as accent

Decorative Elements:	Plantings:	Seasons:
Stylized wooden bridge	Scarlet maple	Photographed in fall
Meandering paths	Cloud-pruned maples	Effective year-round
Large rocks	Pines	Well-established garden
Gravel walks	Azaleas	

**Brooklyn,
New York
Japanese Hill-and-
Pond Garden,
Brooklyn Botanic
Garden**

Site:
Large, open area
*Man-made pond, hills,
and waterfall*
Sun and shade
*Well-drained, moist
soil*

Design Concepts:
Use of sculptured forms
Multilevel plantings
Variety of textures
Bridge as focus
Pond to reflect elements
*Bursts of color amid
cool greens*

Decorative Elements:	Plantings:	Seasons:
Stylized wooden bridge	*Wisteria*	*Photographed in spring*
Bird house	*Japanese maples*	*Effective year-round*
Rocks	*Pines*	*Well-established garden*
	Japanese holly	
	Water flag	
	Japanese irises	
	Azalea	

Winterscapes

By designing a landscape for maximum effect in winter, you can turn a bleak season into one of extraordinary beauty. A winterscape can be planned for any area in which the change of seasons brings cold and its resultant plant hibernation. While a luxuriant layer of radiantly white snow often provides a finishing touch, lending contrast and definition to the landscape, it is not essential. Even in areas where snowfall is rare or nonexistent, you can create a unique garden by choosing plants for their winter appeal.

Nature's Winter Beauty

The winterscapes of nature contain an abundance of riches: the intricate patterns formed by the bare branches of a lone deciduous tree starkly silhouetted against a field or meadow; the interesting textures and character of tree barks; the vivid colors of various shrub canes; the bright berries and fruits of some shrubs and trees; the ever-present dark green of pines and firs often serving to set off and outline plants of contrasting color; and the expanses, large and small, of tall, golden-hued meadow grasses. Topographical features such as rock outcrops, streams, ponds, and hills seem to stand out more strongly in winter, and the horizon is refreshingly open. Any of these natural sights may be adapted to a home garden, no matter how large or small. And with the vast array of winter-hardy varieties and cultivars now available, you can go one step further—installing plants with color, form, texture, and even bloom not to be found in the wild. In a small, well-protected garden—perhaps immediately beyond a window, where there is a warmer microclimate—you can choose from among even more varieties, including some that would not survive in an open area.

Accenting Existing Plants

Whether you desire a small pocket garden or wish to make your entire property as attractive as possible during the cold months, take stock of what is already planted. The concept of designing for maximum winter effect easily accommodates existing plantings, and there may be quite a few specimens in your garden whose winter aspects are prized. Those that are not particularly pleasing may be made so, in many cases, by surrounding them with other plants: a richly textured evergreen ground cover around a bare-branched tree or shrub; a stand of firs backing up and silhouetting a tall, fountainlike spray of ornamental grass; tufts of heath or heather strategically placed amid other plants in an existing bed.

Color, Texture, and Form

In selecting new plants for a winterscape, concentrate on candidates with outstanding color, texture, and form. Bear in mind that the best winter characteristics of some plants are hidden at other times of the year—the bright red canes of dogwood or the gnarled branches of Harry Lauder's walking stick. Do some research and use your imagination. Although you'll probably be planting in spring or fall, you must have a clear idea of what a particular plant will look like in winter before you can place it for best effect.

Flowers in Winter

Are flowers a winter possibility? Unlikely as it may seem, the answer is yes—for all areas within and south of zone 6, that is, and protected sites farther north. To stretch the season of bloom as long as possible, choose species that flower in late winter to early spring—such as winter crocus—and late fall to early winter—witch hazel, for example, with its small yet very fragrant blossoms. These hardy plants will enrich your garden with the rarest of phenomena—bloom amid snow.

A Formal Approach

The mainstays of formal gardens—coniferous trees, boxwood and other evergreen shrubs—remain virtually unchanged throughout the year and so are excellent choices for winter enjoyment. In fact, formal designs lend themselves especially well to small, protected areas of the landscape and should be considered when you contemplate a winter-garden plan. Evergreens trimmed into topiaries are particular treats; they will retain their form and delight all eyes, no matter how forbidding the weather.

Line and Contrast

In mapping out a winterscape, take special heed of the principles of line and contrast. At a time of year when the garden bares its bones, so to speak, strong horizontal, vertical, and angular lines stand out. The degree to which you keep all three types of lines in balance will determine the design's success. Balance the vertical lines of tree trunks with the horizontal configuration of a row of small pines, low-growing shrubs, or ground covers such as English ivy or prostrate evergreens. Offset too many verticals and horizontals with rounded plants, both bare-branched and evergreen.
Play up contrasts wherever possible. Position plants of diverse color, shape, or texture side by side to emphasize the strong points of each. Be sure to include mulches when contemplating color and texture. Pine bark, pine needles, or pebbles—to name a few of the endless varieties available—can provide swaths of ground interest where snow is infrequent.

Winterscapes to Admire

In the following color plates, you'll see how the winter beauty of trees, shrubs, grasses, herbs, and flowers make a dull season come alive. From a row of variously textured shrubs to a single sculptured tree, these winterscapes are subtle and sophisticated.

Surrey, England
Wisley Garden

Site:
Edge of large property
Level lawn
Full sun
Moist, acid soil

Design Concepts:
Horizontal shrub row
contrasts with tall trees
Variety of foliage
Berries as accents
Lawn for contrast

Decorative Elements:	Plantings:	Seasons:
Natural features	Variegated euonymus	Photographed in winter
	Mahonia	Fruit in fall and
	Holly	winter
	Pyracantha	Blooms in spring
	Barberries	Effective year-round
	Viburnum	Well-established garden
	Eleagnus	

Kennett Square,
Pennsylvania
Heath and Heather
Garden, Longwood

Site:
Large, open space
Strong slope
Full sun
Moist, acid soil

Design Concepts:
Contrasting foliage
Evergreens as accents
Path divides area
Bench as focus

Decorative Elements:	Plantings:	Seasons:
Teak bench	Heath	Photographed in late
Fine gravel path	Dwarf evergreen yew	winter
Stone border	Heather	Effective year-round
		Over 5 years old

**Occidental,
California
Western Hills
Garden**

Site:
Open area bordering
woods
Gentle slope
Full sun
Well-drained soil

Design Concepts:
Naturalistic effect
Varied foliage colors
Use of soft textures

Decorative Elements:	Plantings:	Seasons:
Natural features	Blue spruce	Photographed in winter
	Ornamental grasses	Effective year-round
	Heather	Over 5 years old

Port Murray, New Jersey
Well-Sweep Herb Farm

Site:
Large, level area
Full sun
Well-drained soil

Design Concepts:
Knot garden
Use of pruning
Varied foliage colors
Colors echoed in brick

Decorative Elements:	Plantings:	Seasons:
Wooden fence	Equisetum	Photographed in late
Red brick paths	Dwarf barberry	fall
White gravel mulch	Santolina	Blooms in summer
	Dwarf boxwood	Effective year-round
	Scented geraniums	Over 5 years old

| Bronx, New York Rock Garden, New York Botanical Garden | Site: Rocky embankment Full sun Well-drained soil | Design Concepts: Grass as accent Evergreens as backdrop Shrub silhouetted against snow |

Decorative Elements:	Plantings:	Seasons:
Natural features	Azalea	Photographed in winter
	Hinoki false cypress	Azalea blooms in spring
	Prostrate junipers	Grass green in summer
	Ravenna grass	Effective year-round
		Well-established garden

Long Island, New
York
Bayard Cutting
Arboretum

Site:
Open meadow
Full sun
Moist soil

Design Concepts:
Use of silhouettes for
dramatic effect
Rocks, woods as
backdrop

Decorative Elements:	*Plantings:*	*Seasons:*
Natural features	*Oak*	*Photographed in winter*
	Lombardy poplar	*Effective year-round*
		Well-established garden

Gardens by the

The seaside garden sets a mood unique in the landscaping world. Here fragile blooms thrive despite the raw, harsh elements. The sun shines brightly, the tides move rhythmically, and flowers seem to take on deeper colorings, their fragrances becoming sweeter and stronger after dusk. Sun, sea, wind, and salt spray combine to sculpt the plants. The horizon appears an endless expanse, and the stars can be counted on clear, moonlit nights.

A garden at the water's edge can take almost any form. Your tastes and the conditions of your site—open or protected—dictate the types of plants and how they are arranged. There is an astonishingly wide range of plants that will thrive by the sea.

Taking Advantage of the Site
Your garden may be large or small, perched on a rocky promontory or rambling across a flat and open plain. You may decide to create a sheltered enclave with trees and hedges as windbreaks. Or your garden spot may already have considerable shade from seaside trees—pitch pines and oaks along the Northeast coastline, coconut palms in the South, and Monterey cypress on the West Coast. Rocky ledges and outcrops, especially along the coast of Maine, seem to bring the mountains to the sea. Use native alpine hardy candytuft, basket-of-gold, arenaria, and edelweiss to imitate these regions.

Choosing Trees for the Seaside
Dramatically wind-whipped Japanese black pine, slender gray-leaved Russian olive, and fragrant, flowering lilac thrive in cool salty climes. Native pitch pine is a dependable standby, able to survive the harshest winters. Warmer areas of the Atlantic and Pacific enjoy a similarly wide range of trees. Top candidates for these areas are the Australian pine, which invariably leans in the direction of the prevailing winds, the Californian favorite Monterey cypress, and eucalyptus, Norfolk Island pine, Australian laurel, olive, California pepper-tree, shore pine, and the California bayberry.

Flowers by the Sea
The list of small flowering perennials, annuals, and bulbs for seaside gardens seems endless. Daylilies offer yellow, orange, or dark red trumpet flowers arising from slender, arching leaves. Delphinium's tall blue, purple, and white spires will need staking as they follow the whim of each breeze. Other familiar, tried-and-true choices are dahlias, marigolds, petunias, gladiolus, tulips, tuberous begonias, and bee balm. Mix them together, plant in masses on slopes, or try one-color schemes. If you provide some shelter and nourishment, you will be rewarded with a long season of bloom. Always and everywhere by the sea there are roses, climbing and shrubby, to add fragrance and romance.

Sea

Practical Considerations

Whether your garden is large or small, sheltered or exposed to the full brunt of the elements, you will have to contend with light, sandy soils, that must be fortified by organic matter. Wood chips, shredded bark, peat moss, and pine needles are excellent humus for blossoming azaleas, rhododendrons, blueberries, gardenias, and camellias. Heaths and heathers, which form striking ground covers, also benefit from amended soil.

Creating a successful seaside garden is a challenge from start to finish: You must learn to take advantage of the site's topography—the slopes, rocks, hollows, and hills—and to plant what has proven durable there. Some shelter from the elements is usually necessary. Hedges, trees, and even closely-planted perennials can form unusual, attractive windbreaks. Low shrubs, vines, and ground covers will spread quickly to conceal problem areas without obscuring a coveted water view.

Many plants have developed their own protection against the salt air and stiff breezes, adapting their structures for survival. Pitch pines and junipers have flexible branches to bend with the wind. The bayberry's waxy surface and dusty miller's tiny gray hairs help deflect salt crystals and cut down on moisture evaporation. Nature has already done much of the designing, leaving the final composition to your own taste.

Foliage Gardens

A seaside garden can be designed around leaf textures alone. Often this means bringing gray-leaved plants into the tapestry. Merged with the greens of pines, hollies, bearberry, yew, and false cypress, these plants have quiet appeal and a haunting effect, especially on foggy mornings or misty nights.

Enjoying the Beauty of the Beach

The rewards of gardening by the sea come from successfully combining beautiful plants in a harsh environment. On the following pages you will see evocative gardens set in this unique landscape. Coastal dunes dictate a naturalistic design, while a sheltered courtyard protects a sanctuary of colorful delphiniums, irises, and climbing roses. Plants of graduated heights provide a definite border to a lawn at the water's edge, thriving in full sun and sandy soil. A rocky point covered in flowers thrusts dramatically into the sea, the contrasting shapes and textures adding interest and individuality.

See how a well-defined path set in crushed stones harmonizes with the bold, wind-swept shapes of trees in a Japanese-style seaside garden. Finally, observe how an herb garden includes many tones of varied textures, forming a productive, restful enclave by the sea. Each of these gardens reflects one gardener's imagination shaped by a common element—the nearby ocean.

**Martha's Vineyard,
Massachusetts
Private Garden**

*Site:
Coastal dune
.Full sun and wind
Sandy soil*

*Design Concepts:
Naturalistic effect
Use of limited number
of plant types*

Decorative Elements:	Plantings:	Seasons:
Natural features	Rugosa roses	Photographed in
Open view	Northern bayberry	summer
	Japanese black pine	Roses bloom in summer
		Bayberry effective into
		winter
		Over 2 years old

Long Island, New York
Dash Garden

Site:
Small, level yard
Full sun
Protected from wind
Sandy soil

Design Concepts:
Long season of bloom
Maximum use of space
Feeling of enclosure
Variety of foliage
textures and colors
Trees as backdrop

Decorative Elements:	Plantings:	Seasons:
Picket fence	Delphiniums	Photographed in late spring
Block path	Climbing roses	
Ceramic urns	Achillea	Effective spring to late fall
	Irises	
	Astilbes	Over 5 years old
	Yarrow	

Boothbay Harbor, Maine Private Garden

Site:
Level lawn at water's edge
Full sun and wind
Sandy soil

Design Concepts:
Expansive effect
Well-defined beds
Graduated plant heights
Lawn as contrast
Warm colors with cool accents

Decorative Elements:
Simple wooden fence

Plantings:
Lilies
Marigolds
Dahlias
Bluebells
Nemesia
Snapdragons

Seasons:
Photographed in
summer
Effective late spring to
late fall
Over 3 years old

Boothbay Harbor,
Maine
Private Garden

Site:
Rocky shore
Open view
Full sun and wind
Sandy soil

Design Concepts:
Naturalistic effect
Graduated plant
heights
Contrasting flower
shapes
Warm colors
Rocks provide contrast

Decorative Elements:
Natural features

Plantings:
Sumac
Daylilies
Rudbeckias
Gaillardias
Sedums

Seasons:
Photographed in
summer
Most effective in
summer
Over 2 years old

Guilford,
Connecticut
Private Garden

Site:
Rocky shore
Open view
Full sun and wind
Sandy soil

Design Concepts:
Textures soften terrain
Use of dark foliage
Yellow and white
accents

Decorative Elements:	Plantings:	Seasons:
Concrete wall	Yucca	Photographed in
Terrace	Bar Harbor juniper	summer
	Daylilies	Blooms in spring
	Beach plum	Over 5 years old
	Russian olive	
	Lavender	

Mamaroneck, New York
Straus Garden

Site:
Level, open area
Full sun
Sandy soil

Design Concepts:
Japanese-garden effect
Path leads into design
Gravel for contrast
Strong shapes, outlines
Curves for softness
Trees silhouetted in
rear

Decorative Elements:	Plantings:	Seasons:
Crushed stones	Mugo pine	Photographed in fall
Slab path	Japanese pines	Effective year-round
Wooden edgings	Mimosas	Well-established garden
	Junipers	
	Marigolds	
	Sea lyme grass	

Coventry, Connecticut Caprilands Herb Farm	Site: Large, sheltered area Level lawn Full sun Average soil	Design Concepts: Use of silver tones Variety of foliage textures Island plantings break expanse of lawn Stones for contrast Purple accents

Decorative Elements:	Plantings:	Seasons:
Crushed stone paths	Junipers	Photographed in
Brick and stone edgings	Blue fescue	summer
Split-rail fences	Silver mound artemisia	Effective year-round
	Caryopteris	Over 3 years old
	Lamb's-ears	

Gardening in

Unique in appearance and design, a garden filled with dryland plants is a refreshing contrast to more traditional landscape treatments. Its muted colors and bold shapes seem almost sculpted into the landscape. Although these slow-growing plants succeed best in arid climates, you can use them to create this coveted desert feeling almost anywhere by providing the right conditions.

Providing the Right Environment

The natural home for desert plants is an area of little rainfall where harsh conditions conspire to produce tough plants of twisted, twiggy, or bulbous forms. Slender leaves, thorny or ribbed stems, and unusually colored foliage and flowers are clues to how each plant survives the dryness.

You can use virtually any site, apart from a bog or an area of deep shade, for a dryland garden. The key is to provide soil tailored to each plant's moisture needs. Size can range from a container to an entire yard. You may want to combine your planting with other styles, or treat it as a focal point in a larger ensemble. Follow nature's example and add interest with varying levels and some large rocks, or create a dry watercourse with a bed of stones. Terraces or raised beds filled with porous soil will insure the good drainage these plants need.

Creating a Composition

In natural desert and steppe environments around the world there are trees, shrubs, ground covers, woody and herbaceous perennials, and annuals appropriate for your dryland garden. Plants of all shapes grow here—tall, short, columnar, globe-shaped, tight and twiggy, open and rangy, creeping or mounding. There are options for any climate, even where there is extreme cold or snow. Combine them by common characteristics, perhaps placing clumps of thorny plants next to a mound of evergreens. Try grouping plants native to a single area, or plants with other than green foliage.

You might set off a tubular cactus, whose thorns appear among brilliant blooms, with low, woolly-leafed artemisia. Or surround a flowering desert willow with the familiar phloxes, iris, and brooms. Observe the unique characteristics of each plant and imagine how they could be shown to best advantage.

Preparing the Site

Much of the pleasure of gardening in dry sites comes from conceiving and building the garden. Decide how your dryland garden will be viewed—from the street, the patio, or a window; or from more than one vantage point—and structure the plantings and terrain to achieve a natural perspective. If you live in an arid region, this may involve simply clearing the site and doing some slight contouring or placing a few rocks.

If you live in an area of high rainfall, you may need to construct

Dry Sites

terraces and add sand and fine gravel to your soil to make it more porous. Scale the size of your garden to the time and effort you are willing to expend. If you'd like to experiment on a small scale, try a container garden. Drought-tolerant plants do very well in low clay containers, which you can distribute around your deck or patio. Whatever type of site you choose, a natural, comfortable look is the goal.

Establishing Your Garden
It is not always easy to find desert plants for sale, but with a little initiative you should be able to locate your choices in plant or seed. It takes two or three years for most dryland plants to become established, and of course trees will take longer. But once your garden is mature, you'll enjoy low maintenance as an added bonus—no clipping, no mowing, and easy weeding. As your design takes shape, experiment with different plants, replacing those that didn't make it and trying out new combinations. Part of the pleasure of a dryland garden is in the opportunity to observe and nurture plants that have such unique structures and ecology.

Designing with Dryland Plants
On the following pages you will see gardens that successfully use dryland plants in their designs. In one, succulents of dramatic form are interspersed with rocks, driftwood, and red mulch, creating a bold alternative to the suburban front lawn. Note how this composition makes maximum use of space by repeating shapes and varying textures along a level foundation wall.
A wide, Mediterranean-style garden with stepped-back terraces and alternating bands of color is an excellent model for an arid garden in a region where dry summer is followed by wet winter. Dryland plants are perfect on a small scale, too, perhaps to accent a tiny patio. See how combining foliage of contrasting shapes and shades provides year-round interest. Cacti and succulents form an intriguing border to a pathway, a mosaic of green rising above dark volcanic rocks. Finally, note how semidesert plants create a secluded enclave in a moderate climate. A formal plan is enhanced by the definite lines of hedges, planters, and pavings.
These dramatic landscapes may inspire you to re-create them, in part or as a whole. Whatever theme you choose—combining succulents with annuals, using grays and greens, repeating bold shapes throughout a design—your composition will be as unique and attractive as the plants themselves.

**Santa Rosa,
California
Private Garden**

*Site:
Level foundation
planting
Full sun, heat
Alkaline clay soil*

*Design Concepts:
Maximum use of space
Dramatic, repeated
shapes
Varied shades of green
Red mulch for contrast*

Decorative Elements:	Plantings:	Seasons:
Red scoria mulch	Agaves	Photographed in winter
Driftwood	Cereus cacti	Blooms in early spring
Boulders	Echeveria	Effective year-round
Japanese lanterns		Over 5 years old
Gravel path		

**Berkeley, California
Blake Garden**

Site:
Wide, steep bank
leading to house
Full sun
Well-drained soil

Design Concepts:
Mediterranean effect
Terracing contrasts
with vertical slope
Gray foliage as accent
Repeated whites,
yellows

Decorative Elements:	Plantings:	Seasons:
Gravel paths	Dusty miller	Photographed in early
Stone walls	Basket-of-gold	spring
	Gray-leaved euryops	Effective year-round
	Santolina	Well-established garden
	Mexican fleabane	

**Berkeley, California
Private Garden**

Site:
Small, level patio
Partial to full sun
Dry soil

Design Concepts:
Use of contrasting
shapes
Variety of heights
Orange and purple
accents

Decorative Elements:	*Plantings:*	*Seasons:*
Patterned brick patio	Variegated agave	Photographed in winter
Wooden fence and	Crassula	Effective year-round
stairway	Aeonium	Over 10 years old
Concrete walkway	Aloe	
Sandstone boulders	Cereus cacti	
	Opuntia	

Kaui, Hawaii Plantation Garden

Site:
Level area bordering path
Partial shade
Well-drained soil

Design Concepts:
Naturalistic effect
Contrasting plant shapes
Variety of foliage colors
Gray as accent
Dark rocks for contrast

Decorative Elements:
Hard-surfaced path
Porous black rocks

Plantings:
Agaves
Cycads
Euphorbia
Cordylines
Ponytail palm
Trichocereus
Kalanchoe

Seasons:
Photographed in fall
Effective year-round
Well-established garden

Gloucestershire,
England
Mrs. Winthrop's
Garden

Site:
Large, level area
Full sun
Average soil

Design Concepts:
Use of semi-desert
plants in moderate
climate
Geometric plan
Enclosure by hedge
Potted plants for focus
Soft flowers contrast
with bold foliage

Decorative Elements:	Plantings:	Seasons:
Patterned brick paving	Beech, hornbeam, and	Photographed in
Terra-cotta planters	lime hedges	summer
	Yucca	Blooms in summer
	Agaves	Well-established garden
	Cordylines	
	Lady's-mantle	
	Veronica	

A Naturalistic

The invigorating freshness of a mountain forest, the bucolic summer pleasure of a broad meadow, the quiet mystery of a pond filled with water lilies—such natural landscapes are attractive because of their inherent harmony. The plants are perfectly compatible with their settings. We would not expect to see beach grass and rugosa roses growing in a forest or cacti in a marsh. There should also be compatibility in a garden. The goal of naturalistic gardeners is to understand the harmony in forests, meadows, ponds, and mountains and to re-create this beauty in a garden setting.

Natural Inspiration for Any Site
Whether your property is sunny or shady, wet or dry, acid or alkaline, there is some counterpart to it in nature from which you can draw inspiration. Do you have a yard full of shade trees? Look at woodland settings to discover how to fill in with understory trees, shrubs, perennials, and ground covers. Is there a poorly drained site in your garden? Instead of fighting nature by making raised beds or installing drains, create a small bog garden using the intriguing plants that thrive in and around marshes, swamps, ponds, and streams. If you live in an area of low rainfall, cut your water bills by growing plants that grow naturally in dry areas.

Selecting Plants
In naturalistic gardening, it is important to select plants suited to a site not only by cultural needs but also by type. This means using woodland plants in shade, simple sun-loving flowers in a meadow, and desertlike plants in hot areas of low rainfall. When possible, it is a good idea to use true species rather than hybrids. Hybrids are often bred for large, showy flowers or fancy leaves that look out of place in a natural setting.
Matching plant to site does not restrict you to local species—far from it. A meadow garden in Connecticut could include prairie species from the Midwest. A shady garden in New Jersey might include woodland plants from Japan. A naturalistic garden in California's Sacramento Valley would be a good place to use Mediterranean plants. The key is to select plants whose native habitat you can simulate in both climate and appearance.

Flowing Lines
The lines of a naturalistic garden should echo the loose arrangements found in nature. Straight lines and rigid blocks of one particular plant are not the norm in meadows or woodlands. Plants placed in curves and loose groupings give the effect of untouched growth and seasonal spreading. This does not mean your landscape will be undisciplined. On the contrary, a naturalistic garden is perhaps the most difficult type to plan precisely because it involves trying to rival nature, whose designs are more intricate and complex than anything humans could create.

Effect

Each type of natural garden will have its best season or seasons. A woodland garden has its peak bloom in spring, while a sunny meadow garden is most colorful in summer. Rock gardens usually peak in late spring and early summer. Clever additions of a few late-bloomers, evergreens, and plants with bright fall color can stretch these seasons, but make sure their shapes fit naturally into the scheme.

Starting Out

Your naturalistic garden can be as simple as a planting of woodland flowers under a dogwood tree or as grandiose as a whole hillside filled with mountain laurel. If you're new at this type of gardening, begin with a simple treatment of a small area and expand as your confidence grows. The labor required will be the same as for any other type of garden, but once established, this design will be easier to maintain than a formal one. In the wild, no one stakes plants or deadheads flowers, and there is no need to here.

Do not expect the garden to be at its height overnight. Although annuals will give you an effect within a few weeks, it is more difficult to establish them for a year-after-year effect. Perennials will take a couple of seasons to settle in, and trees and shrubs need even longer. It helps to rely on large plants that already exist. After several years, however, the beauty of your new garden will become apparent, and it will grow more lovely with age.

Attracting Wildlife

A bonus of a naturalistic garden is that wildlife tend to recognize it as a place of shelter or source of food. A meadow garden will often bring butterflies, which look like extensions of the flowers themselves. A woodland garden provides shelter and nesting habitat for many species of birds. A water garden brings dragonflies and frogs and can serve as a drinking fountain for other creatures. Watching a landscape that you've designed become a miniature ecosystem is immensely rewarding.

Serene Landscapes

Ranging from bright expanses of multicolored flowers to shady banks cloaked in glossy-leaved shrubs, the gardens on the following pages all have the serene aura of natural scenes. Behind each lies the hand of a knowledgeable designer who has closely observed the compositions of meadows and woodlands in various areas. Notice not only the choices of plants but how they have been arranged to imitate nature's schemes of propagation and growth. By adapting some of these ideas to your own landscape you can bring the beauty of untouched places to your doorstep.

Columbus, Ohio
Public Landscaping

Site:
Large, open area
Very slight slope
Full sun
Well-drained soil

Design Concepts:
Meadow effect
Tapestry of colors
Varied flower shapes
Attracts butterflies

Decorative Elements:	*Plantings:*	*Seasons:*
Natural features	*Cornflowers*	*Photographed in*
	Poppies	*summer*
		Most effective in
		summer
		Over 1 year old

**Westport,
Connecticut
Osborn Garden**

Site:
Large backyard
Gentle slope
High, dappled shade
Humus-rich acid soil

Design Concepts:
Woodland effect
Layered plantings
Pastel colors

Decorative Elements:	Plantings:	Seasons:
Low stone walls	Oaks	Photographed in early spring
	Dogwoods	
	Azaleas	Effective spring and fall
	Creeping phlox	Over 5 years old

**Philadelphia,
Pennsylvania
Gevjan Garden**

Site:
Large backyard
Gentle slope
High, dappled shade
Humus-rich acid soil

Design Concepts:
Woodland effect
Path leads through
design
Use of foliage textures
Nesting habitat for
birds

Decorative Elements:	Plantings:	Seasons:
Wood-chip paths	Oaks	Photographed in early
Simple wooden seat	Dogwoods	spring
Birdhouse	Azaleas	Effective spring and
	Ferns	fall
	Creeping phlox	Over 10 years old
	Trillium	
	Primroses	

New Hope,
Pennsylvania
Benner Garden

Site:
Clearing in wooded
area
Gentle slope
Partial sun
Humus-rich acid soil

Design Concepts:
Meadow effect
Woods as backdrop
Green and white theme
Birdbath as focus
Attracts birds

Decorative Elements:	Plantings:	Seasons:
Birdbath	Oaks	Photographed in spring
	Leucothoe	Effective spring to early
	Rhododendrons	summer
	Bluets	Well-established garden
	Creeping phlox	

Hampshire,
England
Hillier Arboretum

Site:
Open woodland
Gentle slope
Light shade
Average soil

Design Concepts:
Woodland effect
Layered plantings
Variety of textures

Decorative Elements:	Plantings:	Seasons:
Grass paths	Beeches	Photographed in spring
	Paperbark maple	Most effective in spring
	Azaleas	Over 10 years old
	Rhododendrons	
	Pieris	
	Bulbs	

**Swarthmore,
Pennsylvania
Wister Garden**

Site:
Large wooded area
Strong slope
High, dappled shade
Humus-rich acid soil

Design Concepts:
Mountain woodland
effect
Use of foliage textures
Paths lead through
design
Repeated colors
Nesting habitat for
birds

Decorative Elements:	Plantings:	Seasons:
Hard-surfaced paths	Dexter rhododendrons	Photographed in spring
	Irises	Effective spring to fall
	Dogwoods	Well-established garden
	English bluebells	
	Lenten and Christmas	
	roses	
	Epimediums	

Site:
Large, level, open area
Borders on woods
Full sun
Well-drained soil

Design Concepts:
Meadow effect
Woods as backdrop
Red as accent
Attracts butterflies

Decorative Elements:	Plantings:	Seasons:
Natural features	Poppies	Photographed in early summer
	Russell hybrid lupines	Most effective in summer
	Phlox	Over 2 years old
	Grasses	

Landscapes to

Rosalind Creasy

The concept of growing food around the home is certainly not a new one, but for many years, food plants were grown only in inconspicuous areas—behind the barn or garage. It certainly was not fashionable to have vegetables or herbs growing in the front yard or to use edible plants as major components of an ornamental landscape.

In recent years, however, gardeners have broken with tradition by making food plants part of their designs. Even gardeners who prefer to keep a separate plot for vegetables are learning to arrange the plants for beauty as well as bounty. Creating a landscape to harvest, an "edible landscape," is a challenge that rewards you with fresh, unique foods grown in a natural, environmentally sound way. It also widens the range of shapes, colors, and fragrances with which to fill your yard.

Design Guidelines

To compose such a garden, you must think about the overall color, shape, and texture of each plant you want to grow and place it accordingly. Because your landscape will be a living composition in three dimensions that changes with the seasons, you'll need a strong framework of paths, beds, and structures on which to "hang" the design. The success of the garden will depend on three important elements of design: form, line, and color.

Form and Line

Think of your yard and the air space above it as a large piece of stone from which you will carve your design. Each object you carve will have an overall shape—round, cubic, irregular—which is its form. It will also exhibit a two-dimensional line—straight, curved, arching—as seen against the horizon or the ground. For example, a pruned hedge will have a straight line; its form is the three-dimensional shape to which it has been pruned.

In a successful edible landscape, large ornamental perennials and evergreens provide form, especially in the background. These plants will be effective throughout most or all of the year, while annual vegetables will go through various stages of growth and harvesting. For most parts of the country, the best large ornamentals include compact conifers, yews, various forms of juniper, privets, hardy rhododendrons, hollies, and boxwood. If you use these as hedges, prune them so they have sloping sides and narrow tops, to avoid damage from heavy snow. In warmer areas, try pineapple guavas (*Feijoa sellowiana*), citrus trees, or yellow strawberry guava (*Psidium littorale littorale*). Low hedges of lavender are also useful in warm-winter climates.

The lines in a landscape can be defined by rows of plants or by structures such as arbors, paths, edgings, and patios. In ornamental food gardens, the lines of non-plant structures are particularly important. Your neat rows of lettuce will look picture-perfect only

Harvest

until you begin to eat your way through the composition. Planting crops in succession, so that one is still growing while another is being harvested, helps solve this problem. So does planting strips of colorful ornamental flowers among rows of food plants. But the surest way to maintain an overall sense of order is to overemphasize the lines, make them "harder" or more noticeable, by relying on man-made elements. A system of paths or edgings with a pleasing texture or pattern provides interest daily—regardless of weather, pests, or harvesting. The vertical lines of arbors, trellises, and even raised beds add permanent height to your design.

You can supplement and soften the lines of paths by bordering them with plants. Use the easier-to-care-for ornamental perennial herbs, both edible and inedible: lavenders, santolinas, chamomile, thymes, geraniums, alpine strawberries (*Fragaria vesca*), wood betony (*Stachys officinalis*), dwarf boxwood, golden marjoram (*Origanum vulgare* 'Aureum'), wall germander (*Teucrium chamaedrys*).

Color

The most obvious and dramatic element of most landscape designs is color. The eye flows over form and line, but it is caught and held by accents of color. These accents must be used with some restraint to avoid a gaudy or garish look that doesn't allow the eye to rest. It is especially tempting to combine too many colors in an edible landscape because the wide variety of foods you want to grow may not fall neatly into one color scheme. One way to solve this problem is by introducing areas of green—in the form of evergreen backdrops, lawns, or larger groupings of green edible plants such as corn, lettuce, or cabbage. Green is a restful, neutral color that separates and calms brighter patches.

Another way to tone down the riot-of-color effect is to plant your edibles in groups of similar, harmonious hues. For example, plant tomatoes with red bell peppers; parsley with basil; red-leaf chard with red petunias; eggplants with opal basil or purple-podded beans; green-leaf culinary sage with gray, ornamental woolly thyme; and yellow and orange calendulas in front of rows of wheat.

Color can also be used to unify the design of a garden. Try to arrange colorful plants so that several of them will be blooming or showing a particular color at certain times during the gardening season. Yellow, for example, could be sprinkled through the year beginning with spring-blooming tulips, yellow beets, and calendulas; followed by daylilies, yellow tomatoes, and marigolds; then by anise or fennel left to bloom (but not allowed to drop mature seed); and ending with the bright yellow fall color of an apricot or an Asian pear tree.

Choosing a Site

In choosing the best site or sites for your food gardens, you'll have to balance practical and aesthetic concerns, matching the cultural

Landscapes to Harvest

needs of the plants you want to grow with the sun, soil, and temperature conditions in your yard. Pay special attention to soil drainage patterns. Few edible plants can tolerate poorly drained soil. Vegetables require the best soil—fertile and well-drained—in order to be both productive and beautiful. Save the worst-drained areas of the yard for water-tolerant ornamentals.

There are other things to consider, such as how private or public you want the garden to be. Do you want it to create an impact when seen from the street, or would you prefer a more private site to be enjoyed from the house or patio? Are you willing to devote most of the yard to edible plants, or would you rather divide it into smaller areas for various uses? Clarify your needs and desires before beginning any garden construction.

Planning the Beds

Once you have selected your site, you can start sketching ideas for individual beds. You might choose right angles, diagonals, sweeping curves, or more informal shapes within which to arrange plants. The shape of the beds can greatly influence the look and feel of the landscape. For example, irregularly shaped beds will soften the linear architecture of a ranch house; a row of rectangular beds will emphasize and extend it. You can make a small space look larger by placing beds diagonally. Angled or curved beds can lead the eye to focal points in your design.

Consider the practical pros and cons of any type of layout. Long, sweeping curves are wonderful lines in a landscape design, but curved beds without fixed sides can be difficult to work with. When you're dragging the hose around for watering, it tends to creep up onto the beds and knock over seedlings. Putting wooden or masonry sides on the bed will help, but it is difficult and expensive to make them follow a curve. You might compromise by making several individual rectangular beds and placing them in a series to form a sweeping arch. Or use vertical stakes or rotating hose guides every few feet along the convex sides of unedged beds to prevent hose damage to tender plants.

You may want to plan separate beds for annuals and perennials. The intensive soil development that annual vegetables and flowers need is unnecessary or even harmful to woody herbs and some perennials. Creating separate beds will ensure that you don't overwater the woody plants as you cater to the needs of annual transplants or seedlings.

Consider building raised beds for vegetables where drainage is less than ideal, or simply as a design element—to create a sense of height and depth. Build wooden or masonry walls 12 to 24 inches high and fill the raised beds with amended soil. Or simply mound prepared soil to at least 8 inches high, slope the sides 45 degrees, and mulch them or plant them with an attractive ground cover such as thyme, baby's-tears, chamomile, or clover.

The width of each vegetable bed, whether raised or level, should be convenient for you to reach across while harvesting or weeding. The usual width is 2½ to 4 feet, depending on your reach. Pathways need be only 12 to 18 inches wide, but at least every other path should be 3 to 4 feet wide in order to accommodate a wheelbarrow or garden cart.

Building Healthy Soil

Without a fertile, reasonably well-drained soil of good texture, even the most carefully laid out edible landscape will just limp along and fail to produce the desired cornucopia. The importance of taking time to prepare your soil cannot be overstressed. After you've defined the outlines of your garden, turn over and loosen about a foot of soil. Amend it with large amounts of organic matter, such as compost or manure, and add fertilizer if your soil needs it.

Fruit trees generally don't need as fertile a soil as do vegetables and annual flowers, but they do thrive on a deep loam with good drainage to prevent root and crown rots. Unfortunately, many homes are built on soil that is far from ideal for fruit trees. The root systems of such trees are extensive, and it is impractical for home gardeners to prepare the large volume of soil that would be necessary. Unfortunately, using dwarf trees is not always the answer because they are especially intolerant of wet, heavy soils. They also have shallow roots that can be harmed by cold weather. The practical solution is to choose only fruit trees that are adapted to the soil you have. If your soil is shallow or clay, consider planting only those trees that tolerate water and poor drainage. Some recommended types—in order from most to somewhat tolerant—are quinces and pears, apples, walnuts, and plums.

As a measure of protection against root and crown rot in all but the sandiest of soils, plant each tree on a large planting mound, 10 to 18 inches high and 2 to 3 feet wide. This will give the sensitive crown of the root system the drainage it requires. Mulch the mound extra heavily during the first year, to protect the roots from drought.

Choosing Plants

Your family's tastes are the first criteria in choosing what to plant in your edible landscape, but be realistic. Compare the list of favorites with knowledge about what will grow in your climate and soil. Save most of the riskier varieties until you have a number of bountiful gardening seasons under your belt. Do some experimenting but do it on a small scale.

Perennial Edibles

Traditional vegetable gardens include mostly annual plants. Introducing perennial edibles—such as fruit or nut trees, vines,

Landscapes to Harvest

shrubs with berries, or herbs—gives your garden more permanence. The care and harvesting of these plants can be time-consuming, so it pays to choose them carefully. Check with local landscapers, designers, and the regional Cooperative Extension office to find out which plants for your area are free of pests and diseases.

When selecting tree crops and fruiting vines, consider how messy they can be. Such plants shouldn't overhang patios, decks, or sidewalks because ripe fruit will drop to the ground, staining the surface and making it slippery. Avoid figs, mulberries, peaches, nectarines, guavas, cherries, plums, and persimmons in these areas. Try less messy fruits: grapes, kiwis, pomegranates, cactus fruit, firm apple varieties, and pears and avocados.

Some perennial edibles require frequent or messy spray programs to control pests or diseases. If you've chosen some that do, avoid planting them near the walls of your home. Tree crops, shrubs, and edible vine crops that need little or no spraying include alpine strawberry, blueberry, fig, loquat, Japanese and American persimmons, pineapple guava, pomegranate, and most wild plums and cherries.

In choosing perennial herbs, be sure to check on their cold hardiness. Rosemary is a popular seasoning, but it is hardy only in zones 6 to 10. If you live in a colder climate, try it as a houseplant. Some herbs—such as the mints, horseradish, and comfrey—are invasive. Place them far from cultivated plantings or in patio containers, where they can be controlled.

Annual Vegetables

Treat annual vegetable crops as you would annual bedding plants like marigolds and petunias: Plant a selection, plant in small areas, and plant several times throughout the season. Avoid the temptation to plant too much during the peak of springtime enthusiasm. Many vegetables are now sold in "six-pack" containers, but heaven help the small-space gardener who puts in all six zucchini or cherry tomato plants! It is wiser to put in small patches of crops such as lettuce, beets, and radishes every seven to ten days until the heat of summer, so that the harvest is spread out over a convenient length of time.

Separate annual flowers and vegetables into planting groups by looks and cultural requirements. Group those with similar fertility and water requirements—zinnias or marigolds with peppers, white stock with red chard. Or combine plants of complementary colors —red and orange cosmos behind zucchini, calendulas or apricot-colored violas with lettuce, red dianthus with red chard, yellow violas with carrots and lettuce. For an interesting mixture of foliage textures and color, combine plants like johnny-jump-ups with corn salad and chervil or red dianthus with red chard. You can randomly mix such combinations for an informal look or plant them in alternate rows for a more formal design.

Some other combinations to experiment with: Jerusalem sage (*Philomis fruticosa*) with bronze fennel; variegated sage with clove dianthus; carrots planted among bibb lettuce; garlic or shallots or chives poking up through thyme; opal basil surrounded by deep red petunias.

Try some of the new gourmet vegetable varieties that are offered each year. Among the gourmet varieties that have recently become popular are Romanesco broccoli, chocolate brown and orange-yellow bell peppers, Little Gem and red romaine lettuces, Hopi Blue flint corn, Purple Ruffles basil, Moon and Stars watermelon, and Rosa Bianco eggplant.

Planting Fruit Trees

If you have room to grow fruit trees but want to avoid the orchard look, cluster several different varieties together to create a small grove. For example, you might choose three types of apples, each of which matures at a different time. Place trunks randomly, at least far enough apart to allow for the mature width of the canopies. If your space is limited, plant two or three trees, two to three feet apart, in one large planting hole. Prune each so that the trees share, in effect, one full canopy. This bit of extra care in pruning will give the visual effect of one tree while providing a sequence of tasty harvests instead of an overabundance all at once.

In an attempt to combine edible and ornamental gardens, many people plant ground covers around and beneath their fruit trees. While they may be beautiful, thickets of ground covers can create problems.

Generally, the best way to treat the area beneath the dripline of a tree canopy is with an attractive mulch, or with Dutch white clover or hardy annual wildflowers that can withstand harsh conditions and trampling. Place flower borders and ground covers at least five to ten feet beyond the mature dripline of the canopy.

Most fruit and nut trees do not grow well in or right next to a lawn. This includes the popular apples, plums, cherries, chestnuts, figs, peaches, nectarines, and walnuts. The amounts of water and fertilizer needed to keep the lawn happy can create problems for these trees. Mildews, fire blight, crown rot, aphids, and fungal diseases are some of the problems that are encouraged by combining fruit trees and lawns. Place the fruit trees away from the edge of the lawn by a factor of two to three times the width that their canopies will reach at maturity. There are a few productive semitropical trees and vines that will tolerate being near or in a lawn, including kiwi vines, pineapple guava, and loquat.

Garden Structures

The use of structural elements is important, especially in cold-winter areas. They give continuity to a design throughout the year. Consider using well-designed and thematically integrated

Landscapes to Harvest

pathways, patios, trellises, or arbors. Never use more than three types of construction materials in your landscapes. Too many textures will make your design look confused and complicated. A constrained use of materials, such as creating brick walkways transected with railroad ties at certain intervals, helps unify the garden.

Use a limited number of structural elements as focal points or accents. Arbors, small fish ponds, decks, gazebos, permanent paths, benches, patios, and greenhouses can be serviceable as well as attractive. Some are easy to build yourself. Others—especially gazebos, greenhouses, and large pools—should be built by craftsmen under your supervision.

Planting in Containers

Container plants are often important parts of a cohesive design, providing colorful highlights in just the right spots. Planting annual flowers, herbs, and vegetables with different harvest times in containers allows you to rotate their positions in the garden—with the best-looking ones in the most visible spots.

A Small, Mild-Climate Garden

The landscape plan on page 298 represents a restrained use of low-maintenance edible plants for a small yard in zone 9 or 10. General plant types, rather than specific varieties, are indicated on the plan. If you'd like to adapt this scheme to your site, select varieties known to thrive in the conditions you can provide.

A number of ornamental shrubs and trees are included because they add beauty without requiring as much maintenance as fruit trees. If you have a busy life-style, you may want to substitute other ornamentals for some of the fruit trees. The perennial edibles require little maintenance. The only trees that demand an ambitious spray program are the peaches and nectarines. Here, genetic dwarfs have been specified to make the spraying and harvesting easier. The grapes used on the front-porch arbor should be mildew-resistant varieties. A few evergreen trees—pineapple guava and citrus—will provide year-round form to the design. The lawn, which provides a cooler atmosphere for lounging than the patio, has been kept small to reduce maintenance.

Lavender hedges in both the front and back yards create a repeated theme. The backyard hedge guides foot traffic from the kitchen door to the vegetable beds. The vegetable beds and the culinary herbs are close to the kitchen so they are easy to harvest while cooking. Flowers are planted randomly among the vegetables so that the beds look especially attractive from the patio. The vegetable beds are designed to be used only for late spring through summer crops. They are too close to the north side of the house for good winter growth. Instead, a soil-improving cover crop will be planted there each fall.

A Large, Cold-Climate Garden

The plan on page 300 is for a colder climate—zones 4 to 8—and is meant to provide an integrated design without too many perennial crops. Again, only general plant types are specified. Most of the allee along the driveway consists of ornamental shade trees so that fruit drop is not a problem, and the form of the arching branches frames and leads the eye to the entry. The two fruiting trees at the driveway entrance add a highlight and distinguish this yard from others in the neighborhood. The informal cluster of fruit trees south of the lawn is underplanted with a wildflower meadow. The clustering allows the trees to be close enough to pollenize one another.

Again, the vegetable area is placed close to the kitchen. It has a traditional layout because the goal is high production. The planting beds around the patio are more ornamental and fairly easy to care for due to the use of relatively low-maintenance blueberries and grape vines. Wildflower meadows are used extensively throughout the landscape to reduce the amount of mowing and watering. For continual color in the meadow areas, an ambitious reseeding would be required every three to five years. If you prefer a different style, you could choose perennial ground covers. If introducing meadows is frowned on in your neighborhood, you could extend the lawn, but this will increase your maintenance time.

For the best sun exposure and wind protection, all the edibles are planted on the south side of the home. Much of the backyard has been designed as a wildlife-enhancing woodland. Some of the berries could be harvested for exotic jams and jellies or simply left for the birds.

Making Changes

Without a bit of wonder, experimentation, and magic, any landscape can be static and ordinary. In their zeal to beautify every space, beginning designers tend to leave little room for experimentation in their landscapes. Try to be flexible. Combining colorful food plants is like painting—you need some blank canvas on which to work. Reserve an area just for trying out various combinations of unusually colored plants. Discovering what succeeds on this small scale will help you plan new, larger arrangements next year.

Expect to rework various areas of your edible landscape over the years, even if your life-style doesn't change. Your taste in colors or in food may evolve, or you may just get tired of looking at the same view from your kichen window. Your changing landscape will repay your work and attention with a tasty bounty throughout the growing season, and it will be a pleasant place to sit, work, play in, or simply admire. You'll have the satisfaction of gardening in a way that nurtures all the senses. Bon appetit!

Trees and Shrubs	• Plum	1
	• Genetic dwarf peaches	2
	• Semi-dwarf pear	3
	Ornamental evergreen shrubs	4
	• Pineapple guava	5
	• Genetic dwarf nectarines	6
	• Dwarf citrus	7
	• Persimmon	8
	Street tree	9
	Ornamental deciduous shrubs	10
	• Pomegranate	11
Vines	• Wine grapes	12
	• Kiwi	13
	• Grapes	14
	Flowering vine	15
Vegetables and Herbs	• Jerusalem artichokes	16
	• Herbs	17
	• Vegetable garden	18
	• Lavender hedge	19
Ground Covers	Ornamental ground cover	20
	• Strawberry	21
	Mulch	22

299

In this plan for a small garden in zone 9 or 10, low-maintenance food plants, denoted by bullets, are combined with ornamentals.

General plant types are indicated. To adapt the scheme to your site, select varieties known to grow well in your area.

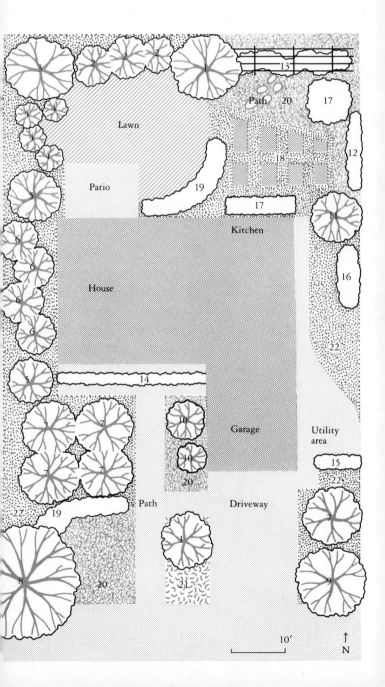

Windbreak and bird habitat	1
Ornamental weeping cherry	2
• Dolgo crabapple	3
Pin oak, small oak, or sweet gum	4
• Pink Pearl apple or American persimmon	5
Low evergreen hedge	6
• Asian pears or apples	7
Sugar maples, oaks, chestnuts, or walnuts	8
Dogwoods (beneath)	9
• Plums, cherries, peaches, or nectarines	10
• North Star cherry	11
Ornamental conifers	12
• Blueberries	13
• Grape vines	14
• Herbs in containers	15
• Vegetable garden	16
• Asparagus	17
Wildflower meadow	18

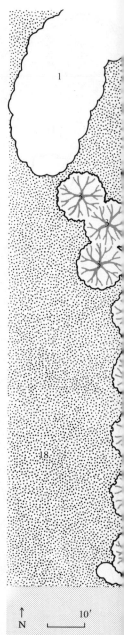

↑
N   10'

This plan for combining food plants, denoted by bullets, and ornamental plants is designed for a large lot in zones 4 to 8.

General plant types are indicated. To adapt the scheme to your site, select varieties known to grow well in your area.

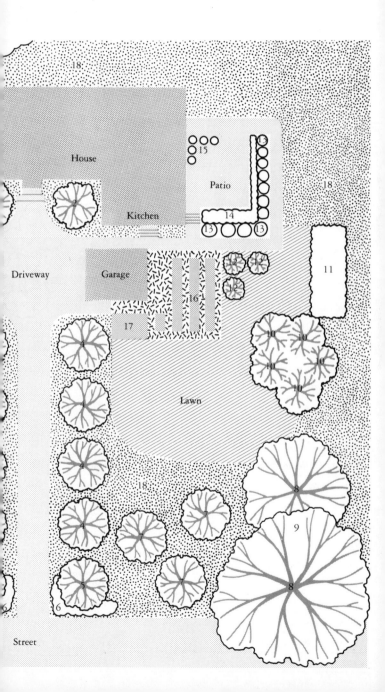

House

Patio

Kitchen

15

13

14

13

13

Driveway

Garage

16

17

11

12

12

12

Lawn

4

4

4

4

5

6

18

18

18

7

7

7

7

10

10

10

10

10

8

9

8

2

Street

Landscapes to Harvest	Listings in the Source column are page references to individual Taylor's Guides. A key to title abbreviations appears on page 11.	Under Zones, W and C indicate warm- or cool-season annuals.

	Source	Zones
Plant Choices		
Actinidia chinensis Kiwi	D-294	8–10
Allium schoenoprasum Chive	V-420	4–10
Amaranthus tricolor Amaranth	V-292	W
Beta vulgaris, Crassa group Beet	V-306	C
Brassica oleracea Ornamental kale	V-344	C
Capiscum annuum Pepper	V-369	W
Cichorium endiva Escarole	V-332	C
Citrus spp. Citrus	D-296	9–10
Cucurbita pepo Summer squash	V-389	W
Daucus carota var. *sativus* Carrot	V-315	C
Diospyros spp. Persimmon	D-294	5–10
Eriobotrya japonica Loquat	T-329	8–10
Feijoa sellowiana Pineapple guava	S-339	8–10
Ficus carica Fig	D-294	9–10
Foeniculum vulgare var. *dulce* Sweet fennel	V-425	C
Fragaria vesca Alpine strawberry	V-393	5–9
Lactuca sativa Lettuce	V-347	C
Lavandula angustifolia Lavender	P-359	5–9
Malus spp. Apple	D-295	4–10
Momordica charantia Balsam pear	V-338	W
Ocimum basilicum Basil	V-410	W
Petroselinum crispum Parsley	V-436	C
Phaseolus vulgaris Snap beans	V-302	W
Poterium sanguisorba Salad burnet	V-414	4–10
Prunus spp. Cherry	S-386	4–8
Punica granatum Pomegranate	S-387	8–10
Pyrus spp. Pear	T-386	4–9
Salvia spp. Sage	V-442	4–10
Thymus vulgaris Thyme	V-446	4–10
Vaccinium spp. Blueberry	G-369	4–9
Vitis spp. Grape	G-410	4–7

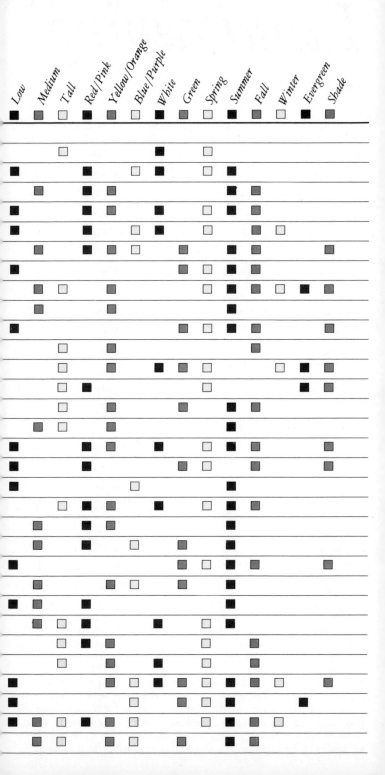

Landscaping

Barbara Damrosch

Imagine, for a moment, that you are creating a real flower bed with just a paintbrush. Dip it in a crimson pigment, splash some bold patches of color across the back of the bed, and large clumps of phlox 'Starfire' appear. Among the patches, trace some tall blue-violet spikes. Now monkshood 'Bressingham Spire' is growing. Next, dip your brush in yellow-gold and make some bright spots just below the blue for daylily 'Star Dream'.

Your garden is now a balanced composition of clear primary colors, but it includes only tall plants and could use some softening. Using white paint, splatter a cloud of tiny dots in the center of the bed and a couple of others toward the sides. Perennial baby's-breath is now growing in the middle ground. Between these clouds, make patches of multicolored dots to produce zinnia 'Cut-and-come-again'. Then anchor the composition in front by painting in blue ageratum, French marigold 'Red Wheels', and marigold 'Lemon Drop'. Your garden is now in full bloom.

Of course, creating a flower garden is not quite that easy. Between the time you dream up the picture and the moment you can actually view it, months or even years may elapse. Those tall perennials will take two years to become established and to reach their full heights. If you are then displeased with the picture, it may take another year or two to adjust it. Meanwhile, some plants may die, or you may discover that some were mislabeled as to color or height. And how does the garden look when it's not at its peak? Is it still full of color and interest? Wouldn't it be more satisfying to just paint pictures instead?

It Pays to Plan

Avid gardeners find that careful planning sparks creativity. Perhaps this is because focusing the rational part of the mind on design principles and plant characteristics allows the intuitive part to roam more freely. While you fiddle with plant heights and sequences of bloom, you'll find that new ideas present themselves. Many of these visual possibilities would not occur to you if the planning process did not take so long.

You can design a simple flower garden fairly quickly. Some of the prettiest gardens contain just one clump of a single, well-placed species. You might plant a drift of forget-me-nots along a path or a sweep of mixed-color daylilies beside a fence. Or try using a few plants in a successful combination, such as tall white cleome, red-orange cosmos 'Diablo', and blue *Cynoglossum* in a tricolor annual bed.

Some gardeners never design their beds at all. They just plant them, putting the tall flowers in back, the short ones in front, and let it go at that. Later, as they buy more plants and accept the odd donations that always come a gardener's way ("You've *got* to take some of my bee balm!"), they just fit the new ones in where there are spaces. Often as not, the colors mix reasonably well, just as

with Flowers

meadow flowers scattered by nature all seem to go together. But the timing may be off. The garden may look gorgeous in June but dismal in July and halfhearted in August.

Most gardeners find that planning really does pay off. A carefully designed garden has great visual impact and clearly expresses its creator's taste. The plan may change as the garden develops, but if it is rooted in sound, workable concepts, adjustments will be easy to make. Besides, planning gardens is fun. Doodling on graph paper is an outlet for the gardener's fantasies, and it can be as rewarding as the resulting garden itself.

What Kinds of Plants to Use

Almost all plants bear flowers, but not all are useful in flower gardens. Most large flowering shrubs, for example, would overwhelm a small garden unless used as a backdrop—such as a lilac hedge that would bloom along with your other spring flowers. Some flowering trees—a flowering crabapple at one corner of the garden, for example—might become part of your color picture. And the most compact flowering shrubs, such as *Deutzia gracilis* or Arnold Dwarf forsythia, could be used in the border. Roses can also be used in flower gardens, though they are more commonly planted in beds all their own. But here we are mostly concerned with annuals, perennials, and bulbs.

Annuals

The easiest group to work with is flowering annuals, so they are best for beginners. Even a child can grow a colorful bed of petunias and marigolds, and many do. An annual plant completes its life cycle in one growing season, leaving behind seeds that will start new plants if the environment is favorable. If your garden is enough like the plant's native habitat, it will self-sow, which may or may not make you happy. If your garden follows a very fixed scheme, these self-sown "volunteers" may disrupt it. On the other hand, you may like working with them—pulling out the ones that come up in the wrong places, leaving the ones that fit in well. Johnny-jump-ups, as the name implies, are self-sowers and are considered assets in gardens where they can naturalize themselves attractively. Unfortunately, many annual hybrids do not breed true to seed. Chances are the volunteers from your ruffled pink petunias will have single purple flowers, like the original species. If you are not sure what a self-sown annual will do, let it bloom, then pull it out if you don't like the result.

The chief virtue of annuals in the flower garden is the showiness of their blooms over a long period of time. In a Connecticut garden, for example, they will last at least three months. In California gardens, annuals are often the mainstay, blooming all winter. In central Oregon, however, where a frost can occur during any month of the year, annuals do not mean reliable color. It is important to

Landscaping with Flowers

know, for design purposes, whether the annuals you're choosing are hardy—that is, can withstand some frost in spring and fall. Hardy annuals can be counted on for a much longer period of bloom.

Perennials
Botanically speaking, perennials are plants that persist from one year to the next in their native habitats. In practical terms, we speak of plants being perennial in some climates and annual in others. Many perennials take a long time to reach flowering size if they are raised from seed, so most gardeners buy them as started plants for an immediate effect. Some do grow well from seed and will even self-sow.

Many people think that perennial gardens are less work than annual ones because they don't have to be replanted each year, but this is rarely true. Once planted, annuals require less maintenance, such as staking and dividing. These tasks are certainly not overwhelming, but it is important not to neglect them. In an unsupervised perennial garden, the more vigorous plants will soon crowd out the less vigorous ones. Furthermore, most perennials bloom for only a few weeks. It is thus difficult to compose a garden solely of perennials and have a mass of bloom all season long. You can provide a sequence of bloom by choosing flowers for every part of the season, but if you put them all in one garden, you should expect patches of greenery between the blooms. Nonetheless, a well-composed perennial garden is a truly glorious sight, and there are a number of tricks that can help you achieve continuous bloom.

Bulbs
The flowering period of bulbs is even briefer than that of most non-bulbous perennials. Their foliage must be allowed to mature and die before it is cut back, so spring bulb foliage will take up space in a garden for the rest of the season. Many gardeners choose to give bulbs a site all their own, but they can be worked into beds of perennials and annuals—at the back of the garden, for example, where their foliage will be hidden by plants that grow tall and bloom after the bulbs have completed their show. Some of the compact summer bulbs—such as lilies, alliums, gladiolus, and dahlias—work beautifully when mixed with other plants in the border.

The Size and Shape of Your Garden
How large you make your flower beds will depend on how much space you have, how much money you want to spend for plants, and how much time you are prepared to spend maintaining them. Large beds take a long time to prepare. Then you must weed and fertilize them, divide the perennials from time to time, stake the tall ones, pinch some to make them bushier, cut others to make them rebloom, and deadhead, or snip off, faded blossoms to

strengthen the plants. It is better to have a small bed that looks
well cared for than a large, messy one.

Also consider the distance from which the bed will be viewed. A
small bed seen from across a wide lawn will not be very impressive,
but the same bed might be charming in a spot near the house, next
to the terrace, or along a fence near the pool.

The shape of the bed will be determined to a large extent by where
it is sited. Unless you are planting a shade garden, try to give your
flower garden full sun—at least six hours of sun a day. Note that
some flowers—such as daffodils, sunflowers, and morning glories—
may turn to the east, south, or southeast to face the sun and be less
effective when viewed from the other side.

The garden also needs a spot with good drainage. If it is on a steep
slope, it should be terraced with retaining walls of stone, brick,
timbers, or some other natural material. Such a garden can be very
beautiful because it achieves, through the slope, the gradation of
heights so sought-after in borders. Just make sure it slopes toward,
not away from, the viewer.

Borders and Beds

What is a flower "border"? We now use the word interchangeably
with flower "bed," but it originally referred to the long,
rectangular bed that so often borders a walk, a lawn, or a pool in
English gardens. True borders often have backdrops of tall
evergreen hedges or masonry walls, or they may be just strips of
garden with lawn on either side. They are especially lovely when set
parallel to each other, with a focal point at one end. The principle
of an English flower border can be carried out just as successfully
next to a split-rail fence in the country, or along the sunny side of
a backyard wall in a tiny city or suburban lot. You might even set
a flower border along the fence of your vegetable garden. You may
also hear the term "herbaceous border." Strictly speaking, this is a
garden composed of soft-stemmed plants, not woody ones. Usually
the word is used loosely to denote a perennial garden.

Flower beds can be much more informal in shape than traditional
borders, following gentle, free-form curves along the edge of a
lawn, or serving as "island" beds in the middle of the lawn, to be
viewed from all sides. In free-form beds, which are not a uniform
width, you must adjust the plant heights accordingly. An island
bed will have tall plants in the center and increasingly shorter
plants as you move out to the edge. A curved border viewed from
one side will have its tallest plants in the wide parts, with more
size gradations than in the narrow sections.

Which style is for you? If your house is old, or built in a specific
style, you may want to adapt the garden style to it, even choosing
plants that suit the specific period of the house—such as Early
Colonial, Georgian, or Victorian. In any case, trust your own
personal taste.

Garden Edgings

As you select the site and decide on the shape of your flower bed, don't forget to allow some room for an edging. If the garden borders a gravel or masonry terrace or walk, that will form the edging. But if it borders a lawn, you may prefer to make a permanent edging in order to avoid constant redefining of the bed's contours. The lawn will not understand that it is unwelcome in the bed; the creeping veronica will not know that the lawn is off-limits. A metal edging strip or a single row of bricks sunk vertically partway into the ground will help, but the best solution is a foot-wide strip of flagstones or bricks that the lawn-mower wheels can rest on. You can even let your plants spill out attractively onto this edging without being shorn. In more formal gardens, you can use low clipped hedges of boxwood, germander, or lavender, but these are more difficult to maintain.

Choosing a Period of Bloom

Suppose you decide that you want a garden composed solely of annuals. You can either buy started plants from a nursery or grow them from seed. Some seeds should be started early indoors; others can be sown directly in the garden. Most of the garden will be planted by late spring, but it will be a while—six weeks, perhaps—before the plants are large and bushy enough to show much color, especially if you are pinching back the stems for more branching and a better show. In cool climates, this will usually mean a garden that blooms from early or midsummer to early fall.

With all-perennial gardens, you have a choice of abundant bloom all at once or less bloom stretched out over a long season. Often a one-season perennial garden makes sense. For example, if you travel during the summer months, you might want to enjoy spring perennials before leaving and fall perennials after your return. Conversely, if you have a country home you visit only in July and August, you could plan a colorful garden for those months. Many people who have had difficulty orchestrating three-season borders decide they prefer several smaller gardens, each for a different season.

Stretching the Season

It is possible, however, to plan a long-season garden. Choose perennials for a sequence of bloom over a long period, making sure that at any one time something will be in flower, either in the front, middle, or back of the border. To minimize the number of gaps, choose perennials that have the longest blooming periods. Plant them in overlapping horizontal drifts rather than solid blocks and make the border at least five feet wide. A wide border allows for more gradations in height and therefore more color in the garden.

Another way to prolong color is to include foliage plants and annuals. Plants with attractive leaves are interesting all season long, whether they are blooming or not, and can be useful accents in the garden in any case. White-leaved plants—such as lamb's ears, artemisias, and annual dusty miller—can either soften a bright color scheme or serve as an integral part of a muted one. Plants with dark red leaves—such as purple perilla, basil 'Dark Opal', or barberry 'Crimson Pygmy'—look beautiful with flowers; so do yellow-leaved plants such as golden thyme. Consider using accent plants with interesting shapes or textures, such as the spiky-leaved yucca and dwarf evergreens; or in southern gardens, the lacy asparagus fern.

Learn to use flowering annuals in gaps in the border or near plants that have already bloomed and left foliage that will either die back, like that of Oriental poppy, or is compact, like that of bearded iris. If you are really ambitious, you can exchange one form of plant for another. Start in fall by planting tulips in all the gaps between perennials. Dig them up and discard them immediately after blooming (they are rarely as productive the second year), then replace them with annuals. After frost, discard the annuals and set in bushy, full-grown chrysanthemums. You may discard these after bloom, or winter them over in a greenhouse or a cold frame, divide them in spring, and grow them in a small nursery plot for fall use.

Colors, Hot and Cold

Preference for color is so personal. No one likes to be told what color "goes" with what. But here are a few basic facts about how color works in the garden and how to use it to advantage. Cool colors such as blue, lavender, and blue-green recede; hot colors such as red, yellow, and orange come forward. So does white. Thus, if you use blue flowers in a border that is far away, you may not see them at all.

Hot colors, on the other hand, are useful when the best site for the garden is a little too far away, because they seem to bring it closer. The rare bright plants that bloom in shade can also be used to illuminate dark corners—red-orange impatiens, for example. White flowers or white-leaved plants, such as hostas and lamiums, also bring out shaded areas. Remember that you need a large mass of a cool color to catch the eye, a smaller mass of a hot one.

Choosing a Color Scheme

People have strong preferences as to cool and warm color schemes. Some gardeners adore a riot of bright color, while others are more apt to create toned-down schemes with pastels, dark purples, and subtle blendings of foliage tones in blues, silvers, and different greens. Some people like a lot of contrast, using strong primary colors next to one another. Others like a narrow gradation: gardens with only rose and blue tones, or with just yellow, orange,

Landscaping with Flowers

mahogany, and rust shades. Even single-color gardens, which are difficult but fun to plan, are always enhanced by foliage tones. White is useful in a garden in almost any situation, whether in the big patches formed by phlox or shasta daisies or in soft-looking areas created by baby's-breath or dusty miller.

Combining Colors

Deciding on your color scheme is only the first step. You must then figure out how to make it work in the garden. The principles behind designing flower gardens are just like any principles of design. You want to make the composition harmonious and balanced, usually by repeating a color throughout at balanced intervals. Balanced does not necessarily mean perfectly symmetrical, but the picture should not be lopsided, with, say, all the red at one end. Sometimes this means forcing yourself to use fewer plants so you can repeat them often enough to tie the composition together. This is difficult to do if you like to grow a lot of different things, but your restraint will be rewarded in the end.

Think hard about which plants you are placing right next to one another, particularly if they will bloom at the same time. If you feel that magenta and yellow clash, or that such a blaze of color destroys the balance of your design, you can separate them with a softer color or even with a patch of green. Some flower colors may enhance one another. For example, pale yellow yarrow is quite attractive next to blue veronica. The gentle contrast lies not only in the colors, but in the flower shapes: The yarrow has flat clusters and the veronica has vertical spikes.

Considering Shape

Remember that flower and plant shapes are as important as their colors. Some plants grow narrow and upright, others are mounded, and still others are low or sprawling. Keep in mind which plants bloom only on top and which bloom all the way up the stalk. If a plant is tallish but its blooms start low, it should be placed in the bed so you can see the low flowers too. The same can be true of drooping plants. Some should be staked, especially in climates where their stems are weak. For example, delphiniums and lupines need staking in Connecticut, but in Maine or Vermont, they may not. You may simply prefer the floppy look of plants such as shasta daisies or Frikarti asters. In that case, put only very low plants in front of them.

Digging In

You may find some of these design decisions hard at first, especially if you are not familiar with the plants you are using. Don't feel discouraged. Even veteran gardeners find it difficult to predict how a plant will respond in a particular setting. It may be very short the first year or unexpectedly tall because of very fertile soil or insufficient sun. And no one can know exactly when a plant will start blooming or how long it will flower. Books and catalogues are rarely precise about this, and with good reason. Blooming times vary so much from place to place. Even a specific cultivar will perform differently in different climates.

Ask gardeners in your area how certain plants have performed for them. Local nurseries can also offer useful tips. But in the end you will work things out by trial and error. Your picture will never be a fixed one. Make notes of what each plant did each year, how tall it grew, and when it bloomed. Take pictures to help you remember what you want to change at planting time. If their placement really bothers you, you can even move most plants during their growing season, provided you lift them with plenty of soil around the roots and water them in well.

To show you how to put all these principles into effect, here are three sample flower gardens. They illustrate the step-by-step process of putting a garden together.

Summer Perennial Garden

A garden planted with only summer-blooming perennials is a challenge, but it can be done, and the reward is a constantly changing array of colors. The garden shown on page 316 is designed to be attractive for three months. In the Northeast, these would be June, July, and August. In warmer climates, it would be earlier and the plant choices would reflect your climate, but the same planning principles apply. In order to ensure plenty of blooms in each month and enough repetitions of each to be effective, the garden is 40 feet long and six feet wide; but you could cut off nine feet on either end and still include most of the plants, since the garden is symmetrical. There would just be fewer repetitions.

Arrange the plants in drifts that are horizontal as you stand and face the garden. This arrangement creates the effect of continuous bloom. At any point in the garden there will be about four drifts of plants overlapping one another, at least one of them blooming. The plant groupings should be kept relatively small—three of the same plants together in most cases, fewer of the largest ones—to make more repetitions and more unity possible.

The color scheme for this garden is cool and muted. Blue and rose tones predominate, along with lavender, purple, white, and in each season, a few red or orange accents. The desired effect is a constant balance of these hues throughout the season, but your garden could, of course, change in color scheme as the season goes on.

Notice that the plants are placed fairly close together. You always have a choice between spacing perennials far apart and waiting for them to fill in or planting them close together and having to divide them sooner. Wide spacing is more economical, but close spacing gives you a full effect sooner, especially if you are not using annuals to fill in gaps.

Landscaping with Flowers

Selecting Plants

In selecting plants for your own garden, you should bear in mind three factors—your color scheme, the heights of the plants, and their blooming times. You'll find it helpful to make up a chart of the flowers you are considering. The chart shown on page 314 is a model for you to follow. It shows how plants were chosen for the Summer Perennial Garden.

First decide on a color scheme and note the color categories in the left column, leaving space under each color heading for a list of flower names. Next, indicate across the top several height categories and the blooming times. Then, as you think of plants you'd like to include—by finding them in catalogues or books, or seeing them in other gardens in your area—write their names under the appropriate color category. Do some research to determine whether each plant will grow in your area, how tall it gets, and when it blooms. Make check marks in the appropriate height and season categories. Many of your choices may bloom over more than one of the intervals you are planning for—simply check all that apply.

Once you have a substantial list, look at the pattern of check marks you've made. Are there at least several flowers included in each height category, or are almost all of them three to four feet tall? Will some flowers of each color be blooming in each part of the season, or does it look like late summer will be barren of color? Add and subtract plant names until your chart, like the one here, shows a good balance of colors in each height and season category. Let the list run deliberately long for now. You can cross off some names as you fill in your garden plan—the next step.

Sketching the Plan

Draw a plan of the garden and begin filling it in with plants from your chart. This has been done in the drawing labeled Planting Scheme, on page 316. The outline of each grouping shows how many plants it contains. Start with the taller plants, filling up the back of the border, and then work toward the front. You can check to make sure you have produced a pleasing arrangement for each season by superimposing a piece of tracing paper on the master plan and sketching only those plants that will then be in bloom. The three drawings shown under the planting scheme are the results of such tracings. In some cases they account for sporadic as well as full bloom. As you sketch, you may notice that you've bunched too many plants together in one spot and left a gap in another. Rearrange them, making changes on the master and adjusting the other tracings.

While you are doing all this, try to picture in your mind what the garden will look like from one week to the next. You'll learn to predict it fairly well but never perfectly; some species will always surprise you. Length of bloom time is particularly hard to predict, and long bloom in this sample garden depends partly on how attentive you are about cutting back spent flower stems on plants that rebloom—especially coral bells, pinks, feverfew, pyrethrum, and delphinium.

Color in Early Summer
Early summer in this sample garden brings blues and purples of Siberian iris and delphiniums, along with purple clustered bellflower. For rose tones, there are a long-blooming species of pinks and gas plants. Coral bells are a small, darker pink accent; lily 'Enchantment' a strong red-orange. The pyrethrum clumps will throw flowers of assorted pinks and reds; the lupines are in mixed shades of pink, blue, and rust. Phlox 'Miss Lingard' and feverfew are the white accents. For feverfew, look for the tall species—not the shorter German chamomile (*Matricaria*).
Possibilities that were eliminated were a tall and a short shasta daisy—because they are more short-lived than the self-sowing feverfew—and peonies, poppies, and columbines—because of their short blooming periods. In warmer climates, eliminate the lupines and delphiniums but try gloxinia penstemon (*Penstemon gloxinioides*) and carnations (*Dianthus caryophyllus*). By the sea, try common thrift (*Armeria maritima*).

Midsummer Blooms
For the midsummer picture, there is pink-flowering heather 'County Wicklow', a dark rose yarrow, pink musk mallows, and pink and lavender shades of phlox. Sea-lavender provides dainty lavender-colored clouds, Frikarti aster a mass of violet blue, wild bergamot another patch of lavender. The tall, daisylike purple coneflowers are rose-purple with a rust center, and a variety of loosestrife makes purple spikes. The bluebells lend a touch of lavender-blue. Daylilies selected are melon-toned, butterfly weed a bright but not garish red-orange. The white accents of early summer, feverfew and Carolina phlox 'Miss Lingard', are still blooming stalwartly; and the pinks, coral bells, and pyrethrum are producing scattered blooms.
Plants reluctantly crossed out for midsummer were blue scabiosa, pretty but not very showy in a big border; *Centranthus,* which though long-blooming was too much like the pink yarrow; and tall blue globe thistle, which also might be too subtle to be seen from a distance. In warmer climates you might try the bulbous lily-of-the-Nile (*Agapanthus africanus*), various lavenders, or mealy-cup sage (*Salvia farinacea*). Near the ocean, try *Erigeron* hybrids.

Flowers for Late Summer
In the last month of the border, some earlier plants will still be blooming—namely Frikarti aster, heather, bluebells, feverfew, coneflower, pink and lavender phlox, sea-lavender, loosestrife, and musk mallow. Others may still be throwing a few blooms—pinks,

Chart for a Summer Perennial Garden   *The numbers after each plant refer to plants in the garden plan.*

Blue to Purple Flowers

Garden phlox (1)	*Phlox paniculata* 'Lilac Time'
Purple loosestrife (2)	*Lythrum salicaria* 'Dropmore Purple'
Delphinium (6)	*Delphinium elatum* 'Bluebird'
Siberian iris, purple (7)	*Iris sibirica*
Wild bergamot (8)	*Monarda fistulosa*
Delphinium (9)	*Delphinium elatum* 'Summer Skies'
Siberian iris, blue (10)	*Iris sibirica*
Delphinium (11)	*Delphinium elatum* 'King Arthur'
Frikarti aster (19)	*Aster × frikartii* 'Wonder of Staffa'
Danesblood bellflower (23)	*Campanula glomerata* 'Superba'
Sea-lavender (26)	*Limonium latifolium*
Bluebell (28)	*Campanula rotundifolia*

Red to Orange and Mixed Flowers

False sunflower (4)	*Helenium autumnale* 'Moerheim Beauty'
Lily hybrid (12)	*Lilium* 'Enchantment'
Russell hybrid lupine (13)	*Lupinus* 'Russell Hybrid'
Daylily (15)	*Hemerocallis* 'Abstract Art'
Daylily (18)	*Hemerocallis* 'May Hall'
Pyrethrum (21)	*Chrysanthemum coccineum*
Butterfly weed (22)	*Asclepias tuberosa*

Rose to Dark Pink Flowers

Purple coneflower (3)	*Echinacea purpurea*
Garden phlox (5)	*Phlox paniculata* 'Dresden China'
Gas plant (16)	*Dictamnus albus* 'Purpureus'
Musk mallow (17)	*Malva moschata*
Yarrow (24)	*Achillea* 'Red Beauty'
Coral bells (25)	*Heuchera sanguinea*
Heather (27)	*Calluna vulgaris* 'County Wicklow'
Allwood pink (29)	*Dianthus × allwoodii*

White Flowers

Carolina phlox (14)	*Phlox carolina* 'Miss Lingard'
Feverfew (20)	*Chrysanthemum parthenium*

Plan for a Summer Perennial Garden

Planting Scheme

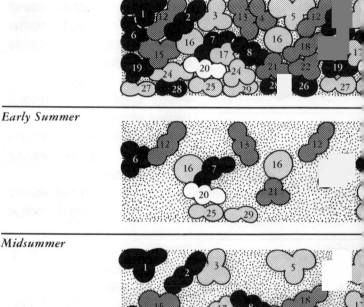

Early Summer

Midsummer

Late Summer

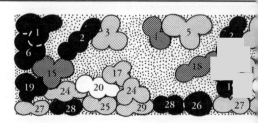

Plants over 3 ft.
1. Garden phlox
   'Lilac Time'
2. Purple loosestrife
   'Dropmore Purple'
3. Purple coneflower
4. False sunflower
   'Moerheim Beauty'

5. Garden phlox
   'Dresden China'
6. Delphinium
   'Bluebird'
7. Siberian iris, purple
8. Wild bergamot
9. Delphinium
   'Summer Skies'

10. Siberian iris, blue
11. Delphinium 'King
    Arthur'
Plants 2–3 ft.
12. Lily 'Enchantment'
13. Russell hybrid
    lupine
14. Carolina phlox
    'Miss Lingard'

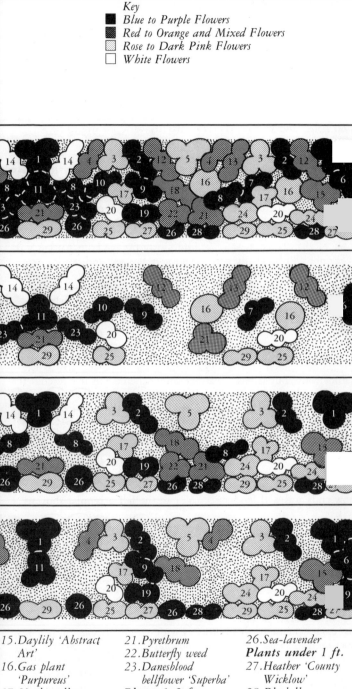

Key
■ Blue to Purple Flowers
▨ Red to Orange and Mixed Flowers
▨ Rose to Dark Pink Flowers
□ White Flowers

15. Daylily 'Abstract
    Art'
16. Gas plant
    'Purpureus'
17. Musk mallow
18. Daylily 'May Hall'
19. Frikarti aster
    'Wonder of Staffa'
20. Feverfew

21. Pyrethrum
22. Butterfly weed
23. Danesblood
    bellflower 'Superba'
Plants 1–2 ft.
24. Yarrow 'Red
    Beauty'
25. Coral bells

26. Sea-lavender
Plants under 1 ft.
27. Heather 'County
    Wicklow'
28. Bluebell
29. Allwood pink

coral bells, and yarrow. The two daylily varieties would be reblooming; and the delphiniums, which should be cut back after their first bloom, would be showing once again. Their new flowering stems would be shorter, however, so they were not placed too far back in the border. The only strictly late-blooming plant added was an August-flowering variety of helenium, for a bronze-red accent. If there were space, you could add some rose- and salmon-toned dahlias. In the South, you might work in some Stokes asters (*Stokesia laevis*).

Some of the plants chosen are notoriously piggy about garden soil. Bergamot and bluebells will spread very quickly and need restraining. The feverfew and lupines will be short-lived but will self-sow prolifically. That's fine; you can just eliminate any you don't want. But over time, these spreading plants will help the border lose some of its symmetry and take on a softer, more natural look.

A Three-Season Garden

The border shown on page 322 is the same shape and size as the summer one, but it has a warmer color scheme and it stretches the blooming season even further. It begins with three late spring perennials: Oriental poppies, peonies, and bearded iris. And it finishes with fall perennials: sedum, chrysanthemums, asters, great burnet, and azure monkshood. In between, there is a show of annuals: bachelor's buttons, snapdragons, French marigolds, annual baby's-breath, golden coreopsis, and zinnias. All the annuals chosen can withstand some frost at either end of the season, so they will already be showing color when the rather brief spring perennial show ends and will lend some color to the fall perennial show as well.

It would be very difficult to span spring, summer, and fall with an all-perennial garden. But the use of annuals in summer makes this scheme work. Since these are hardy annuals, they can be planted in spring along with the fall perennials. The bearded iris should be planted in late summer, however, and peonies and poppies in fall.

A Multicolored Scheme

The color scheme of this border is wide-ranging. You might describe it as "multicolored but not garish." All the peony, iris, and poppy colors blend well together, ranging from orange through red, pink, purple, and white. Care was taken to arrange all the varieties to avoid a lopsided concentration of one color, since the bloom periods of these three overlap somewhat. They are also roughly the same height, forming a band across the middle of the border, with later plants filling the spaces behind and in front of them. This is a rather different arrangement from that of the summer border, where a tapestry of overlapping drifts creates the effect and there is always something blooming in the front, middle, and rear of the bed. (This bed really has three, almost separate seasons.) In warm climates, you might substitute Louisiana iris for the bearded type.

The annuals include some strong primary colors—red marigolds and blue bachelor's buttons. There is also multicolored red/gold/brown coreopsis, frothy white baby's-breath, and zinnias and snapdragons in a mixture of shades, including dark reds and pinks.

The annuals were chosen for variety in height and flower shapes as well as color, adding extra interest for the summer show. The marigolds, with their neat, rounded petals, contrast with the bachelor's buttons, whose heads of small, tubular flowers appear spiky. The coreopsis looks similar to the marigolds, but its slender leaves lend an airier look. The baby's-breath is a welcome break of light texture and color among the strong red and orange flowerheads, and the zinnias echo the marigolds in shape farther back in the bed. The distinctively shaped snapdragons, with their pouched, tubular flowers on long stalks, add vertical accents amid the more rounded forms of the other annuals.

For fall, both short and tall chrysanthemums were chosen in several shades of yellow and red. The tall asters in back range from warm pinks to cool blues and purples. They are mixed with dark blue spikes of azure monkshood and white spikes of great burnet. Sedum 'Autumn Joy', in front, blooms carmine-rose in late summer to early fall, then graces the garden with mahogany seed heads that are beautiful all winter long. The peony foliage, handsome green mounds in summer, will be yellow in fall—a fine addition. The less attractive poppy and iris foliage will be hidden by the summer and fall plants.

Substitutes for Different Climates

This border was charted and sketched out in the same way the Summer Perennial Garden was. The color scheme was selected, and then the plants were chosen according to color, height, and bloom time. The list was adjusted to give the balanced categories shown in the chart on page 320. Finally, the plants were carefully placed on the plan.

Among the annuals eliminated but still worth considering were ageratum, candytuft, portulaca, *Cynoglossum,* larkspur, white *Nierembergia,* and for foliage accents, annual dusty miller and purple perilla. Lantana would also be a fine addition, especially in warm climates where it is perennial. Siberian iris, lupines, and columbines might also have been included for late spring—and Louisiana irises in the South. Dwarf asters, snakeroot (*Cimicifuga simplex*), and *Helianthus* × *multiflorus* would be good substitutions for fall. In warm areas you could also try the tall, lavender Staunton elsholtzia, red-hot poker (*Kniphofia*), or the bulbous common montbretia (*Crocosmia* × *crocosmiiflora*).

Chart for a Three-Season Garden   *The numbers after each plant refer to plants in the garden plan.*

Blue to Purple Flowers

Azure monkshood (4)	*Aconitum carmichaelii*
Michaelmas daisy (5)	*Aster novi-belgii* 'Marie Ballard'
Michaelmas daisy (6)	*A. novi-belgii* 'Eventide'
Michaelmas daisy (7)	*A. novi-belgii* 'Sailor Boy'
Bearded iris (21, 22, 24)	*Iris* hybrids
Bachelor's button (29)	*Centaurea cyanus*

Red to Orange and Mixed Flowers

Michaelmas daisy (8)	*A. novi-belgii* 'Crimson Brocade'
Peony, double (9, 12)	*Paeonia* hybrid
Peony, single (14)	*Paeonia* hybrid
Oriental poppy (16, 17)	*Papaver orientale*
Common zinnia, mixed (19)	*Zinnia elegans*
Common snapdragon (20)	*Antirrhinum majus* 'Rocket'
Chrysanthemum (27, 30)	*Chrysanthemum × morifolium*
Autumn Joy sedum (31)	*Sedum* 'Autumn Joy'
French marigold (32)	*Tagetes patula* 'Red Wheels'

Pink Flowers

New England aster (1)	*Aster novae-angliae* 'Harrington's Pink'
New England aster (3)	*A. novae-angliae* 'Alma Potschke'
Peony, double (11)	*Paeonia* hybrid
Oriental poppy (15)	*Papaver orientale*
Bearded iris (23)	*Iris* hybrid
Chrysanthemum (28)	*Chrysanthemum × morifolium*

Yellow Flowers

Golden coreopsis (26)	*Coreopsis tinctoria*
Cushion chrysanthemum (33)	*Chrysanthemum × morifolium*

White Flowers

Great burnet (2)	*Sanguisorbia canadensis*
Peony, single (10)	*Paeonia* hybrid
Peony, double (13)	*Paeonia* hybrid
Oriental poppy (18)	*Papaver orientale*
Bearded iris (25)	*Iris* hybrid
Annual Baby's-breath (34)	*Gypsophila elegans*

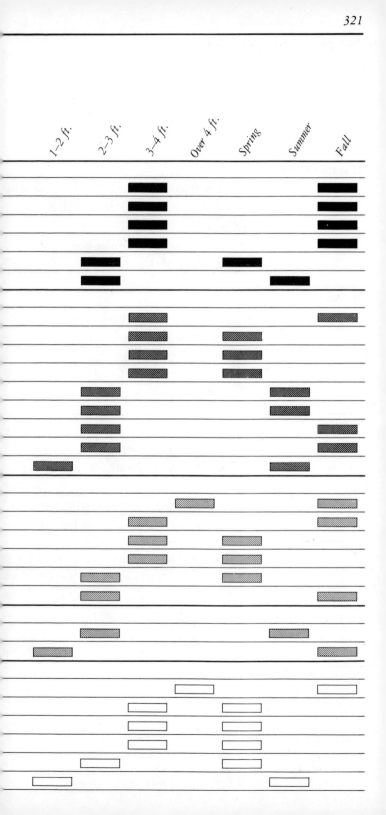

Plan for a Three-Season Garden

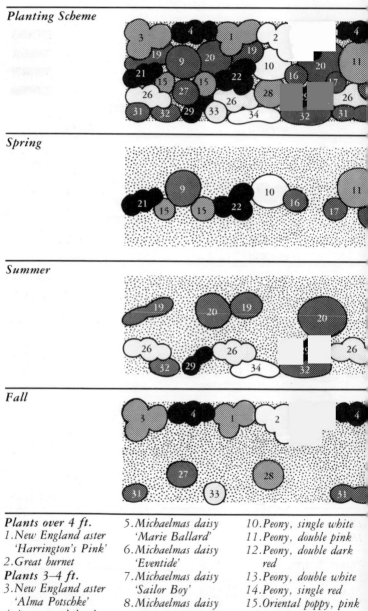

Planting Scheme

Spring

Summer

Fall

Plants over 4 ft.
1. New England aster 'Harrington's Pink'

Plants 3–4 ft.
3. New England aster 'Alma Potschke'
4. Azure monkshood

5. Michaelmas daisy 'Marie Ballard'
6. Michaelmas daisy 'Eventide'
7. Michaelmas daisy 'Sailor Boy'
8. Michaelmas daisy 'Crimson Brocade'
9. Peony, double red

10. Peony, single white
11. Peony, double pink
12. Peony, double dark red
13. Peony, double white
14. Peony, single red
15. Oriental poppy, pink
16. Oriental poppy, orange

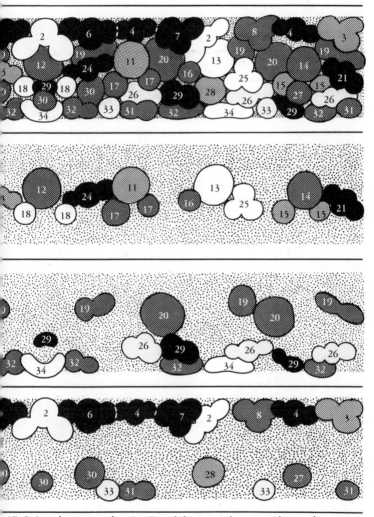

Key

■ Blue to Purple Flowers
▨ Red to Orange and Mixed Flowers
▦ Pink Flowers
▢ Yellow Flowers
□ White Flowers

17. Oriental poppy, red
18. Oriental poppy, white

Plants 2–3 ft.
19. Common zinnia
20. Common snapdragon 'Rocket'
21. Bearded iris, blue
22. Bearded iris, purple

23. Bearded iris, pink
24. Bearded iris, lavender
25. Bearded iris, white
26. Golden coreopsis
27. Chrysanthemum, red
28. Chrysanthemum, pink
29. Bachelor's button

30. Chrysanthemum, bronze
31. Autumn Joy sedum

Plants 1–2 ft.
32. French marigold 'Red Wheels'
33. Cushion chrysanthemum
34. Annual baby's-breath

Landscaping with Flowers

Spring and Summer Garden

In the three-season border, early spring was given somewhat short shrift. You might want to create a garden with just spring bulbs and early perennials, then interplant them with annuals that will last until frost.

The spring garden shown on page 328 is an island bed 22 feet long, in a free-form shape. While there is at least one carefully placed repetition of each plant group, repetition and balance are a little less important here. The bed is seen not all at once, but as you walk around it. It combines spring bulbs, perennials that bloom in spring and early summer, perennial foliage plants, and summer-blooming annuals. The bulbs would be planted in fall. The perennials could be planted either in fall or very early spring. Most of the annuals would be planted after danger of frost.

The color scheme consists of yellow, yellow-green, blue, blue-green, purple, white, and a few touches of red-orange. This time the "early" column on the chart included white and purple common crocus, blue glory-of-the-snow, yellow rock cress and English primroses, purple-blue bulbous iris, and Kaufmanniana tulips, which grow four to eight inches tall and are generally bicolored (choose one in which red predominates). Then came a yellow-and-white daffodil mix, including the poet's narcissus with a red-edged center.

Color in Late Spring

Late spring in this garden will start with Darwin hybrid tulips, one clump of a yellow variety and one of a red. Soon several perennial foliage plants will start to be effective—blue fescue, a grass that makes a fine blue hummock; molinia grass, which is green-and-yellow striped; the woolly-white *Artemisia stellerana;* gray-leaved santolina; and blue-leaved rue. Lemon daylilies will appear. Neither the santolina nor the rue will show their yellow blooms until early or midsummer, but the foliage will be attractive earlier. A number of late spring perennials will be blooming: a bright red-orange helianthemum; doronicum, euphorbia, and trollius—all of them yellow but with a variety of flower shapes; red-and-yellow common columbine; and blue Jacob's ladder.

A Display of Annuals

While these are blooming, the annuals will be gathering strength for their display, beginning with white sweet alyssum, followed by a dark blue edging lobelia, orange calendulas, tall spikes of blue salvia, and Iceland poppies in mixed shades of yellow, orange, red, and white. The alyssum and calendulas can be sown right in the garden in early spring. The lobelia, salvia, and poppies should be started indoors and set out after danger of frost—or started as purchased seedlings. In addition, Japanese iris will bloom—one clump in a purple shade and one clump in a blue. All the foliage

plants will still be effective as well. After the early summer
perennials have finished blooming, the garden will still be showy
because of the annuals and the foliage plants, which will last all
summer.

All these plants are arranged with regard to height within each
season, with the low plants along the edge of the bed, the tall
ones in the center, and the medium-height ones in between.
(Early-blooming plants such as narcissus may then have taller, late-
blooming plants in front of them.) Other additions to this garden
might be: snowdrops and winter aconites, which are both very
early; basket-of-gold (*Aurinia saxatilis*); yellow-leaved *Origanum;*
purple *Anemone pulsatilla,* which leaves lovely white clouds of seed-
heads; white *Iberis;* Siberian iris; yellow goldenstar (*Chrysogonum
virginianum*); *Oenothera missourensis,* the low-growing, non-invasive
sundrop; blue spiderwort (*Tradescantia*); shasta daisy 'Little Miss
Muffet'; coreopsis 'Goldfink'; *Campanula carpatica; Alchemilla
vulgaris;* yellow yarrow (*Achillea*); white-leaved, blue-flowered
Veronica incana; blue and white *Campanula persicifolia;* the intense
blue Chinese delphinium; lavender 'Munstead Dwarf'; lavender-
flowered catmint (*Nepeta mussini*); and the long-blooming yellow
Coreopsis verticillata. In warmer climates, try the tall, yellow foxtail
lily (*Eremurus stenophyllus*); and some warm-weather bulbs such as
Persian buttercup (*Ranunculus asiaticus*) for early spring and tiger
flower (*Tigridia pavonia*) for summer.

Limitless Possibilities

This long list of perfectly appropriate "rejects" illustrates how many
possibilities occur when you are working within a particular color
scheme. This list could easily be tripled.

Following these examples, you can choose plants according to color,
height, and bloom time to create compositions unique to your taste
and site. The types you select and the shape of the flower bed itself
can be altered to give your garden a casual or formal look.

Your flower garden can include features other than plants to
heighten its drama. You might build it on a series of terraces held
by handsome stone walls. Or plant a perennial border on either side
of a brick path, making the color and pattern of the brick part of
the design. Consider placing an elegant fountain or statue in just
the right spot, or create a garden that consists entirely of flowers in
containers set around a pool.

Whatever style you decide on, reevaluate the design periodically.
You may see that some of your experiments with color or height
combinations didn't work, or you may simply want to try
something new. Your own taste and imagination will always
suggest new and different designs. Don't you sometimes wish you
could have a hundred gardens?

Chart for a Spring and Summer Garden

Blue to Purple Plants

Edging lobelia (4)	*Lobelia erinus* 'Crystal Palace'
Bulbous iris (7)	*Iris reticulata*
Glory-of-the-snow (8)	*Chionodoxa luciliae*
Common crocus, purple (10)	*Crocus vernus*
Blue fescue (18)	*Festuca ovina glauca*
Jacob's ladder (24)	*Polemonium caeruleum*
Mealy-cup sage (25)	*Salvia farinacea*
Common rue (26)	*Ruta graveolens*
Japanese iris, blue (27)	*Iris ensata*
Japanese iris, purple (29)	*Iris ensata*

Red to Orange and Mixed Plants

Iceland poppy, mixed (6)	*Papaver nudicale*
Rock rose (9)	*Helianthemum nummularium* 'Fire Drago
Water lily tulip, red (11)	*Tulipa*, Kaufmanniana hybrid
Common columbine (13)	*Aquilegia canadensis*
Pot marigold (14)	*Calendula officinalis*
Darwin hybrid tulip, red (23)	*Tulipa*, Darwin hybrid

Yellow Plants

English primrose (1)	*Primula vulgaris*
Rock cress (3)	*Draba densiflora*
Leopard's bane (12)	*Doronicum cordatum*
Common globeflower (15)	*Trollius europaeus*
Purple moor grass (17)	*Molinia caerulea variegata*
Cushion spurge (19)	*Euphorbia epithymoides*
Daffodil (22)	*Narcissus* hybrid
Lemon daylily (28)	*Hemerocallis lilioasphodelus*
Darwin hybrid tulip (30)	*Tulipa*, Darwin hybrid

White Plants

Common crocus (2)	*Crocus vernus*
Sweet alyssum (5)	*Lobularia maritima*
Beach wormwood (16)	*Artemisia stellerana*
Lavender cotton (20)	*Santolina chamaecyparissus*
Daffodil (21)	*Narcissus* hybrid

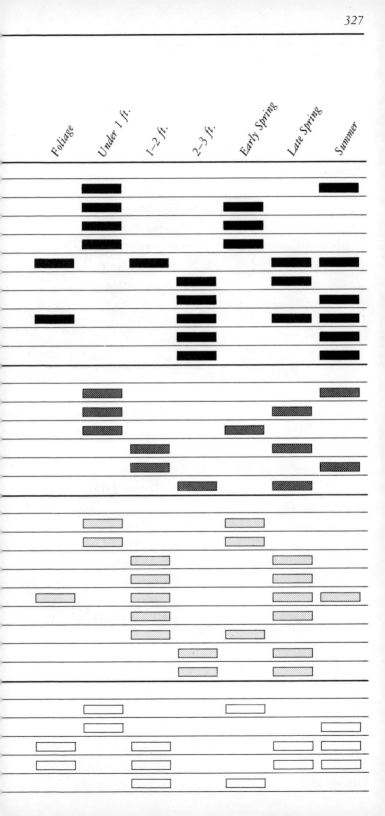

Plan for a Spring and Summer Garden

Planting Scheme

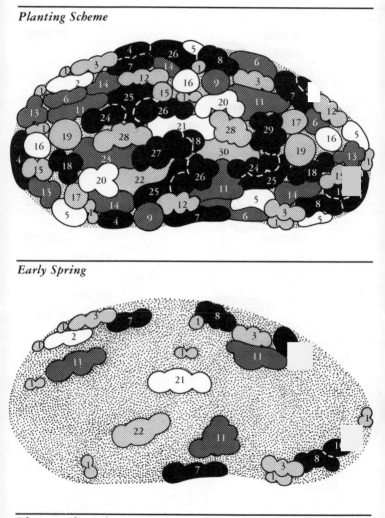

Early Spring

Plants under 1 ft.
1. English primrose
2. Common crocus, white
3. Rock cress
4. Edging lobelia 'Crystal Palace'
5. Sweet alyssum
6. Iceland poppy, mixed
7. Bulbous iris
8. Glory-of-the-snow
9. Rock rose 'Fire Dragon'
10. Common crocus, purple
11. Water lily tulip, red

Plants 1–2 ft.
12. Leopard's bane
13. Common columbine
14. Pot marigold
15. Common globeflower
16. Beach wormwood
17. Variegated purple moor grass
18. Blue fescue

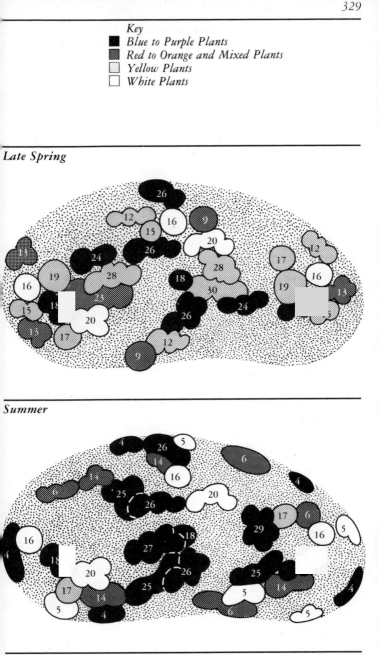

Key
- Blue to Purple Plants
- Red to Orange and Mixed Plants
- Yellow Plants
- White Plants

Late Spring

Summer

19. Cushion spurge
20. Lavender cotton
21. Daffodil, white
22. Daffodil, yellow

Plants 2–3 ft.
23. Darwin hybrid
    tulip, red
24. Jacob's ladder
25. Mealy-cup sage
26. Common rue
27. Japanese iris, blue
28. Lemon daylily

29. Japanese iris, purple
30. Darwin hybrid
    tulip, yellow

Landscaping with Flowers

Listings in the Source column are page references to individual Taylor's Guides. A key to title abbreviations appears on page 11.

Under Zones, W and C indicate warm- or cool-season annuals.

	Source	Zones
Plant Choices		
Achillea spp. Yarrow	P-274	3–9
Agapanthus africanus Lily-of-the-Nile	B-275	8–10
Antirrhinum majus Common snapdragon	A-284	C
Aquilegia spp. Columbine	P-287	4–8
Campanula spp. Bellflower	P-303	3–8
Centaurea cyanus Bachelor's button	A-303	C
Cleome hasslerana Spider flower	A-308	W
Coreopsis spp. Coreopsis	P-314	4–9
Crocosmia × *crocosmiiflora* Montbretia	B-299	7–10
Dahlia pinnata hybrids Dahlia	B-306	W
Dianthus spp. Pinks	P-319	4–8
Echinacea purpurea Purple coneflower	P-326	4–9
Erigeron hybrids Fleabane	P-329	5–7
Gypsophila spp. Baby's-breath	P-343	4–8
Hemerocallis hybrids Daylily	P-347	4–10
Heuchera sanguinea Coral bells	P-349	4–8
Ipomoea nil Morning glory	A-347	W
Iris spp. Iris	P-354	3–8
Kniphofia uvaria Red-hot poker	P-357	5–8
Monarda spp. Bergamot	P-371	4–8
Narcissus spp. Daffodil	B-357	4–7
Paeonia spp. Peony	P-376	4–7
Papaver orientale Oriental poppy	P-378	4–7
Penstemon spp. Beardtongue	P-378	4–9
Phlox spp. Phlox	P-381	4–8
Primula spp. Primrose	P-388	5–8
Stokesia laevis Stokes aster	P-406	5–8
Tagetes spp. Marigold	A-407	W
Tigridia pavonia Tiger flower	B-372	8–10
Tropaeolum majus Nasturtium	A-414	C
Tulipa spp. Tulip	B-374	4–6

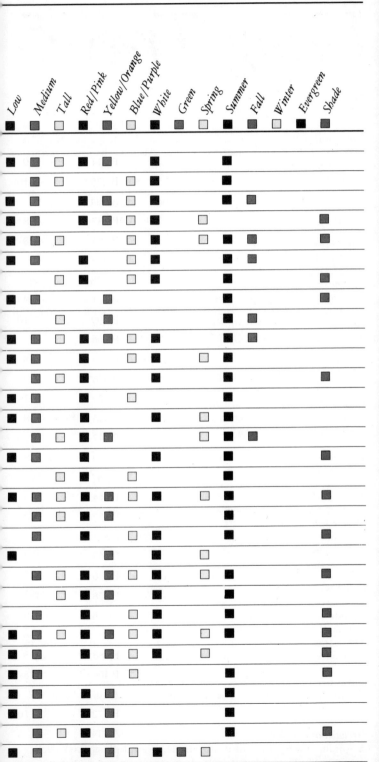

Using Trees &

Joseph Hudak

Trees and shrubs are the foundation of any landscape design. You may select them for a practical purpose, such as shading a terrace or screening a view, or just for their colorful attractions. Because of their great heights and widths, extensive root systems, extraordinary longevity, and often slow growth, trees should be the first plants you consider when planning a new layout. Shrubs come next, filling in the lower levels and helping mask raw foundations.

An Array of Choices

Trees and shrubs fall into three groups by leaf type: needle-leaf evergreens, broadleaf evergreens, and deciduous. Their natural outlines are delightfully varied: rounded, vase-shaped, pyramidal, columnar, open, weeping, prostrate, and more. Each seems to have an individual character—rugged or delicate, flamboyant or somber, wistful or elegant. Within these outlines are colorful flowers, fruits, and foliage that add accent and changing interest.

With thousands of trees and shrubs known and grown for garden use, you may feel that choosing and arranging them is an overwhelming task. But you can narrow the field quickly by focusing on what purposes you want these plants to serve. Combining that knowledge with information about whether the plants you admire will grow in your general climate and on your particular site will lead you to reliable, rewarding choices.

Practical Uses of Trees and Shrubs

The architecture of trees and shrubs is not only beautiful but functional. To block out a view into your neighbor's yard, you might select an informal hedge of lilac, spirea, or forsythia—stalwart flowering shrubs that thrive in most soils but bloom best in full sun. In shadier sites, evergreen trees like hemlock, arborvitae, or American holly are useful for privacy. They adapt well to modest shade if watered consistently. Tough and reliable needled evergreens, such as the sizeable spruces and pines, are durable windbreaks, especially useful for diverting drifting snow or strong sea breezes. On a smaller scale, tall shrub yews or junipers make attractive enclosures and barriers to noise, wind, and intruders. You can trim them into neat hedges or allow them to assume their natural, informal shapes.

Shade trees can help lower your air-conditioning costs by reducing glare and heat penetration in summer. In winter, tall deciduous shade trees such as oaks or maples allow the sun to filter through and provide heat. Firs and other evergreens will shade your house all year long, so they are best used close to the house only in warm-winter areas.

Ornamental Uses

A specimen tree or shrub is any single, beautifully shaped, well-grown example of nature's craft. It is meant to be a focal point—an

Shrubs

accent—so its site should be prominent and uncrowded. A dramatic hibiscus or delicate flowering dogwood needs no support from neighboring plants. A glistening holly or rich Japanese maple is a solitary gem in the landscape, set off by only the surrounding green lawn. Specimens require careful maintenance—watering, fertilizing, and pruning—to keep them in top form. Treasure and preserve any tree or shrub specimens already on your property, designing the rest of the garden around them. Removing such plants to make way for your own design can be a mistake, especially considering the many years it will take for a new tree or shrub to reach its ornamental peak.

The imposing forms of trees and shrubs can work together handsomely in groupings or masses, as backdrops to lower-growing plants, or standing alone as accents in the landscape. You can plan a mass of plants to give spectacular color in one season—a spring-blooming garden of dogwood, azaleas, and rhododendrons, for example—or to stretch the interest over a longer period, with spring and summer flowers followed by berries and foliage that persist into winter. It is best to combine plants of similar type rather than create a polka-dot effect by sprinkling them throughout a design.

At lower levels in the landscape, use prostrate shrubs such as sun-loving creeping juniper or cotoneaster to make welcome textural contrasts to lawns and nearby shrubs. For semishaded locations there are handsome evergreens: creeping mahonia, fragrant sarcococca, or euonymus 'Emerald Gaiety'.

Low shrubs have functional purposes as well. They can save you the trouble of mowing an embankment by replacing lawn with a carpet of color. Try memorial rose or Chenault coralberry in full sun; creeping St. Johnswort or prostrate abelia in semishade. There is a long list of shrubs that make attractive ground-cover beds in sun or shade.

Foundation Plantings

One of the most important functions of small ornamental trees and shrubs is as foundation plantings. These groupings should be sensitively selected to emphasize and embellish the features of your house and to hide exposed concrete or to cover architectural flaws. Coordinate the colors, textures, and styles of house and plants harmoniously, considering nearby walls, fences, outbuildings, or pavements as integral parts of the design. Choose durable plants that will act as a unifying element in all seasons.

Design Principles

Whether you choose trees and shrubs for function or beauty, knowing some simple design principles will help you decide how to combine and place them. The concepts most important in arranging these plants are repetition, sequence, and balance.

Artful Repetition

Repetition is the most fundamental concept and the easiest to achieve. A simple example is a row of several of the same plants—a hedge of Hatfield yew or border forsythia, a driveway lined with equally-spaced sugar maples or beeches. The reappearance of one color, shape, texture, size, or arrangement in various areas throughout a design is a more subtle form of repetition. For example, pink might be repeated in azaleas near the house, roses along the fence, and a dogwood in the front lawn. There might be a theme of weeping shapes created by a willow, a forsythia, and the foliage of daylilies. A staggered row of spruces or pines might echo a flower border in shape. Such repetitions tie the scheme together.

Sequence

By arranging plants in sequence, you lead the eye in one direction. This can be done with the progressive change of at least one plant characteristic in a grouping, such as the sizes of leaves or flowers. A border of rhododendrons with different foliage and blossoming times is one example. Such a sequence might include only one of each plant type or many, depending on your space and inclination.

Balance

The arrangement of objects in relation to a vertical axis is called balance. When objects on both sides of the axis are mirror images of one another, there is symmetrical balance. If the arrangement is unequal, there is asymmetric, or informal, balance. Trees and shrubs placed in either manner can be attractive, depending on the setting.

If your house is of Georgian style, for example, it probably has an equal number of matched front windows flanking a pillared doorway. The entrance planting you design ought to be similarly formal. Neat-growing, dense shrubs such as box or Japanese holly would be appropriate, along with Kwanzan Oriental cherry and Swiss stone pine for tree accents. Contemporary homes are far more casual in design, so the landscape treatment that looks best is naturalistic and informal.

Perspective

As you arrange trees and shrubs for repetition, sequence, and balance, you must also keep in mind the effects of distance and perspective, which alter the perceived features of all objects. For example, the fine-leaved Carolina hemlock seems to lose its texture at a great distance; only its feathery silhouette gives a clue to its identity. Plants placed close at hand in the landscape can be appreciated for their details but not for the effect of their full outlines on the horizon. Identify the dominant feature of the plant you are considering—detail or overall shape—and place it in the landscape accordingly.

If you have a specific site in mind, rather than a specific plant, it helps to realize that plants with coarsely textured foliage, such as horse-chestnut or Siebold viburnum, will project toward your eye; those with finer textures—heather or cedar of Lebanon, for example—will recede. Knowing this trick of perception allows you to design a particular space so that it seems larger or smaller than it actually is. Use fine-leaved plants in small spaces, where they will appear to recede, adding a sense of distance. Place a large-leaved plant far back to bring the background closer.

Colors can prove useful in the same way. Cool colors such as blue, purple, or green retreat; the hot tones of red, orange, and yellow advance.

Planning for Seasonal Interest

Like flowers, trees and shrubs bloom at different times of the year, so it is possible to design a garden in which something is flowering from early spring to fall. But because flowers are only one of the many attractions of these plants, it makes sense to use trees and shrubs that have appeal in more than one season. For example, the orange-and-gold fall color of witch hazel, the sparkling fruit clusters of fire thorn at Christmas, and the blood red stems of Siberian dogwood against new snow bring you bonuses long after spring flowers have faded. Evergreens remain constant, dominant forms year-round, earning their reputation as aristocrats of the landscape. Because designs that rely exclusively on them tend to become gloomy, dull, and a bit overpowering, while groupings of only deciduous plants seem sparse and leggy in winter, strive for an agreeable mix of both.

Choose shade trees that offer seasonal extras—birches whose clean white trunks stand out in summer, mountain ashes whose brilliant red or orange fruits last well into winter, or maples that turn vibrant red in fall. For year-long interest, add needle-leaf evergreens of unusual color, such as blue Atlas cedar, white fir, or golden thread cypress.

Know It Before You Grow It

Once you are aware of the many design possibilities involved in growing trees and shrubs, you need to learn to avoid some practical pitfalls. One of the most common mistakes gardeners make is to underestimate the ultimate sizes of these plants. Somehow it is difficult to think ten or twenty years down the line when you're staring at a barren lot. But those years will pass much more quickly than you can imagine, leaving you with the undesirable options of removing a bad choice or deforming its shape by excessive pruning. For example, an evergreen such as Norway spruce or southern magnolia placed too close to your house will become a deformed caricature of its true self in a short time as you prune to let light in the windows or to clear access to the door. If your space is

Using Trees & Shrubs

restricted, keep in mind that nurseries today are well stocked with dwarf and compact varieties of many popular plants.

Resistance to pests and diseases should rate high on your list of what to know about the trees and shrubs you admire. Every growing area has its special problems, so ask local nursery owners and neighbors what pests and diseases they've had to battle and how. Even if it means giving up one of your first choices, avoid plants that have bad track records. Remember that a sickly tree is not easy to hide.

Trees and shrubs with messy habits are just as unwelcome as those plagued by diseases and insects. Most mulberries, for example, drop their dark purple fruits all summer, permanently staining any pavement below. Choose a fruitless variety to avoid this problem. Boxelder and Siberian elm seem to rain twigs with every heavy wind. Willow, poplar, and silver maple have brittle stems that are easily shattered by ice and snow storms. These stems not only create litter, but are dangerous when flying through the air. Keep such trees far away from buildings and high-use areas.

Be aware that some shrubs termed "low-maintenance" can actually become nuisances if placed incorrectly. For example, the twiggy, ground-hugging stems of prostrate cotoneasters and creeping junipers adapt easily to a variety of locations in bright light, making them very attractive as ground covers. But they seem to attract fallen leaves from nearby plants, calling for constant raking or hand-picking. Oaks are prized for their large, durable leaves; but because the leaves require at least two years to decay, they may discolor or suffocate any low shrubs on which they fall. Avoid these difficulties either by choosing taller shrubs or by using flat ground covers only under trees and shrubs with smaller, easily decayed foliage.

In areas where heavy snowfalls are common, choose durable and flexible shrubs for flanking driveways and walks. Deciduous plants generally have more resilient stems than evergreens, but any low-branched tree or tall shrub next to a traffic way can be broken when it is laden with ice or snow. The best solution is to plant either a grassy strip or a late-blooming perennial bed where snow is likely to pile up in quantity.

Effects of Shade

Large trees provide shade, but many smaller trees and shrubs grow in the shade. As your garden matures, it will probably become shadier, causing blossoming trees and shrubs to become weak-flowered and spindly. Even azaleas, rhododendrons, and mountain laurels—shrubs known for great shade tolerance—diminish in flowering effect as shadows become very dense.

Shade may be only part of the problem. The soil in dark areas may have become drier and less rich in humus as the large trees robbed shallow root zones of moisture and food. Beech and maple are particularly greedy, as are most low-branching evergreens. Even weeds have a difficult time growing under such trees. These problems may be alleviated by pruning overhead growth and amending the soil, but you might have to accept the changes of time and replace failing plants with new ones that will tolerate deeper shade.

There is a modest but useful list of shade-tolerant trees and shrubs. Flowering types need plenty of sun, so in shady areas it pays to rely on foliage textures and silhouettes for interest. Broadleaf evergreens such as Japanese aucuba, drooping leucothoe, the many forms of Japanese holly, andromeda, and camellia are good foliage plants in shade. Relatively few needle-leaf evergreens are happy in deep shade, but Japanese yew, Harrington plum-yew, and hemlock do very well as long as the soil is kept moist. Consider them especially if you are planting on the north side of your house.

Choices for Wet or Dry Areas

Most evergreens require some special treatment, including consistent moisture all year long to keep their foliage in good shape. Broadleaf evergreens, in particular, will languish on rocky, dry, exposed sites. But one group of needle-leaf evergreens—the junipers—is remarkably versatile, which explains their widespread use. Available in tree, shrub, or ground-cover forms, junipers are adaptable to dry or wet sites, high wind, and blazing sun or semishade—and they grow in almost any climate.

In general, deciduous trees and shrubs do far better in soggy conditions than do evergreens. Red maple, willow, river birch, and bald cypress are sterling examples of trees at home with wet feet. Some of the best shrubs for moist soils are swamp azalea, common winterberry, vernal witch hazel, and snowberry. Although it is possible to force plants to adapt to adverse conditions, it is much easier on you and them if you match their needs to your conditions.

Putting Your Knowledge to Work

Armed with a reasonable, practical and aesthetic knowledge of the trees and shrubs you admire, you should be able to match site and selections reliably. One of the first areas you may want to tackle is the front yard, where trees and shrubs form the living architecture that complements your house style and structure.

Designing Entrance Plantings

The entrance to your property is the beginning of your landscape development—the face you present to the world. You want it to express your taste and to welcome visitors.

The trees and shrubs to choose from in designing entrance plantings are so numerous and varied that it is much more practical to suggest features to avoid than to list particular "best" choices. After you've made sure the plants you are considering will grow in your

Using Trees & Shrubs

climate and conditions, anticipate and avoid the following possible problems.

What should be an open view from the street or driveway to your door can become quickly obscured if you don't consider how fast your entrance plantings will grow. Such plants as Hetz juniper or pine will require constant cutting back, ruining both your weekends and their shapes. For obvious reasons of comfort, keep thorny plants like barberry and hawthorn away from walks and entryways. Remember to space plants so they do not overhang these areas, since no one enjoys brushing up against dusty, wet, or icy foliage.

Although entrance plantings should soften the architectural boxiness of your house, take care that they don't entirely obscure its outlines. Plants should frame windows, not make them invisible. Think about the view from inside the house, as well. If a window is completely blocked, or if you peer out and see only bare, leggy stems, it's time to prune or transplant. Try to anticipate such problems and avoid this extra yard work.

A common mistake of new homeowners is to line up foundation plants strictly parallel to the walls of their houses. This creates the impression that the house is resting on a green pillow, with no connection to its setting. It is much better to enlarge the bed and include at least two rows of plants in graduated heights.

If you wish to screen your front yard from that of a neighbor, for privacy, place the tall screening plants as far as practical from the house. That way you'll have something to look at rather than through. Consider placing a bed of colorful shrubs like Carolina rhododendron, gold mop cypress, or hydrangea 'Hills of Snow' in front of such a screen as a bonus for the eyes.

Keep evergreen or deciduous shrubs at the entryway in scale with the house. A one-story house looks best adorned with horizontal or low-growing shrubs, while a two-story dwelling can accept larger, vertical accents, particularly at the corners. In snowy areas, position plants far enough out from the roof so they won't be damaged by sliding snow. Remember that deciduous shrubs suffer less from snow damage than evergreens do, and they recover growth more quickly. Arrange trees to give adequate shade to both house and parking areas. Choose deciduous types for more winter light and warmth, which hasten the melting of snow.

Starting from Scratch

A raw, undeveloped house lot presents quite a challenge to the beginning designer. Start by dressing up the foundation with shrubs and a few shade trees. Tackle one area at a time to avoid scattering your energies, and plants, all over the lot. Half the plants you purchase initially should be large enough to look attractive as soon as they're installed. These will "carry" your design while the other plants gather strength.

Improving Established Landscapes

At some point, trees and shrubs planted decades ago become
oversized or tired-looking. This is the time for a rejuvenation of
your landscape. Transplanting is often costly, and even if you can
afford it, your yard may be too crowded to accommodate equipment
large enough to handle the job. Ripping out and starting over takes
courage, but it can give your landscape a whole new lease on life.
Consider saving any attractive plants that could become anchors in
the new scheme, particularly if you can reshape them by pruning.
Then choose new plants that complement these survivors in colors,
textures, and growth habits.

Maintaining Your Design

Your new trees and shrubs will require thorough and consistent
watering during the first year after planting or transplanting. It is
also important to provide adequate water to both established and
new plantings just before they go dormant in winter, particularly if
the fall has been dry. Annual fertilizing, followed by a good
soaking to distribute the fertilizer and prevent root burn, is also
necessary to maintain health and disease resistance. Spray for insect
pests as soon as you see any signs of them.

Pruning is also necessary to establish tidy growth, to remove dead
or broken branches, and to rejuvenate overgrown trees or shrubs.
Your goal in pruning should be to produce a naturalistic effect, not
to create green blobs that sacrifice flower buds and handsome
silhouettes to rigid heights and widths. If you do not have time to
handle these chores personally, hire a reputable firm to manage the
pruning on a regular schedule. Make a yearly timetable for all your
maintenance tasks instead of waiting until major problems develop.
In the long run it will cost less and your grounds will look well-
tended in every season.

Designing a Shrub Border

A shrub border is an informal, harmonious grouping designed to be
attractive over a long season. It is relatively easy to add to a new or
existing landscape and can be designed on a large or small scale.
The border is a display area, attractive when viewed from the street
or seen from the house. You might choose some of the plants with
the idea of using branches indoors as well. The showiest flowering
borders are those that grow in full sun, but the challenge of relying
on other, more subtle, features in shady sites can be very
rewarding.

The following drawings of two simple shrub borders illustrate how
to plan for seasonal interest in two different sites. The first is
planned for a southern exposure in the northeastern part of the
country. The second is arranged for a semishaded plot in the
Southeast. Individual spacing between shrubs takes into account the
expected growth of moderate-sized plants. You should buy the

Using Trees & Shrubs

This shrub border is designed for a sunny site in the North. The plants provide a sequence of colorful flowers, fall foliage, and fruit from spring to winter.

Needle-leaf screen	• American arborvitae	1
	Thuja occidentalis 'Techny'	
Foliage shrubs	• Blue Princess holly	2
	Ilex × meserveae 'Blue Princess'	
	Blue Prince holly	3
	Ilex × meserveae 'Blue Prince'	
	• Crimson Pygmy barberry	4
	Berberis thunbergii 'Crimson Pygmy'	
Pink- to lavender-flowering shrubs	• Rose daphne	5
	Daphne cneorum	
	• PJM rhododendron	6
	Rhododendron 'PJM'	
	Miss Kim lilac	7
	Syringa patula 'Miss Kim'	
	• Blaauw's Pink azalea	8
	Rhododendron 'Blaauw's Pink'	
	Redvein enkianthus	9
	Enkianthus campanulatus	
	Palibin lilac	10
	Syringa meyeri 'Palibin'	
White-flowering shrubs	Slender deutzia	11
	Deutzia gracilis	
	• Polar Bear azalea	12
	Rhododendron 'Polar Bear'	
Crimson-flowering shrubs	Froebel spirea	13
	Spiraea × bumalda 'Froebelii'	
	Stewartsonian azalea	14
	Rhododendron 'Stewartsonian'	

341

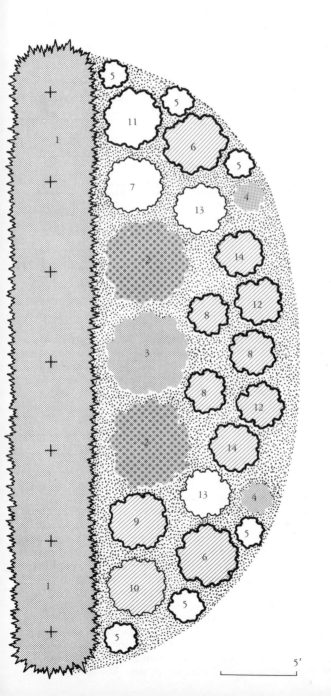

Bullets denote evergreen or semi-evergreen plants.

Outline Key
- Needle-leaf evergreens
- Spring-flowering
- Summer-flowering

Screen Key
- Foliage plants
- Colorful fall foliage
- Colorful fruit

5'

←N

background hedge plants in larger sizes so they will serve as effective backdrops right away.

A Sunny Border for the North

This 40-foot-long bed is 18 feet wide at the center and faces due south in an open space in zones 5 or 6. It is presumed the soil is well-drained, acid to slightly alkaline, and of normal fertility and good tilth. Compost, rotted manure, or peat moss incorporated into the entire bed would help ensure success. Add fertilizer only after a plant is established and growing well.

As a shield from northerly winter winds, and also as a unified backdrop, the plan shows a hedge of the tidy American arborvitae, which matures at about ten feet and carries needlelike, bluish green foliage. The foreground evergreen and deciduous plants are arranged for sequential blooming or for long-lasting winter fruit. The flowering parade begins in April with the evergreen PJM rhododendron, whose blossoms are bright lavender-pink. The three-inch foliage turns bronze in winter. Nearby, the emerging deep red foliage of the pygmy Japanese barberry will add its flush of color. May brings the scented bloom of the low-growing evergreen rose daphne, along with white accents from the evergreen azalea 'Polar Bear,' the bright blooms of the semi-evergreen azalea 'Blaauw's Pink,' and the subdued red of the spreading semi-evergreen azalea 'Stewartsonian.' Each of these azaleas also has colorful fall foliage. At the same time, the tall, pink-toned, deciduous enkianthus will develop pendulous clusters of blueberrylike flowers to coordinate with the deciduous white deutzia at the other end of the bed. Although the deutzia has no autumn coloring, the enkianthus will blaze forth in a combination of red, orange, and yellow.

Early June brings the fragrance of two medium-sized lilacs: 'Miss Kim' and 'Palibin'. Both are prized for their resistance to leaf mildew. 'Miss Kim' is much sweeter-scented than 'Palibin' and grows to about eight feet. Its leaves drop without fall color, but the wavy-edged leaves of 'Palibin' become bronzy in fall, and the plant reblooms sporadically by September.

From July into September, the deciduous Bumald spirea 'Froebelii' displays flattened heads of crimson flowers. New growth—with flowering—neatly covers up spent blossoming. By this point, the evergreen female blue hollies will carry green fruit that will mature to a glossy red by September. The male plant will remain glossy green, but both male and female types will develop purplish stems and a purplish green overcast to the leaves by winter.

A Semishaded Border for the South

This border is of the same size and shape as the sunny one, but it faces east and includes plants that profit from some shade to look their best. The border will get early morning sun but will be protected from damaging heat later in the day. The neat-growing hedge of the Oriental arborvitae 'Texanus Glaucus' provides the shade, along with some shade from nearby deciduous trees. Here, too, it is presumed the area drains water easily and that the soil has been well prepared.

The background hedge plants are pyramidal, with blue-green needle-leaf foliage. They can reach a height of 20 feet. As in the northern border, the foreground shrubs are arranged for sequential blooming or for long-lasting fruit. The majority of them are evergreen.

The flowering begins in March with clusters of bright yellow blossoms on the glossy evergreen Oregon grape holly. By midsummer this shrub will develop sizeable bunches of tiny gray-blue fruit, much like the true grapes it is named for. In late fall its green leaves will change to red-bronze for the winter.

The nodding white flower strands of the evergreen pieris appear by April and have a tantalizing scent, much like that of ripened grapes. The emerging foliage appears in rosettes and is bronze-toned. At about this time the everblooming abelia begins to show tiny lavender-pink, funnel-shaped blossoms in small clusters. Seed pods, which add to the appeal, are bright red and persist after the flowers drop. The small-leaved native rhododendron from the Carolinas also blooms in April and can vary in color from pale pink to lavender.

In May the cinnamon-colored, arching branches of the deciduous spirea 'Snowmound' will become covered with creamy white flowers and small blue-green leaves. The yellowish white blossoms of skimmia will also appear, as sweetly scented as those of lily-of-the-valley. By August the females will display large clusters of durable, bright red fruit.

June brings the showy, scented white flowers of the large-leaved, evergreen Japanese viburnum, followed later by small clusters of red fruits. Also in June, the intriguing heavenly bamboo will produce spikes of white flowers that evolve into glossy red fruits. New growth on this shrub is a striking bronze-red.

By early June, the semi-evergreen Iveryanum azalea will produce showy white flowers flecked with rose. By late fall, its leaves will turn crimson or red-purple. From July to October the evergreen St. Johnswort 'Hidcote' carries fragrant yellow blossoms with prominent stamens. The August-flowering gardenia rounds out the blossoming season with heavily perfumed white flowers.

Summing Up

Our lives are enriched through all the seasons by the bounty of trees and shrubs. They provide buffers from intense sunlight, create barriers to distracting noise and movement, mask unwanted views, modify intense winds, please the senses with their colors and scents, and bring beauty and value to any property. We could not do without them.

Using Trees & Shrubs

Needle-leaf screen	Oriental arborvitae	1
	Thuja orientalis 'Texanus Glaucus'	
Yellow-flowering shrubs	Oregon grape holly	2
	Mahonia aquifolium	
	Hidcote St. Johnswort	3
	Hypericum patulum 'Hidcote'	
Pink-flowering shrubs	Edward Goucher abelia	4
	Abelia 'Edward Goucher'	
	Carolina rhododendron	5
	Rhododendron carolinianum	
White-flowering shrubs	Heavenly bamboo	6
	Nandina domestica	
	Snowmound spirea	7
	Spiraea nipponica 'Snowmound'	
	Dwarf azalea	8
	Rhododendron indicum 'Iveryanum'	
	August Beauty gardenia	9
	Gardenia jasminoides 'August Beauty'	
	Japanese skimmia, female	10
	Skimmia japonica	
	Japanese viburnum	11
	Viburnum japonicum	
	Japanese skimmia, male	12
	Skimmia japonica	
	Taiwan andromeda	13
	Pieris taiwanensis	

*Fall interest comes from
fruits and colorful
foliage. Most of the
shrubs are evergreen or
semi-evergreen.*

Outline Key
- Needle-leaf evergreens
- Spring-blooming
- Summer-blooming

Screen Key
- Colorful fruit and fall foliage
- Colorful fruit
- Colorful fall foliage

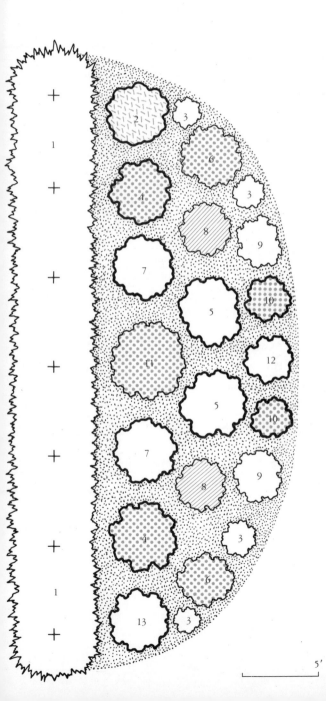

5'

↑
N

Using Trees
& Shrubs

Listings in the Source column are page references to individual Taylor's Guides. A key to title abbreviations appears on page 11.

	Source	Zones
Plant Choices		
Abies concolor White fir	T-290	4–7
Acer spp. Maple	T-293	3–9
Aucuba japonica Japanese aucuba	S-298	7–10
Betula nigra River birch	T-307	5–10
Camellia spp. Camellia	S-309	8–9
Cedrus atlantica 'Glauca' Blue atlas cedar	T-313	6–9
Fagus spp. Beech	T-334	3–9
Forsythia spp. Forsythia	S-339	5–8
Hamamelis spp. Witch hazel	S-346	4–8
Ilex opaca American holly	T-345	5–9
Juniperus horizontalis Creeping juniper	G-334	3–9
Leucothoe fontanesiana Drooping leucothoe	S-363	4–6
Magnolia grandiflora Southern magnolia	T-355	7–9
Picea abies Norway spruce	T-372	3–7
Prunus serrulata 'Kwanzan' Oriental cherry	T-383	5–8
Pyracantha spp. Fire thorn	S-388	5–9
Rhododendron spp. Rhododendron/azalea	S-391	4–8
Spiraea spp. Spirea	S-405	4–8
Symphoricarpos × *chenaultii* Chenault coralberry	S-409	4–7
Syringa spp. Lilac	S-410	3–8
Taxodium distichum Bald cypress	T-398	5–10
Viburnum sieboldii Siebold viburnum	S-419	4–7

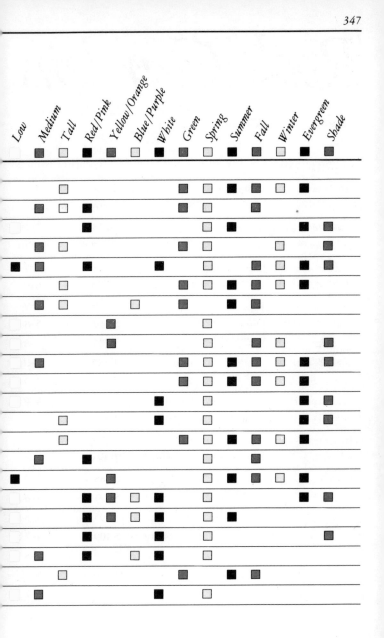

Rock Gardens

Panayoti and Gwen Kelaidis

The inspirations for rock gardens come from such beautiful wild settings as woodland glades, flowering meadows, and alpine slopes. In these wild areas, compact plants carpet the ground, often growing around, or tucked among, rocks of all sizes and types. Such harmonious natural designs are easy to re-create in your own garden. You can plant a steep, gravelly bank with tiny high-mountain, or alpine, perennials; build a stone wall and tuck plants into its intricate crevices; or cover a gentle slope with mat-forming ground covers and low perennials. You might even create a small rock garden in a container to grace a patio or entryway.

Because rock-garden plants are usually small, it is possible to grow literally hundreds of different kinds on a small lot. For much of the spring and early summer, your garden can be ablaze with mats and cushions of jewel-like blooms. Summer-, fall-, and even winter-blooming flowers can extend the season of interest through the calendar. Variations in ground level and in the heights of the rocks themselves add vertical interest. In addition, the surfaces of the rocks set off the form and texture of the plants. Imagine the delicate tracery of ferns against dark, elemental granite; or the silvery foliage of artemisia against red sandstone.

Selecting a Site

Most people who live in urban or suburban settings have small gardens and rectangular yard plans. In order to incorporate a rock garden into such a site, first determine which part of the yard is best suited to the naturalistic style of the garden. Some people feel it should be removed from the immediate area of the house, so as to seem closer to nature. Others point out that a garden containing small plants and relatively minute details of design should be placed close at hand, to be viewed from a window or patio, for example. A bonus is that wherever you place your rock garden, with its many evergreen plants, it will have visual interest even in the winter.

Look carefully at how the ground slopes in various areas. It is easy to build a rock garden where natural changes in grade already exist. Steep banks sloping down into your yard or the problem slope from lawn to sidewalk—hard to mow and to water—are perfect sites for rock gardens. If you have a natural rock outcrop, you may be able to remove weeds, do a bit of soil preparation, and plant into the existing structure. If there are no natural grade changes and the yard is very small, consider using rock work and ground covers to replace a lawn, filling the small space much as an Oriental carpet can fill a room.

In larger flat areas, use rocks to build raised beds or berms. A berm, a mound or small hill of earth, can create a sense of boundary along the edge of a lot or give a feeling of enclosure as it curves around a corner. Raised beds bring small plants closer to the eye of the observer and provide a sense of intimacy to the garden.

The crevices between the rock walls of a raised bed, which are filled with soil instead of mortar, serve as perfect places in which to tuck small plants.

Assessing Your Microclimate

Once you have selected a site, determine what microclimate prevails there. What is the nature of the soil? How much sun will the site receive in midsummer and at other times of year? How much moisture will fall there? When you begin to choose plants, you will want to be aware of these conditions so you can avoid trying any that will not tolerate the soils, moisture, and aspect you provide.

Preparing the Soil

All rock garden plants require soils with plenty of air space and good drainage. If you live in a moist climate, such as in the coastal regions of the United States, you'll need to incorporate a healthy proportion of sand or gravel, or both. A mixture of one part sand, one part gravel, and one part humusy loam is a good formula. In drier climates, use soils with a good deal more clay, but be careful to avoid overwatering, which will drown the plants by depriving their roots of air. In very wet climates, use almost pure grit and gravel or sand. This will allow you to choose plants that would normally grow only in drier climates or in the rock crevices of high mountains. If you are mixing a soil, be sure to mix it thoroughly, either with a shovel by the wheelbarrow load or—for big jobs— with a cement mixer.

After you've planted your garden, apply a small gravel mulch around the plants. This helps to keep the crowns of the plants dry, cool the soil, retain moisture, prevent washout, and keep weeds down. It also gives a neat, uniform appearance to the garden surface.

Choosing the Rocks

Selecting rocks that look natural together will give you a harmonious effect. Some gardeners succeed in combining rocks of similar colors, such as limestone and granite, but it is usually safer to stick to one type of rock. The repetition of its color and texture throughout the garden helps unify your design.

Some of the most popular rocks for gardens are sandstone, which can vary from white to tan or red; limestone, granite, and gneiss, which are shades of gray or even pink; and porous rocks such as lava and tufa. For the most natural look, choose a type of rock that is native to your area. A bonus to using native rock is that it will probably be easy to obtain.

There are several ways to go about getting rocks. In the best of scenarios, someone with especially rocky property may be looking to sell or give away a truckload. Somewhat battle-scarred rock is often free for the taking at construction or highway sites. In some regions, quarries are especially good, inexpensive sources of large rocks. Consider hiring someone to pick up and place the rocks for you. Most larger metropolitan areas have rock yards—places that sell rocks for landscape use at reasonable prices. Be sure to ask what hauling and placement will cost.

Placing Rocks for Beauty and Safety

Natural appearance is the goal in rock gardening, so you should look to nature for clues on how to place rocks. Take pictures or make sketches so you can imitate natural effects in your own design. Notice that part of each rock is usually underground, that rocks occur in groups, often touching each other, and that limestones and sandstones tend to occur in layers and lines. Sketch out ideas for situating the rocks in your particular site. Or, using small rocks of the type you plan for the garden, build a scale model in a box of sand. The time you spend constructing a model will save much backbreaking rearrangement later.

Once you've decided where the rocks should go, be sure you move them carefully and set them firmly. With a little ingenuity and the help of someone with a mechanical sense, you can move surprisingly heavy rocks. Very large ones should be placed by a professional. On a steep slope, bury a portion of the rock rather than laying it on top of the ground. It is a good idea to tilt the rock slightly back into the slope. Water will then run back into the ground, benefiting the plants, rather than cascading off the front of the rock and washing out the soil.

When you think a rock is stable, test it by stepping on it. If you can wiggle it by standing on any edge, try again. Changing the position slightly or adding more soil under one side or another will probably cure the problem. Frost is likely to heave slightly shaky rocks, so check for stability each spring.

Building a Raised Bed

Raised beds are useful for ensuring quick drainage and for adding height to your garden. You should consider this option especially in low-lying areas or if your soil is clay.

First decide on the outline of the bed and dig a trench about ten inches deep in the correct shape and size—round, rectangular, or free-form. Set large, flat stones in the trench at a slight angle, using soil as you would mortar to fill the spaces between rocks. Put garden soil inside the wall up to ten inches from its rim and fill in with the same mixture of sand, gravel, and loam you would use on ground level. Plant in this layer, and add a gravel mulch for drainage and a tidy appearance.

Remember to tuck some small plants into the crevices in the wall for a more natural look. Try a raised bed near a patio or walkway, where it will be sure to get attention from visitors.

To create a rock garden
on a slope, partially
bury rocks at an angle.
Water will run back
into the soil and benefit
the plants.

Rock Gardens

To build a raised bed, dig a trench about 10 inches deep. Set flat rocks in at an angle, using soil as you would mortar to build a wall 2 to 3 feet high. Fill the bed with garden soil up to 10 inches from the rim. Then add a mix of sand, gravel, and loam. Plant the bed and add a layer of gravel mulch. Tuck a few plants in crevices in the wall.

Choosing the Plants

Now you are ready to embark on the delightful task of plant selection. As you design your rock garden, keep in mind height; flower color and season of bloom; foliage color, shape, and texture; and aggressiveness of spread.

Height

Most of the height in rock gardens comes from varying the levels of soil and stones. In traditional alpine gardens, most plants are less than a foot high. In larger gardens, it helps to include a few taller plants to give vertical interest. Even in small gardens, an occasional spike of cardinal-flower, larkspur, or foxtail lily provides a dramatic counterpoint to mounds and mats. Many spike-bloomers flower late, extending the season of the garden and therefore doubling their worth. Among the best of these are the many species of true lilies, which include smaller sorts that fill the later half of the growing season with spectacular blooms. At the lower levels, very flat mats like the thymes may be combined with slightly taller mounds, such as clove pinks, or with plants that have basal rosettes of leaves but throw up taller bloom stems, such as coral bells and penstemons.

Flower Color

Coordination of flower color is not as complicated in rock gardens as in perennial and annual gardens. Rock garden plants are of such delicate textures and tints that they rarely clash as do the heavier cultivars used in traditional flower beds. And rock gardens tend to change color with the seasons. Many of the late-spring flowers—the phloxes, primulas, and pinks—are in the pink-white-lavender color range, so these tend to be the dominant colors in this season of heady bloom. Early summer often takes on blue and lavender tones from the predominant campanulas, gentians, and mint family plants. Later in the summer, many of the flowers available, such as helichrysums and sunflower relatives, are warm tones of yellow and orange.

Consider arranging flowering plants in groups for masses of color. Use a great many of an individual plant, such as a chosen form of creeping phlox in spring, a large group of campanulas in summer, or a bank of dwarf asters in early fall. Or use many species of the same genus—a show of yellow drabas in early spring, some bright red tulips later on, or clumps of tall blue delphiniums in midsummer.

Instead of pooling masses of colors, you might sprinkle them throughout a garden, creating a tapestry effect much as we see in an alpine meadow or a prairie. This can unify a diversified planting, satisfying designer and plant collector at the same time. Use plants that do not spread laterally too much—such as the annual poppies, the smaller geraniums, and all manner of bulbs.

Accent Colors

Colorful plants can also be used as accent touches. The California fuchsia creates a brilliant focal point of red in late summer, while specimen plants of butterfly weed can serve the same purpose a bit earlier. Establish other bright spots with euphorbias, dwarf rhododendrons, gentians, or winter-blooming violas.

With some experimentation and experience, you can eliminate plants that do not appeal to your color sense and learn to combine those that do. The garden should please the gardener, and this is never more important than in choosing color schemes.

Bloom Season

In the high mountains, most alpines bloom in a sudden rush with the melting of the winter snows. It's hardly surprising, then, that many traditional alpine gardens are glorious in the spring but quickly bloom themselves out in the warmer months. There are a few bona fide alpines that bloom later in the growing season, but you must be resourceful to discover them. It is a good idea to include one summer- or fall-blooming plant for every two spring-bloomers you plant in your garden. Some especially intricate and rich in color are aster, astilbe, campanula, coreopsis, gentian, lavender, ipomopsis, and helichrysum.

Using Annuals

Although most rock gardens are planted primarily with perennials, annuals are useful to grow in the bare ground where early bulbs have become dormant. Avoid those with large and double flowers that seem out of harmony with the delicate perennials and the austere texture of the rock. The principle that should guide your use of annuals is constraint: Choose those with delicate form and an air of wildness about them. Some, like *Anagallis linifolia,* are as graceful as any rock garden perennial, and easy to grow, too. Others, such as *Linaria alpina,* self-sow a bit too easily and can become pests.

Some annuals must be planted each year but pay dividends by giving a continuous spot of color throughout the summer. Suggestions might be browallia, emilia, diascia, Dahlberg daisy, monkey flower, nemophila, nierembergia, or the single signet marigolds. Others will self-sow and require no replanting—just thinning from time to time or removal of the plants after they are finished blooming. The variation in numbers coming up from year to year adds a whimsical temporal dimension to the garden. Plants in this self-sowing group include many biennials, too. A few might be the faithful California poppy, other poppies in many colors and sizes, wallflowers, larkspurs, and gilias.

Foliage

Even the longest-blooming flowers last only a fraction of the garden

Plants that spread fast can overtake a rock garden in a surprisingly short time. Ten types to avoid are Aegopodium podagraria, Campanula rapunculoides, Cerastium tomentosum, Glecoma hederacea, Lamium amplexicaule, Lysimachia nummularia, Oxalis corniculata, Polygonum reynoutria, Sedum acre, and most Viola species.

year. The most exquisite flowers often have unsightly foliage for the remaining eight to ten months. Fortunately, most rock plants have attractive leaves and habits. In some, the foliage may be even prettier than the flowers. It is important to group plants in such a way that the various mounds and mats complement one another in shape, texture, and color. For example, the scalloped and mottled leaves of a coral bell might look attractive next to the pale, waxy blues of pinks or the lacy foliage of a bleeding heart. The fuzzy cushions of an edelweiss would look good next to the glossy dark green leaves of moss campion or spring gentian. The fine, airy texture of a sandwort softens the heavier architectural leaves of dwarf iris or sea-lavender.

There are many rock plants with evergreen foliage, and these should be used liberally, since in the snowiest and coldest parts of the country there will be months when the garden will lie bare and these plants can be appreciated. The end of the bloom season and the coming of frost do not signal the end of the rock garden year, but rather a quieter season when one can better appreciate plant form and combination.

Some of the most useful foliage plants for evergreen effect are the hardy succulents such as sempervivums, sedums, and in southern regions, dudleyas and ice plants. Saxifrages are valued farther north for their symmetrical rosettes and intricate patterning. Other plants—like creeping phloxes, pinks, and yarrows—have decorative mats that last through all the seasons.

Spreading Plants

One remaining criterion to consider in selecting plants is how fast they are apt to spread. Nothing discourages a gardener more than some innocuous seedling spreading to fill every nook and cranny of rock work with pervasive runners or seeds. Every region has its special *Index Expurgatorium* of weeds that raise the blood pressure of serious gardeners. Once any of these are established in rock work, they can be very difficult to remove without undoing most of the labor you put into the garden in the first place. Observe all new plants carefully for several years and do not hesitate to remove any plant that spreads beyond its bounds. There are many fine plants with which to replace it.

There are times and places to use highly aggressive plants, such as in areas where nothing else will grow because of harsh exposure, heavy use, or lack of irrigation. It is a good idea to combine plants with similar temperaments, though: Put the aggressive ones together and separate them completely from those of more restrained growth.

Planning Your Design

To come up with an approximation of your design, try the following "paper" method. Keeping in mind the microclimate of your site, copy from catalogues or books the names and general descriptions of appropriate plants that pique your interest. Read up to see that they are suited to your region; or better yet, visit as many gardens in your area as you can. Rare indeed is the gardener who will not welcome an interested stranger, and you might find yourself richer by many a plant—and friend. Be sure to take careful notes of which plants look the best—not just in bloom, but in foliage as well.

The Right Plants
Keep adding to your list of plants until you have many more than you will need. Be sure the plants you pick require the microclimate you have in your garden and are complementary in their rates of growth. It is reasonable to assume that a newly built, small rock garden will require at least one plant for every square foot of planting space. In larger gardens (more than 200 square feet), use several of each kind of plant to avoid a spotty look.

Create a drawing as accurately to scale as you can manage without wasting too much time. (Remember, the garden itself is what matters.) Sketch in the approximate location of the larger rocks and any other immovable objects in the garden. The first thing you must place in both your drawing and the garden are architectural plants: dwarf conifers, shrubs, and focal-point plants that will become the backbone of your garden and serve as the backdrop for the showier carpet plants and mounds. A tiny potted plant may become a monster, so read up on the ultimate height of your "slow-growing" plants. The ultimate height comes more quickly than beginning gardeners ever dream possible.

Now select from your list one-third of the total number of plants you will need in the final garden, choosing only those that bloom after the middle of June. Using construction paper of the approximate color of each, cut out a piece in about the size and shape of the planting you want to make and write on it the name of the plant. It will probably also be useful to write in the bloom season and the ultimate dimensions you expect your plants to reach—both height and width.

Pick from your list an equal number of plants that have outstanding foliage effects year-round. Cut these out of the appropriate color paper, label, and set aside. Then select from among the plants remaining on your original list those you think best complement the ones already chosen, including of course those plants you do not want to be without. These make up your third set of cutouts.

Arranging the Plants
Begin to arrange your garden with these slips of paper, placing plants with complementary flower colors in proximity—if they are to bloom in the same season, that is—and separating those that

would look unattractive in juxtaposition. Shorter, spreading plants can be placed next to paths; taller mounds may be put toward the back of the garden to form a backdrop. Once you have put all the pieces of your puzzle in an arrangement that pleases you, paste them in place, and you have an attractive, sensible landscape design for your rock garden.

Save this original design for historical interest but keep sketching new ones and observing how the plants you have installed like their homes. Rock plants have a way of rearranging the planting scheme, selecting the places they like best to grow. Do not hesitate to move them or to break up unsatisfactory combinations. The real work of garden design does not take place with pen and paper, but in the garden, with trowel and shovel.

Special Effects

The drama of rock work offers some special opportunities to the garden designer. You can drape plants over rocks with lovely shawl-like effects. Genistas, prostrate willows, the creeping plum, and some cotoneasters may lend themselves to this treatment, as will, on a smaller scale, campanulas, thymes, or the glamorous larger androsaces. Use a rock as a backdrop to emphasize the stately upright form of plants such as astilbes or verbascums. Or place a low rock ledge so that it provides a frame for the delightful rosettes of silver sage or lady's-mantle. Fill in rock crevices with rosettes of sempervivums or saxifrages or the tiny leaves of a campanula. "Lawns" can be created within the rock garden with plants that are resistant to wear, like the thymes, cotulas, and antennarias. If you want to use flat green spaces strictly for visual effect, you may choose any species that maintain a beautiful, year-round appearance, without considering the effects of trampling. Such plants include many of the prostrate veronicas, ajugas, sweet woodruff, small sedums, and tiny shrubs like pine-mat manzanita and kinnikinnick.

Tucking Plants

A simple planting technique called the tuck can do wonders to naturalize the appearance of the garden. Notice that in nature plants on rocky slopes tend to grow right next to the rocks rather than in the middle of the open space. Presumably it is easier for seedlings to get started there, out of the wind and weather and out of the way of small rock and mud slides. At first it seems counterintuitive to those of us who are used to planting in the middle of open spaces. Nevertheless, you will find that rock plants not only look better but grow better when tucked in.

Dry Streambeds

A dry streambed is an imitation stream that you can create in an area of drainage through the garden, such as where a downspout empties. Arrange rounded rocks of various sizes in a way that rapidly moving water might leave them. Or line a low contour of the garden with a mat-forming plant that hugs the ground and "flows" down the slope in imitation of water. This is an easy and unique way to give a sense of motion and flow to your rock garden.

Water Features

Few facets of a rock garden generate more interest, expense, and trouble than water features. Nothing can be more delightful than a tumbling natural stream bordered by graceful wildflowers—until torrential rains transform it into a roaring river that washes half the garden into the nearest ocean. Even a simple pond can be a breeding ground for algae and mosquitos and a veritable watering hole for the neighborhood raccoons. It may leak and will need to be cleaned periodically.

Despite these drawbacks, an artistically built water feature can provide a refreshing focal point for a garden. Bog plants will revel in the leaks, goldfish can eat the mosquito larvae, and water lilies will fill the summer nights with wonder. If you are contemplating such a feature, visit at least five gardens that contain them and find out how the best ones came about. Refer to the Water Gardens chapter of this book for more details.

Sample Gardens

Here are ideas for how rock gardens could be incorporated into two different but fairly common types of sites. Most of the plants suggested will grow well in a wide range of climates.

A Sunny Garden

Perhaps you have a sunny bank facing south along the back patio of your house. This is a perfect site for a rock garden. You will simply need to amend the soil with gravel and sand, and topdress it with a mulch of stone chips after planting. Since this garden is next to a patio where the family spends considerable time, it should have year-round interest, color, and appealing textures.

Choose plants that will complement and contrast with one another in bloom and in leaf: Try a silvery blue fountain of blue fescue (*Festuca ovina* var. *glauca*) rising from a dark green mat of finger poppy mallow (*Callirhoe involucrata*). Include some metallic mounds of rue combined with dark green mats of rock rose (*Helianthemum numullarium*). For texture contrast as well as color, choose the airy panicles of emilia against a dark mound of dwarf pines.

For a long flowering season, include crocuses and species tulips that will brave the late frosts. Continue the colorful procession in mid-spring with yellows, such as basket-of-gold (*Aurinia saxitilis*), genista, or rock roses. For summer, plant the purples and mauves of verbena, germanders, lavender, or catnips. Late-blooming plants to include are blazing star and lavender cotton, gaillardias and butterfly weed, or asters and emilias. Most of the perennials in this garden have persistent or evergreen foliage that continues interest throughout the winter months.

A Partly Shaded Garden

If you have a flat, conventional city lot, you can still have an alpine garden. Consider building a berm around the base of a tree. This will create a shady corner for plants that don't like full sun. If the soil is porous and well drained, top-dress it with a neat layer of crushed rock.

Combine plants for foliage effect as well as for bloom. Try *Geranium dalmaticum*'s neatly rounded leaves alongside the spiny mats of drabas and narrow leaves of campions. *Androsace sarmentosa*'s silvery balls would look intriguing alongside the starfish rosettes of edelweiss and dark green cushions of common thrift. Consider daphnes, dwarf balsam fir, or Japanese holly to create neat domes of evergreen branches and provide architecture to the garden in all seasons. To achieve a long progression of bloom, plant colorful masses of phlox, aubrieta, and arabis for early to mid-spring, followed by a long season of such novelties as *Anagallis* (with cobalt-blue flowers), geraniums, and dianthus. Even autumn can be colored with the tall, willowy spikes of *Gentiana asclepiadea* and airy coral bells.

Enjoying Your Rock Garden

Whether you build a rock garden on a small city lot or in a sprawling open area, you'll be constantly pleased by its changing colors and intricate textures. A careful design can transform your yard into a microcosm of the world's high places. After you've taken time to learn about the needs of the plants you've chosen, you can sit back and enjoy while others are busy weeding and pruning their conventional gardens. Don't be surprised if a few of them stop by to ask how you created such a beautiful, low-maintenance landscape.

Rock Gardens   *Listings in the Source column are page references to individual Taylor's Guides. A key to title abbreviations appears on page 11.*   *Under Zones, W and C indicate warm- or cool-season annuals.*

	Source	Zones
Plant Choices		
Androsace spp. Rock jasmine	A-283	C
Arctostaphylos uva-ursi Kinnikinnick	S-297	2–6
Aster spp. Aster	D-358	2–7
Astilbe spp. Astilbe	P-296	5–7
Browallia spp. Browallia	A-295	W
Campanula spp. Bellflower	P-303	3–8
Cheiranthus cheiri Wallflower	A-305	C
Cotoneaster spp. Cotoneaster	G-312	5–8
Delphinium elatum Candle larkspur	P-318	4–6
Diascia barberae Twinspur	A-321	C
Dicentra spp. Bleeding heart	P-320	3–8
Draba densiflora Rock cress	P-325	3–6
Dyssodia tenuiloba Dahlberg daisy	A-324	C, W
Emilia javanica Tassel flower	A-327	C
Euphorbia epithymoides Cushion spurge	P-332	5–8
Galium odoratum Sweet woodruff	G-321	5–8
Genista pilosa Broom	G-323	6–8
Gentiana spp. Gentian	P-338	5–7
Geranium sanguineum Blood-red cranesbill	P-340	4–7
Heuchera sanguinea Coral bells	P-349	4–8
Ipomopsis rubra Standing cypress	A-349	C
Lavandula angustifolia Lavender	P-359	5–9
Leontopodium alpinum Edelweiss	P-360	3–6
Lobelia cardinalis Cardinal-flower	P-364	3–8
Mimulus guttatus Monkey flower	A-369	C
Phlox stolonifera Creeping phlox	P-382	4–8
Salvia argentea Silver sage	P-396	5–8
Saxifraga spp. Saxifrage	P-399	6–8
Scabiosa caucasica Pincushion flower	P-400	4–7
Sedum spp. Stonecrop	P-400	4–8
Veronica prostrata Rock speedwell	G-372	4–7

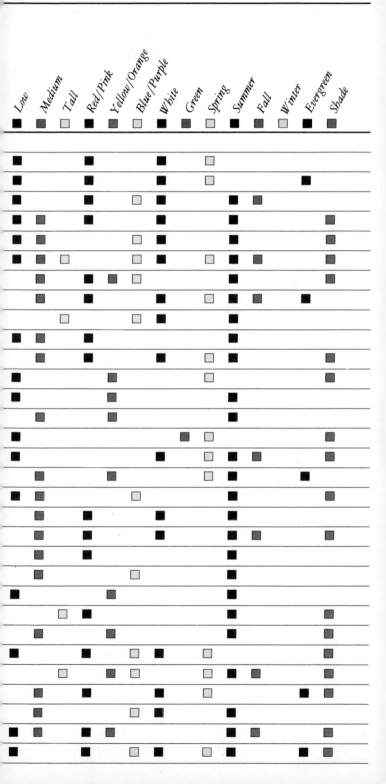

Traditional

William D. Rieley

Interest in traditional gardens has grown greatly in recent years. Many people have realized that these gardens are based on principles that have evolved over hundreds of years and are relevant and inspiring today. Also, the increased appeal of preserving and restoring older houses has led to a desire to create appropriate period landscapes.

Two Design Families

Our heritage in garden design can be divided into two general families, commonly referred to as "formal" and "informal." These terms are misleading, however, since both approaches depend on form and structure for their success—both are organized and composed. They are simply arranged differently. It is more accurate to use the terms "geometric" instead of "formal" and "naturalistic" instead of "informal."

Geometric gardens are structured along clearly patterned lines. They delight and refresh through their order and regularity. Variety in color, light and shade, and shape are all carefully controlled to support and enrich the overall plan. While their patterns varied, gardens throughout most of civilization—Ancient Egyptian, Roman, Moorish, Persian, Indian, and European—were all organized according to geometric principles.

Naturalistic gardens are not symmetrical like geometric gardens, but they must be balanced. There is a succession of carefully composed views along a prescribed path, giving the observer a sequence of scenes. Mystery and anticipation play a greater role than in the geometric garden, and the naturalistic garden often takes up a larger area.

Most traditional American gardens reflect both geometric and naturalistic elements. Many of the great garden designers of the last century were masters of both schools of design and knew how to combine and apply the principles of each as the situation required.

Historical Influences

Garden styles throughout history have expressed the philosophies of their creators. In much of early America, landscape treatments reflected those of England, except in the Southwest where the Spanish influence was felt. Most early American designs reproduced the small, simple geometric gardens of the English Tudor and Elizabethan periods. They were useful as well as ornamental, and their clear, simple patterns symbolized the settlers' belief in the dominion of men in the natural world.

By the time of the American Revolution, geometric styles had decreased in popularity, and there was great interest in the naturalistic English landscape style. The inspiration for these gardens came from poets and landscape painters of the 18th century who espoused a mystical view of the aesthetic and moral power of

Gardens

nature—a very different perception of man's place in the natural world than those of the early American colonists.

It was not until the turn of the century, the Gilded Age, that geometric gardens came back into vogue. Architects began looking back at classical forms, and garden designers turned to ancient traditions, particularly as reflected in the wonderful Italian Renaissance gardens, for inspiration. They once again related the site to the building by extending architectural organization into the landscape.

Gardens of the early 20th century were often influenced by preceding traditions, but there was innovation due to a variety of newly available plants. In particular, the perennial flower border was raised to new aesthetic heights by the English garden designer, Gertrude Jekyll. Her compositions were masterpieces of color, texture, and shape. In collaboration with the great architect Edwin Lutyens, Jekyll created some of the most inspired and beautiful gardens in western civilization. They have the order and structure of geometric gardens, the sweeping irregular lines of naturalistic gardens, and the exuberance and vitality of original works of genius. Jekyll's work was widely appreciated and emulated in this country and continues to have wide appeal and charm today.

Design Principles

There are fundamental design considerations that gardens of all periods and styles share. These explain the way plants and objects arranged in space create different aesthetic effects.

Enclosure and Vistas

One of the first steps in planning a garden is to define its boundaries. A geometric garden is distinctly separate from surrounding areas. Buildings, walls, hedges, and fences are used alone or in combination to partially or completely enclose the space. A completely enclosed garden leaves the designer free to concentrate efforts on the interior area. If the garden is partially enclosed, views beyond it must be carefully incorporated. In naturalistic gardens the boundaries of enclosure are generally more subtle and irregular than in geometric ones. Outside views are important, and they should be carefully framed and composed.

A concept related to enclosure is that of the vista, or focused view. Whether a garden is completely enclosed or open to the surrounding landscape, it should be designed to draw attention to important objects or scenes. In geometric gardens, the vista often ends in a structural focal point: A row, or *allée,* of trees may lead to a central pavilion, for example. In naturalistic gardens, vistas frame particularly beautiful landscape arrangements. In both cases, the vista magnifies the importance of a scene by defining its boundary and excluding extraneous views. In any garden, a focal point must be sufficiently important to justify the use of a vista.

Balance and Repetition

The perception of balance in a composition comes from sensing an equality of form on either side of a focal point. In geometric gardens, balance is often symmetrical—a virtual mirror image—but such strict symmetry is not required. Asymmetrical balance, often associated with a more naturalistic look, is accomplished by placing dissimilar elements so that the sum of their effect on the viewer is generally equal.

Repetition is fundamental to garden design, unifying and bringing harmony to a composition. It may be expressed through shapes, as in the reappearance of columns or trees, or with color, as in a perennial garden of only blue flowers. Of course, too much repetition leads to monotony; it must be balanced with variety. For example, geometric gardens are unified by their overall regularity and repetition of forms, but they contain a great variety of colors and textures. A naturalistic garden may have a complex plan and varied forms held together because of a repeated use of green.

Scale and Perspective

The size of one object in relation to another is its scale. Decorative elements in a landscape are generally of a greater scale than furnishings in a house because they are measured against much larger surroundings. The perception of scale is distorted by perspective. Objects far removed from the eye look smaller than those in the foreground. Designers can exploit this principle, making plants or structures appear more distant by reducing their scale, or closer by increasing it. Generally, however, giving the viewer a true sense of scale is more satisfactory than creating illusions. Using such objects as benches, steps, and gazebos allows viewers to judge scale correctly.

Color and Texture

One of the most enjoyable and challenging aspects of garden design is using color effectively. Unlike the colors in a painting, those in a garden change continually with the seasons. This means the blooming season, flower color, fall leaf color, and winter habit of all the plants in a plan must be considered. It is best to limit the colors showing at any one time to those that are effective in combination. Areas of profuse and varied color should be confined to separate, clearly delineated beds within the garden.

In plants, texture is chiefly a function of leaf size. Like color, it should be used wisely to accent or give definition to different areas within a plan. For example, let the smooth, even texture of a lawn give way to the coarser texture of a ground cover. Some of the most striking changes in texture are not between different plants, but between plants and structures. A perennial border next to a stone wall, for example, is attractive because of the juxtaposition of very different textures.

Constructed Features in the Garden

Traditional gardens rely on constructed features as well as plants to create harmonious effects. The largest and most important features are the ground plane itself—which can be manipulated through grading—and the house, which may be linked to the landscape by an appropriately designed porch or patio. In successful designs, views from major windows and doors and access between indoor and outdoor space are carefully considered.

Pavilions, Gazebos, and Pergolas

A pavilion is a garden structure, usually enclosed, that provides a resting and observation point in a carefully chosen site and is also a beautiful object in itself. Pavilions were quite popular during the late 18th and early 19th centuries.

The gazebo, or summer house, is a roofed but otherwise open garden building, often of a polygonal floor plan. It is used in much the same way as a pavilion, but because it is not enclosed, it has a shorter useful season in cold climates.

A pergola, sometimes called an arbor or bower, is an open overhead structure held up by posts or columns that usually supports climbing plants. It is a very useful design feature in the garden because it frames views architecturally and provides a pleasant sitting area, or simply a lovely accent.

Walls, Fences, and Gates

The principle of enclosure can be satisfied by plants, but walls and fences are more permanent and unchanging than hedges or trees. Walls can enclose and define perimeters, extend the architectural character of the house into the garden, or make transitions between grade changes. In traditional gardens they are commonly constructed of brick, stone, wood, or concrete. Fences and gates in a wide range of types and styles can be used functionally or as ornaments. Picket fences are the most common. They were originally used to keep animals out of private yards, but because they are near the house, they had to be more refined than other utilitarian fences.

Gates are important transition points in the garden, and they should be ornamental as well as functional. The design of a gate should harmonize with that of the fence and other structures.

Paths and Walks

A regular pattern of paths and walks reinforces the configuration of a geometric garden, while a winding pattern creates a more naturalistic effect. Paths can be made of such varied materials as turf, sand, quarry dust, crushed shells, gravel, brick, concrete, or stone. The materials, like those for other structural elements, should be carefully selected to harmonize with the design and serve a specific purpose.

Traditional Gardens

Water

The unique effect of water in the garden delights the senses of sound and sight. Many traditional gardens include pools, fountains, or waterfalls. The shape and scale of a pool is determined by the composition of the garden, but it should almost always be a major focal feature. The water should be kept at or slightly below ground level, except in very small basins such as wall fountains.

Other Structures

Benches and other types of seats may provide comfortable, attractive resting places. They should be located to give the best views of the garden and surrounding landscape. The effects of sun, shade, and wind will also influence the placement of seats. There are many styles appropriate to traditional gardens, from rustic to ornate, in materials such as wood, metal, masonry, or cast stone.

Sculpture makes an effective focal point in a formal garden. Small pieces can serve as accents beside pathways or steps. Any sculpture should match the garden's style, enhancing but not overwhelming it.

Planting Design

There are three uses of plants in the garden—for structure, ornament, and utility. Structure is the most important to the designer because without it, a garden becomes merely a collection of plants. As wall, floor, and ceiling define the space in a house, plants can create the confines of outdoor garden "rooms."

After placing plants for structure, a designer can make careful, limited selections of plants for ornament. These should serve to support and enrich an entire composition. If some plants are to be grown for utility—vegetables, herbs, and fruit, for example—they can be incorporated attractively. In early American gardens, fruits, vegetables, and herbs were grown in the same beds as ornamentals. Of course, the most effective gardens are those that use plants for structure, ornament, and function compatibly.

Two Garden Plans

The plans on pages 370 through 373 are examples of how the principles and elements of garden design can be orchestrated in two different ways. The first, based on a design for "The Deanery" by Gertrude Jekyll and Edwin Lutyens, is a simple plan organized around the extension of the center line of a window in the house into the garden. This line is emphasized by a pool of water that runs the length of the garden, from a wall fountain below a broad terrace, past a sculpture, to a low pool with a central single jet. A gate and bench are centered on the statue at the central cross-axis of the garden. The plants used are chosen for their cool colors, contrasting textures, and long period of bloom in the summer, when this garden is most colorful.

The second plan, adapted from Alden Hopkins's design for the Pavilion VII garden at the University of Virginia, contains elements of both the geometric and naturalistic families of landscape design. The central panel of turf is symmetrical, and the winding outside paths connect the corners of the garden, which are designed to be quiet, secluded areas. Large trees shade the paths and define the open space, and a high evergreen hedge on the perimeter encloses the garden. A variety of native flowering plants embellishes the walks.

Creating a Period Garden

With the right information at hand, it is possible to create a traditional garden to match or complement the style of a house. The physical characteristics of the site and the uses the garden will serve should be considered, as is true in creating any garden. But of particular importance in designing a traditional garden is historic research.

First, the specific history of the site itself should be investigated through old photographs, paintings, or descriptions from family papers. The locations of previous roads, drives, and outbuildings can often be obtained from such sources as old insurance maps, and a simple metal probe can help in searching for old walks or foundations. This site-specific research can be great fun and may turn up important information to influence the garden plan.

The second type of historical research is to determine which traditions are most appropriate and useful. Most often, design plans should be based on traditions reflected in the house. For example, it is usually most effective to design a garden for a Victorian house within the design vocabulary of the period.

Among the wealth of period styles from which to choose, three that are especially adaptable to many American homes are the colonial, Victorian, and classical revival.

Colonial Gardens

Gardens in colonial America were designed to provide food—and even medicine—as well as ornament. A large, flat area of the yard was typically enclosed with a fence, wall, or hedge. Within this outline, paths were laid out geometrically, breaking the space into square or rectangular planting beds. Low plants—often boxwood in the South—were used to outline the beds, and a wide variety of annual and perennial flowers, herbs, and vegetables were grown within this frame. When both ornamental and food plants were included, flowers and herbs were placed toward the outside of the beds, with vegetables—such as artichokes, beets, carrots, celery, cress, garlic, lettuce, onions, radishes, spinach, and turnips—in the center. Fruits were incorporated, too—raspberries, gooseberries, and blueberries as hedges along the enclosing fence or wall, and tree crops in small orchards just outside the geometric garden.

Traditional Gardens

A grid of paths between the planting beds was often made of gravel, quarry dust, crushed shells, or brick. Fences or walls might be lined with flowering shrubs or roses. Sometimes, in place of the traditional boxwood edgings, herbs were used along the walks. Bee balm, fennel, germander, hyssop, lavender, mint, parsley, sage, rosemary, and thyme were widely grown in colonial gardens.
Flowers favored in pre-Revolutionary days included such bulbs as daffodils, irises, lilies, and tulips. Perennials included columbine, daisies, daylilies, foxglove, hollyhocks, larkspur, peonies, phlox, pinks, primrose, sweet william, and violets. Some widely used annuals were gillyflower, marigolds, nasturtiums, pansies, and snapdragons.
The open landscape outside the geometric garden was treated very simply. A common mistake homeowners make in designing period landscapes for older houses is to use foundation plantings, which did not become popular until well into the 20th century. Houses built prior to that time were designed to have their own architectural bases. The grounds near houses were planted very simply, usually with grass or ground covers and trees, and the more elaborate plantings were reserved for the enclosed formal garden.

Victorian Gardens

While geometric colonial gardens were designed as separate and distinct areas, Victorian gardens of the late 19th century were typically integrated treatments of the whole landscape. The two styles are alike in being organized by a system of paths, but in a Victorian garden the paths tend to meander, revealing a series of carefully composed views. Such a walk might wind along the perimeter of the garden, providing sweeping views across a "greensward," or open lawn, to the house.
Oval, round, or irregularly shaped flower beds were often placed at important locations in the lawn adjacent to the walk. They were sometimes constructed as low mounds with a concentric pattern of flowers or unusual foliage plants. When these mounds were located in particularly significant spots, such as on both sides of an entry walk, they were often steep and topped with upright plants such as cannas or ornamental grasses.
The Victorian period was a time of lavish and eclectic taste in all the arts. In garden design, there was an intense interest in a variety of previous styles and in combinations of forms, textures, and colors. Many exotic plants, first introduced to Europe and America in this period, were used for their striking effects.
The list of flowers used by the Victorians is very long, but some of the favorites included: alyssum, anemone, butterfly weed, caladium, Christmas rose, chrysanthemum, crocus, daffodil, dahlias, daylily, forget-me-not, fountain grass, geranium, hen-and-chickens, hosta, iris, jonquil, lily, marigold, nasturtium, New England aster, periwinkle, phlox, pinks, portulaca, snowdrop, spirea, tulips,

*Photographs of
traditional gardens
appear in the color
section entitled
Time-Honored Styles.*

verbenas, yucca, and zebra grass. There was also an affection for
conical evergreens such as the firs, spruces, and hemlocks. They
were arranged on the outside of the walk, serving as accents and
screening any incompatible surroundings. Native shade trees were
also widely planted, as were newly introduced trees of unusual habit
such as the ginkgo, weeping beech, weeping willow, and lombardy
poplar.

Shrubs played a much more important role in the Victorian
landscape than they had in previous eras. Beautyberry, euonymus,
hydrangea, jasmine, kerria, lilac, mountain laurel, osmanthus,
photinia, rhododendron, shrub honeysuckle, spirea, sweet
pepperbush, sweet shrub, viburnum, or weigela might be planted
around the perimeter of the lot or featured closer in as specimens.
Only at the very end of the Victorian era did foundation plantings
begin to appear.

A Victorian landscape was not complete without some structure for
the support of vines, so greatly admired by gardeners of the period.
Boston ivy, clematis, Dutchman's pipe, English ivy, morning
glory, trumpet creeper, and wisteria were all widely popular. Many
gardens also included gazebos in the style of the house or in a
popular "rustic" style of debarked cedar poles. Ornate cast-iron
fences might also be used along the front and sides of the property.

The Classical Revival Style

Around the turn of the century, many architects and landscape
designers turned from the busy Victorian style to look back at the
refined forms of the classical and Renaissance periods. Classical
gardens were usually built in courtyards, completely enclosed and
focused inward. Their lines echoed and extended those of the
buildings they adorned and often created long vistas. They were
characterized by formal balance, carefully composed color schemes,
and a refined use of ornaments such as pools, fountains, and
sculpture.

The plants in gardens of classical-revival style were selected from a
very large palette. Some of the most popular annual and perennial
flowers included: rock aster, baby's-breath, basket-of-gold,
bleeding-heart, candytuft, chrysanthemum, columbine, coreopsis,
daylily, delphinium, hosta, indigo, iris, larkspur, lobelia, pansy,
peony, phlox, pinks, poppy, sea-lavender, speedwell, sweet
william, tulip, and yarrow varieties.

The Rewards of Traditional Gardens

Traditional gardens require careful thought and research to plan and
some effort to maintain, but they offer many rewards. Following the
principles of design that have earned the approval of generations of
our forebears, the home gardener can achieve a delightful balance
between precedent and individual taste, between unity and variety,
and between art and nature.

Traditional Gardens

Plants over 3 feet	Roses:	1
	Blanc Double de Coubert	
	Saratoga	
	Paul's Lemon Pillar (in corners)	
	Rocket ligularia	2
	Ligularia × przwalskii 'The Rocket'	
	Globe thistle	3
	Echinops exaltatus 'Taplow Blue'	
Plants to 3 feet	Musk mallow	4
	Malva moschata 'Alba'	
	Ladybells	5
	Adenophora confusa	
	Fernleaf yarrow	6
	Achillea filipendulina 'Coronation Gold'	
Plants to 2 feet	Bluebell	7
	Campanula rotundifolia	
	Golden flax	8
	Linum flavum	
	Mist flower	9
	Eupatorium coelestinum	
	Perennial flax	10
	Linum perenne	
	Shasta daisy	11
	Chrysanthemum × superbum	

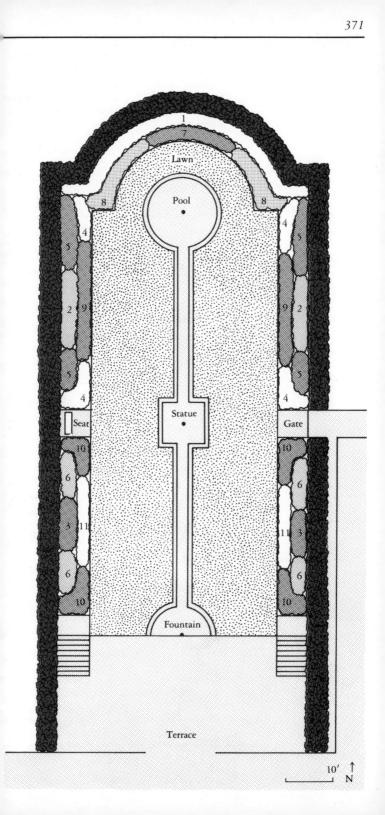

Traditional Gardens Evergreen Trees
and Shrubs:
1. American
   arborvitae
   (*Thuja occidentalis*)
2. Mountain laurel
   (*Kalmia latifolia*)

Trees and Shrubs:
3. Flowering
   dogwood
   (*Cornus florida*)
4. Vernal witch hazel
   (*Hamamelis vernalis*)
5. Franklinia
   (*Franklinia
   alatamaha*)

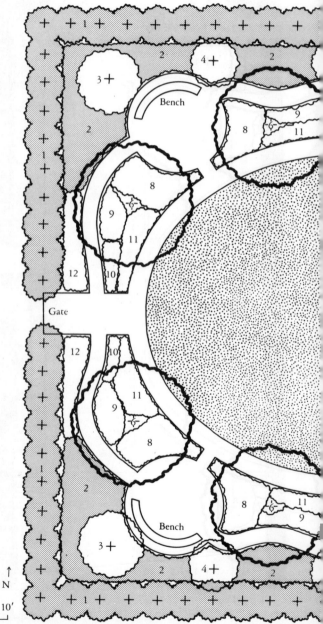

6. White ash
   (*Fraxinus americana*)
7. Silver-bell tree
   (*Halesia carolina*)
8. Oakleaf hydrangea
   (*Hydrangea quercifolia*)

9. Flame azalea
   (*Rhododendron calendulaceum*)
10. Common winterberry
    (*Ilex verticillata*)

Groundcovers:
11. Creeping phlox
    (*Phlox stolonifera*)
12. Alleghany spurge
    (*Pachysandra procumbens*)
13. Foamflower
    (*Tiarella cordifolia*)

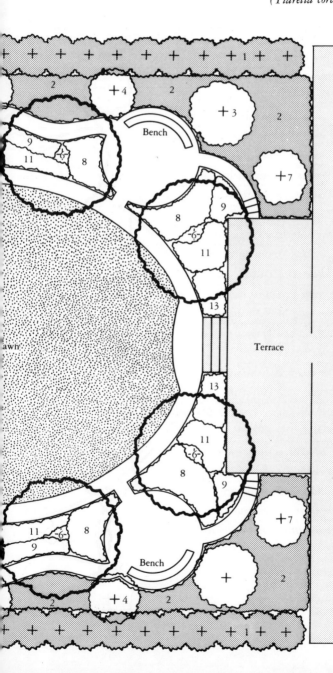

Traditional Gardens *Listings in the Source column are page references to individual Taylor's Guides. A key to title abbreviations appears on page 11.*

	Source	Zones
Plant Choices		
Adenophora confusa Ladybells	P-278	4–7
Chrysanthemum × superbum Shasta daisy	P-311	4–8
Cornus florida Flowering dogwood	T-321	4–9
Daphne odora Fragrant daphne	S-330	7–9
Echinops ritro 'Taplow Blue' Globe thistle	P-327	4–8
Eupatorium coelestinum Mist flower	P-331	5–8
Fatsia japonica Japanese aralia	S-338	8–10
Fraxinus americana White ash	T-339	4–9
Halesia carolina Silver-bell tree	T-344	5–8
Hydrangea quercifolia Oakleaf hydrangea	S-351	5–9
Kalmia latifolia Mountain laurel	S-358	5–9
Linum flavum Golden flax	P-363	5–7
Linum perenne Perennial flax	P-363	5–7
Malva moschata Musk mallow	P-368	4–8
Osmanthus fragrans Fragrant tea olive	S-375	8–9
Pachysandra procumbens Alleghany spurge	G-348	5–9
Raphiolepis indica Indian hawthorn	S-389	8–10
Rosa banksiae lutea Lady Banks rose	R-292	7–9
Rosa × hybrida 'Blanc Double de Coubert'	R-320	3–8
Rosa × hybrida 'Elegance'	R-310	3–8
Skimmia japonica Japanese skimmia	S-404	7–9
Thuja occidentalis American arborvitae	T-399	3–7
Tiarella cordifolia Foamflower	G-368	5–8
Viburnum tinus Laurustinus	S-419	7–10
Vitex agnus-castus Lilac chaste-tree	S-420	7–9

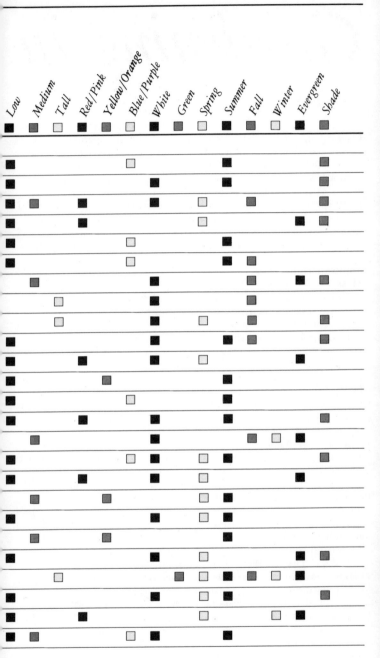

Low | Medium | Tall | Red/Pink | Yellow/Orange | Blue/Purple | White | Green | Spring | Summer | Fall | Winter | Evergreen | Shade

Gardening in

Victoria Jahn

Offering an unexpected haven from hectic house, apartment, or street, a small garden is an intimate retreat designed to personal taste. It is able to reflect your life-style to a much greater degree than a landscape removed in form and function from your home. While careful planning is essential to all successful gardens, in a small space it can make the difference between a serene refuge and a crowded, cluttered area. You will be pleasantly surprised at the many ways plants, flowers, and structures can be arranged to expand your garden without losing its welcome sense of seclusion.

Manipulating Space
Most owners of small gardens view the space within their boundaries as fixed and limited . . . and they are wrong. By carefully choosing and placing masses of plants, ornaments, and architectural features such as pergolas, fences, steps, and walls, you can manipulate the space within the garden to give a sense of intimate enclosure or to visually expand it beyond the edges of your property. Often it is desirable to do both in the same design.

Designing a Framework
You can create a feeling of enclosure through a uniform design. In general, the constructed framework of the garden should be simple. Using edgings for paths and planting beds ties the composition together and defines separate areas of the garden.
Try to limit the use of curves in favor of straight lines—particularly when laying out paving. Straight edges can always be softened by the gentle curves of plants. To keep attention focused within your design and away from neighboring eyesores, use plants with rounded, weeping, or horizontal shapes and avoid those with cones, spires, and assertively upright forms—these tend to lead the eye up and out of the garden.
To expand the garden, use the principles of perspective to your advantage. Deepen shallow spaces by gradually reducing plant height toward the back of the area. Elongate your space by manipulating perspective with a wooden fence of stepped slats— make the slats highest near the house, lower farther away. If a path is part of your scheme, narrow it slightly at its farthest reach. And when using color, place strong, hot tones nearest the foreground and soft, cool pastels farther away, so they appear to fade into the mist.

Evaluating Your Site
To tie the garden design to the house, construct features that will provide privacy as well as a sense of space. They should be useful as well as attractive, so begin by making a list of how you intend to use various areas of the garden—perhaps for cooking, dining, and entertaining; for children's play; or for tool, toy, or trash storage. Evaluate your site thoroughly: Are your expectations realistic?

Small Spaces

Creating a Sense of Space

Small gardens can be planned to give the illusion of larger landscapes through tricks of perspective or by taking advantage of far-off vistas. Because small gardens are almost always adjacent to the house, it is vital to maintain harmony between the two by manipulating two architectural concepts—space and volume. Begin with the architectural framework—fences, terracing, walls, paving, and steps—adding trees, shrubs, herbaceous plants, bulbs, and ground cover, in roughly that order.

When planning the placement of plants and structures, consider traffic patterns. Try to lengthen the route through the area, which will create the illusion of a larger garden. Added levels in the form of terraces, berms, or even a raised deck will make your walk a bit more lengthy and cause the eye to travel a greater distance. Steps act in the same way and, when made of rough-hewn stone, provide an extraordinarily effective focal point.

If your space is long and relatively narrow, separate it into two or more distinct areas. Screen each area from the next with plants, a trellis, or both. Arrange doorway views through each compartment to entice further exploration. Paths leading to a false gate in a fence are a good way to suggest the existence of other gardens beyond.

Fences and Walls

Nearly every small garden is surrounded by some kind of fence. Regarded as purely utilitarian by many, fences are crucial to a garden design in a small space, especially because so much of the structure is usually highly visible. Replacing a deteriorating fence once the garden is planted can be tricky, so choose a wood that will not decay quickly and make sure it is built to last for many years. This is an area you may wish to splurge on.

Redwood and cedar are excellent although costly; left untreated, they weather to a soft silvery gray. Pressure-treated wood is also durable, but its vapors can be toxic to some plants. Let a fence of pressure-treated wood weather several weeks before planting anything near it. Space posts six feet apart for strength. If you are using paths, consider running the paving right up to the fence, to let visitors fully appreciate its beauty.

Fences with vertical lines work well in small areas. Avoid strongly horizontal fences such as split rail, which are more appropriate to the wide open spaces of the countryside. Usually a fence just above eye level is best, but if you are enclosing a particularly narrow area, a fence of that height can make you feel as if you're in a canyon. In this case, make the bottom two-thirds a vertical board fence and the top third a trellis for an airy effect.

Low, knee-high walls are perfectly in scale in most small gardens. A dry stone wall, constructed without mortar, is an unexpected reminder of a larger country garden. If you are thinking of sinking

Gardening in Small Spaces

When using bricks in a patio or path, consider the effects of various patterns. Five popular designs are shown below.

Straight bond

Ladder weave

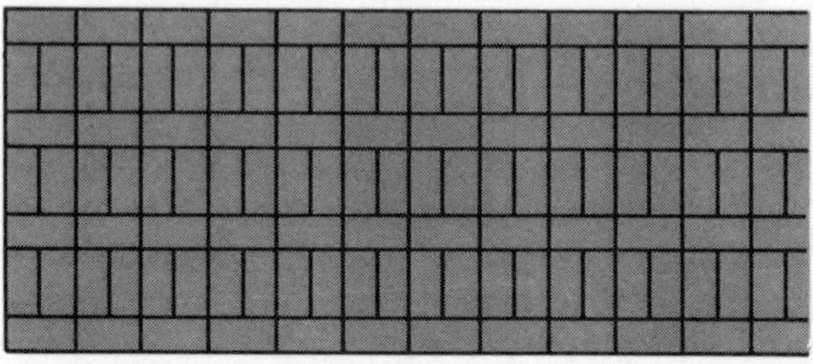

Basket weave

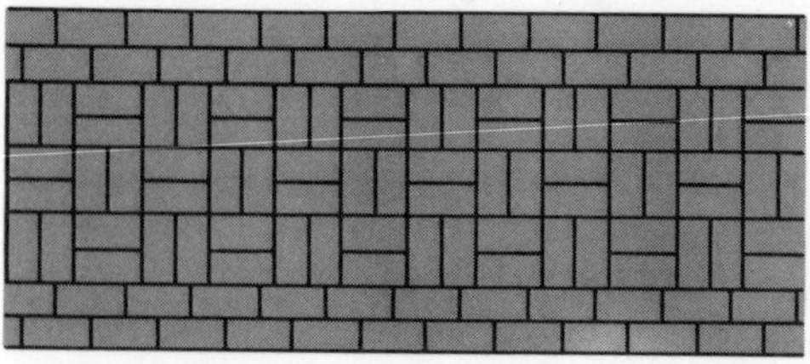

Diagonal

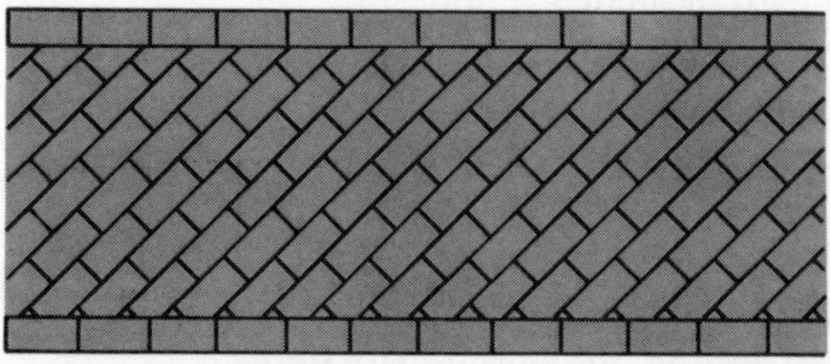

Diagonal herringbone

one area of the garden and using the excavated earth to raise another, a low wall is a logical border between them.

Pavings and Paths

To make an area of limited space appear larger, focus the eye inward and downward by adding visual interest at ground level: a decorative paving, some ground cover with pleasing colors and textures, or even a lily pond. Paving is usually a necessity because a great deal of foot traffic is concentrated in a very limited space. In constructing paths, make sure they follow some logical arrangement. If you would like the path to change direction, curve, or stop, see that there is a reason for doing so.

You can make paths of shredded bark over a compacted soil base— excellent in woodland gardens. For a more formal effect, pave paths with brick pavers, bluestone, or, in frost-free areas, tile. Try to integrate your choice of material to complement the walls of the house.

When laying brick, slate, or bluestone, install them over a gravel-and-sand base with timber, steel, stone, or brick edging to prevent joints from spreading. This makes the path easy and flexible to maintain—just lift out and replace damaged sections. As the garden matures, you can change the paths' layout without costly demolition.

Patterns in Brick

Paving patterns can vary according to the effect you wish to achieve, creating illusions of space. Bricks, with their small and uniform shapes, can appear to expand an area. Lay them in different ways to help set the tone of your garden. Placed horizontally across a path or angled in a herringbone pattern, bricks seem to widen the walk, because they slow the eye down. In contrast, bricks running parallel to the direction of the path lend a sense of speed and dynamic tension. There are many patterns to try; experiment to find which best suits your space.

Choosing Plants

There is no list of best plants for a small garden because the selection is inextricably tied to your environment and preferred garden style. But there are some basic guidelines to choosing plants that will enhance your space without overwhelming it. First, identify the plants that will suit your location: sunny, shady, wet, dry. Many gardeners are drawn to the most eye-catching plants in the nursery yard; but in a small garden, unusual, variegated, and large-leaved plants must be used sparingly.

To avoid the error of purchasing plants on impulse, it is always advisable to go to the nursery with a list. If you are knowledgeable, your list can be quite specific, detailing plants, quantities, and sizes desired. But even if you are a novice, listing the kinds of plants

Gardening in Small Spaces

you want will be enormously helpful in narrowing down the available stock.

For example, you may need three 10-foot conifers to block a view of a neighbor's clothesline, one deciduous tree over the patio for summer shade, five flowering shrubs to screen a toolshed, and some 50 ground cover plants that will thrive in deep shade.

Identify those that will suit the location. Then, unless you are planting a lavish perennial garden that requires contrast, limit the number of varieties you choose and plant them in masses to give your garden some order. Remember that in a small space, plants with strong personalities make the garden appear cluttered.

Selecting Trees and Shrubs

There are many ways to use large plants to enclose an area or to make it seem more spacious. Because the simplest way to unify a small garden is to enclose it, use tall hedges or cluster plants to screen the clutter of neighboring views—clotheslines, picnic benches, barbecue grills, and play equipment—and to make a cozier, more intimate space. Group trees and shrubs to enclose small areas within the design—in effect, building "rooms." Or place a tree near the garden entrance where it frames the vista beyond, making it appear more distant.

To provide privacy quickly, evergreens are ideal year round. Good choices to consider include false cypress, Arizona cypress, Japanese cedar, and Japanese black pine. Use shrubs such as azaleas for attractive flowers and foliage. Try a Japanese holly for its glossy green leaves.

Bear in mind that too many evergreens can make your yard look dark. To lighten the mood, add small- to medium-sized deciduous trees. They cast a marvelous dappled shade on seating areas and give a garden surrounded by tall buildings the feeling of intimacy without making it gloomy. Small flowering cherries and plums, star and sweet bay magnolias, and Japanese snowbell are all well-behaved candidates for limited spaces. For a more natural effect, plant deciduous trees in small groves.

When selecting deciduous trees, keep the mature size of the tree in mind and avoid large shade trees such as Norway maples and lindens. Large trees can be used effectively to screen views and fill empty spaces quickly, but they will outgrow the allotted space in five or ten years and will need to be removed. Eliminate any trees on your list with one or more of the following characteristics: mature height over 50 feet; a spreading, shallow root system; messy fruit; a very dense canopy producing excessive shade; seeds that will sprout all over the garden.

Use dwarf plants sparingly too. Just because the garden is small doesn't mean you have to use plants scaled to landscape a dollhouse. Dwarf alpines, although charming clinging to Himalayan cliffs, will not hide your neighbor's trash cans.

Using Vines

To create height without width, use vines. They soften walls and
fences, anchor the house and architectural features to their
surroundings . . . and do the job quickly. Clematis, jasmine,
passion-flower, wisteria, and even grape vines are ideal candidates
for training on a trellis or an arbor.

Clinging vines such as *Schizophragma hydrangeoides,* climbing
hydrangea, Virginia creeper, and English ivy are also effective, but
do not train them on any structure that requires regular painting.
Their hairlike holdfasts are very difficult to remove. For temporary
bursts of color, try annual vines such as scarlet runner bean,
morning glories, or climbing gourds.

Choosing Flowers

Flowers add colorful accents amid the cool greens of small gardens.
Daffodils and tulips can be literally at your doorstep in spring, to
be enjoyed in the open air or brought inside. Impatiens are favorites
for their cheerful, generous displays, and they do especially well in
shade. Summer bulbs such as dahlias bloom in pink, blue, white,
and yellow hues summer through fall. Velvet-petaled pansies can
add a distinctive border to a small bed.

If you use your garden a great deal at night, consider white and
scented flowers. White is more visible after dark, and aromatic
blossoms can be appreciated best in close quarters. Given the right
growing conditions, you should be able to create your own
flowering bower by choosing among many favorite blooms.

Rooftop Gardens

Terraces, balconies, and rooftops, unlike their ground-level
counterparts, are usually blessed with glorious views. Unexpected
hideaways above the busy streets, these havens are ideal for
entertaining or for recapturing that rare commodity of urban
life—solitude.

But this type of garden also has special challenges to overcome—
intense summer heat from reflective building surfaces, wind, and
dryness. Cold is magnified in gardens exposed to bitter northern
winds. And remember that too many sweeping views can create an
exposed, off-balance mood. Screen some views with trees and
shrubs, and use plants to frame other vistas to create a more unified
retreat.

Before beginning work on your garden, make sure the surface of
the roof will stay watertight. Be aware that tar paper is easily
punctured by chair legs and sharp heels and needs to be covered
with some multipurpose material. Glazed tile is an attractive
choice, but it cannot be used where winter temperatures dip below
freezing. Brick pavers half the usual thickness are another option to
consider.

Another possibility is to use the new stone-and-resin-composition

Gardening in Small Spaces

pavers, which look like granite but are not as heavy; they can be supported over the roofing material on a plastic grid that will hold up the corner of each block.

Before adding any heavy plant, such as a tree in a tub, find out the weight-bearing capacity of the roof or balcony. Check local ordinances and building codes regarding fire access and fireproof building materials before constructing fences, trellises, or decks. There is no point in putting time and effort into a project that will have to be torn down for safety purposes. Also, if there is no direct access to the street, you will have to bring everything through the house. Measure doorways, halls, and tight turns before ordering.

Large containers holding trees should have removable sides so you can prune the roots to prevent them from splitting the planter. Because soil in containers dries out rapidly, a drip irrigation system is a good idea, especially for the gardener who travels.

In the North, plants that will stay out through the winter need to be in planters at least 18 inches in diameter. Smaller containers leave plant roots open to greater temperature extremes and frost heavings.

Very exposed locations need a fence to act as a windbreak and prevent the plants from drying out. To lessen wind resistance, let some air pass through. Be sure to anchor plants securely, especially newly-potted plants without established roots; even heavy, substantial trees have been known to topple to the street in high winds.

Special Considerations for City Gardens

Creating spacious enclosures close to your house will provide you with a multitude of uses—for entertaining others and as a focal point for your family. A backyard patio or bower can be both a haven for serene contemplation and an outlet for overflowing energy. While rooftop and balcony gardens must suffer extremes of exposure, ground-level city gardens must deal with conditions that are quite the opposite.

Be aware that gardens on the ground—surrounded by row houses, high-rises, tall fences, or other structures—suffer from poor air circulation. Plants in these gardens invariably suffer from a host of fungal diseases, from powdery mildew on leaves to root rots. Disease control under such circumstances is usually a losing battle, so do your homework and select only plants that staunchly resist fungus attacks.

Air pollution is another problem. Make sure your garden is hosed down regularly—at least once a week. Thick deposits of soot and grime screen sunlight from leaf surfaces, interfering with photosynthesis and weakening the plant over time. Slow-growing plants lack sufficient vigor for these problem locations. Rugged individuals with an extra-vigorous, almost weedy, capacity for

Photographs of small gardens appear in the color sections entitled City Gardens and Gardens in the Suburbs.

growth can survive adverse conditions and compensate with phenomenal growth the following season.

Finally, cast a critical, unsentimental eye on existing plants and features. You may love that unruly briar rose every time it blooms, but it is probably far too aggressive and thorny to use in close quarters. Aimless narrow paths, concrete bed dividers, many fences, and awkward patios should be removed at the start to give you an uncluttered canvas on which to create your new design.

Testing the Soil

A soil test is essential for smaller landscapes, which often contain buried building rubble, dumped subsoil from the foundation, or other hostile composites left over from construction. The barren, compacted soil of neglected yards needs generous helpings of peat moss, compost, shredded leaves, or other organic matter before you can start planting.

Many gardeners, in a rush of enthusiasm and impatience, neglect the labor and expense of careful soil preparation. Do take the time. Given the marginal environmental conditions of city gardens, the proper soil can make all the difference in achieving a successful garden.

A Tailor-made Garden

Tricks of perception, beautiful plants framing spectacular views, and well-placed structures screening unsightly ones will help enlarge and enhance a small space. Remember to design the area so that it also serves your life-style. With a healthy mixture of imagination and common sense, you can create a garden more satisfying than the grounds of the largest estate—because it has been made specifically to suit you.

Gardening in
Small Spaces

Listings in the Source
column are page
references to individual
Taylor's Guides. A key
to title abbreviations
appears on page 11.

Under Zones, W and
C indicate warm- or
cool-season annuals.

	Source	Zones
Plant Choices		
Chrysanthemum spp. Chrysanthemum	P-309	3–9
Clematis spp. Clematis	G-385	4–9
Cornus kousa Kousa dogwood	T-321	5–8
Cosmos spp. Cosmos	A-313	W
Cryptomeria japonica Japanese cedar	T-325	6–8
Cupressus arizonica Arizona cypress	D-380	7–10
Dahlia pinnata hybrids Dahlia	B-306	W
Jasminum polyanthum Pink jasmine	G-395	7–10
Magnolia virginiana Sweet bay	T-355	5–9
Malus spp. Crabapple	T-356	4–10
Narcissus spp. Daffodil	B-351	4–7
Passiflora spp. Passion-flower	G-402	7–10
Pinus thunbergiana Japanese black pine	T-378	5–9
Prunus subhirtella 'Pendula' Weeping cherry	T-383	6–8
Rhododendron spp. Rhododendron/azalea	S-390	4–8
Styrax japonica Japanese snowbell	D-380	5–8
Tulipa spp. Tulip	B-374	4–6
Viola spp. Pansy	A-417	C
Vitis coignetiae Crimson glory vine	G-410	5–8
Wisteria spp. Wisteria	G-411	5–9

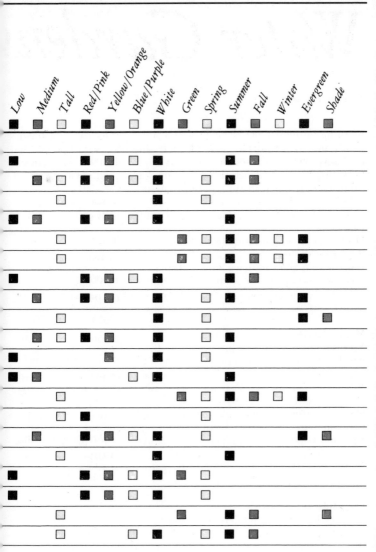

Low	Medium	Tall	Red/Pink	Yellow/Orange	Blue/Purple	White	Green	Spring	Summer	Fall	Winter	Evergreen	Shade
■			■	▨	□	■			■	▨			
	▨	□	■	▨	□	■		□	■	▨			
		□				■		□					
■	▨		■	▨	□	■			■				
		□				■	□	■	▨		□	■	
		□				■	□	■	▨		□	■	
■			■	▨	□	■			■	▨			
	▨		■	▨		■		□	■			■	
		□				■		□				■	▨
	▨	□	■	▨		■		□	■				
■				▨		■		□					
■	▨				□	■		□					
		□				■	□	■	▨		□	■	
		□	■					□					
	▨		■	▨	□			□				■	▨
		□				■		■					
■			■	▨	□	■	▨	□					
■			■	▨	□	■		□					
		□				■		■	▨				▨
		□			□	■		□	■	▨			

Water Gardens

Charles Thomas

Nothing quite matches the appeal of a water garden. Even a small pond can give a landscape new life, refreshing it with a special kind of beauty. Graceful irises and rushes whisper in the breeze, delicate water lily blossoms dance above floating leaves, and open patches of calm water reflect lush surroundings. A rocky waterfall or a babbling brook can be the finishing touch to a woodland garden, and a formal pool with a fountain will turn a small courtyard into a cool oasis.

High expense and long maintenance hours once kept many people from considering water gardens, but improved technology in construction and care have largely displaced such concerns. Add to these advancements the tremendous number of new aquatic plant hybrids that are available today, and you begin to realize that water gardens are within the reach of almost any home gardener.

Water Gardens for Any Site

You can create a captivating design in an area as small as half a whiskey barrel, displayed on a patio deck or even perched on an apartment balcony. If you have a whole yard to work with, there are all sorts of options. A pond or pool can be lined with concrete or with a sheet of polyvinyl chloride. There are also preformed fiberglass structures available that you simply lay in an excavated site. Of course, if you are lucky enough to have a lake, a stream, or a natural pond on your property, you can create an aquatic paradise with minimal construction. Regardless of your circumstances, there is almost certainly a way that a water garden can add a special touch to your landscape.

Deciding on a Theme

A water feature is a dramatic addition to the landscape and often becomes its focal point. Your planning should involve making sure this new element will be compatible with the rest of your garden style. If you are starting your landscape from scratch, the choices are much wider. You can design what you consider the perfect water garden and then develop the remainder of your landscape around it. A large open space might be ideal for a naturalistic pond; a small, square patio would be a nice setting for a formal pool, perhaps with a central fountain. A secluded corner could be accented with a small informal pond, including a rock waterfall.

The Best Site

You can locate some type of water garden almost anywhere in your landscape as long as there is enough sunlight. Most water plants require a minimum of six hours of full sun daily; without it, they will bloom very poorly or not at all. Stay away from areas close to deciduous trees. Aside from providing too much shade, they cause maintenance problems. Many an hour will be spent scooping leaves from your pond.

Other considerations in choosing a site include easy accessibility for viewing and the proximity of such necessities as running water for refilling a pond and electricity to operate pumps or lights. The grade of the landscape is also a factor. Steep slopes usually require more expensive construction than do flat areas. Locating your water garden in a low area of the landscape can also result in problems. Ground water may run into the pool, carrying dissolved insecticides or herbicides that can upset the pool's ecological balance. You can stop this by building up the edge of the pool an inch or two higher than the surrounding soil. If the site is subject to too much runoff, ground water can float a pond or pool out of its foundation.

Building a Pond
Most water gardens begin with an excavation, but from that point on, the approach can vary greatly. There are four basic types of ponds: earthen, concrete, ponds made with plastic liners, and preformed fiberglass ponds. Which type will be best for you depends on how much money you want to spend, how durable you expect the pond to be, and what shape you desire.

Earthen Ponds
It is possible to leave a hole unlined and fill it with water to create a pool. This is called an earthen, or earth-bottom, pond. Earthen ponds are inexpensive to create, but there are quite a few disadvantages associated with them. Most soils do not hold water very well, so you may end up with a mud hole instead of a water garden. Also, aquatic plants tend to take over the bottom of such pools through unimpeded rooting.
If your soil does not percolate well—if it holds water instead of allowing it to pass through, as clay soil does—you may be able to create an earthen pond. You can test for water retention yourself. Simply dig a small hole in the desired area, fill it with water, and wait several hours. If there has been no appreciable lowering of the water level, you can go ahead with construction. If the water seeps away, however, use concrete or a liner.

Concrete Ponds and Pools
The advantages of lining pools with concrete include strength, longevity, and freedom of shape. Disadvantages range from expense to the fact that most concrete ponds eventually develop leaks as a result of annual freezes and thaws. Most large ponds and, of course, swimming pools are built of concrete, and it makes sense to leave this work to professionals. Many landscape companies now offer pool installation among their services. Ask for references from the builder and be sure he knows exactly what you want.
An unused swimming pool can be converted into an aquatic garden, and there are companies that specialize in such work. Again, ask for references before choosing a builder.

Water Gardens

PVC-lined Ponds

A third and increasingly popular method of pond construction makes use of a PVC liner—a sheet of polyvinyl chloride, a plastic—laid directly into an excavation to hold water. A PVC liner will work in a pond of any shape and is relatively inexpensive. Unlike concrete, however, it will probably require replacement within 10 to 15 years.

Preformed Fiberglass Ponds

You can install a preformed fiberglass pond quite easily. Like PVC-lined ponds, these are less expensive than concrete. But fiberglass ponds last a lifetime. The best ones are one-quarter inch thick. Your choice is limited, however, to the shapes and sizes on the market—available through mail-order water-garden firms, water-garden specialists, and some garden centers and nurseries. These pools hold up very well to winter extremes.

Due to their low cost and ease of installation, PVC liners and preformed ponds are probably used to construct 99 percent of small, backyard water gardens today. For that reason, simple instructions are provided here for only those methods. If you choose to install a concrete pond or pool, you should seek the advice of a professional landscape contractor.

Installing a PVC-lined Pond

The first step in planning any water feature is to see if there are any local ordinances regulating pools in home landscapes. Check with your city or county government zoning board or building permit agency by calling or writing and describing what you'd like to do. You can construct your water garden anytime from the beginning of spring through fall and plant it from spring until 30 days before the average first-frost date. If you plant hardy aquatics early enough, you can expect blooms the first year.

To begin construction, decide on the shape of your pond. Drag the garden hose to your chosen site and use it to outline various shapes until you find the perfect one. It is best to keep it simple and avoid right angles.

Now you are ready for the heavy work—excavating. Before you dig in, decide where on your property you will use the excavated soil or arrange for its removal. Excavated soil can come in handy in landscaping around the pond or in building a waterfall or a rock feature.

The best pond depth is approximately 18 inches. You may want to cut one or more steps into the sides of the pool, where you can place those plants that cannot tolerate more than a few inches of water above their "feet." Once you've removed soil to about 18 inches in roughly the shape you desire, refine the sides of the pond, making them slope toward the center. This provides additional strength, which is especially important in cold parts of the nation

To construct a PVC-lined pond, dig a hole about 18 inches deep, cutting shelves into the sloped sides if desired.

Line with ¹/₂ inch of sand and press the plastic liner into the contours. Fill the pond and trim back all but 1 foot of excess liner. Hide this flap under a paver set in reinforced mortar.

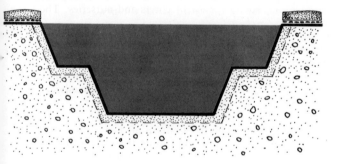

where winter freezes and thaws might otherwise cause damage. Next, remove all debris in the hole that might eventually rupture the liner. For added protection, line the excavation with a half-inch cushion of damp sand or other protective material, such as scraps of carpet.

Leveling the Pond

The final step is to ensure that the top of the pond is level all around. An error can result in a pond that overflows at one end while resting shallow at the other. First, set wooden pegs into the soil around the pool, spaced about three to four feet apart. Use a level to ensure that the tops of the pegs are level with each other. Then lay a long piece of lumber across the pool, positioning it on two opposite pegs, and check that it is level. Perform this last step several more times, laying the board across the pond at different angles and adjusting the edges as necessary to make them level.

Installing the Liner

To determine what size liner you will require, measure the maximum length and width of the excavation. Add to each dimension a figure equal to two times the maximum depth, to account for the sides and shelves, plus two feet, to create a one-foot overhang on each side of the pool. Liners are available in standard sizes, which will cover the needs of almost all home gardeners, but some firms will take custom orders. Ordinary scissors work fine for any necessary trimming. Should you need a very large liner, glue several together with a glue designed specifically for flexible PVC. The glue that is commonly used for hard PVC pipe fittings will melt a hole in a PVC pool liner.

Once you have a liner of the correct size, drape it over the hole, weighing it down with smooth stones or bricks at several points where it overhangs the pool rim. Then get into the pond, in stocking feet or sneakers, and press the liner into the contours to make it fit snugly. Climb out of the pond and begin filling it with a hose. The weight of the water will cause the liner to fit tightly into every contour of the excavation, but anticipate wrinkles. Use your hands to spread the creases carefully.

The only task remaining is to trim back and cover those portions of the liner that overhang the excavation. Leave one foot of excess, anchoring and hiding this flap beneath sections of sod or large rocks, ornamental brick, flagstone, or tile set in reinforced mortar, or whatever seems appropriate for your garden style.

Installing a Preformed Pond

The method for installing a preformed fiberglass pond is similar to that just described for PVC-lined ponds. Dig a hole of roughly the correct shape and depth, and line it with sand. Rest the pond on the sand, checking that its edges are level. Fill in around the

To be certain your pond is level, set pegs at 3-foot intervals around the rim, checking that the top of each is level with the next. Then lay a board across opposite pegs and make sure it is level.

Do this at several different angles across the pond, adjusting the edges if necessary before proceeding with sand and liner.

sides with soil while the pond is filling. This equalizes pressure inside and outside of the pool. Camouflage the edges of the pond with sod, sand, gravel, large rocks, or other appropriate materials.

Special Effects

You may want to add drama to your water garden by installing a special feature such as a fountain, a waterfall, or a stream. Mechanical fountains are available from specialty nurseries and water-garden firms, and they come with fairly simple instructions for installation and use. Waterfalls and streams require a bit more expertise; it is best to call in a professional if you're considering these features.

For safety, always use a ground fault circuit interrupter with any electrical appliance—pump, fountain, or lights, for example. This device, available from electrical supply houses, water-garden firms, and some nurseries, shuts off power immediately if there is an electrical leak. It should be installed by an electrician.

Plants for the Water Garden

There are a tremendous number of beautiful plants with which to adorn your new pool or pond. Because few local nurseries carry a wide range of aquatic plants, watch for advertisements of specialty nurseries in gardening magazines. You may also want to contact a nearby botanical garden or arboretum, or a national plant society—such as the Water Lily Society or the American Horticultural Society—for information on sources of aquatics in your area.

If you live near a water-garden supplier, you may be able to buy potted aquatic plants that will give your garden an immediately "finished" look. Plants from mail-order nurseries and ferns generally arrive bare-rooted and take six to eight weeks to mature.

The number of plants you will need depends on the total surface area of your pool and on the sizes of the plants themselves. Most suppliers' catalogues indicate the maximum area required by each plant.

Aquatic plants fall into three main categories: submerged plants, floating-leaved plants, and emergent plants.

Submerged Plants

One of the magical qualities of a water garden is that it has depth; its beauty does not stop at ground level. Beneath the water's surface, submerged plants carpet the floor of a pond, providing hiding places for fish, frogs, and snails, and at the same time giving texture to the pond's interior. The delicate foliage of these plants absorbs mineral salts and nutrients in the water and thereby discourages the growth of algae, which will cloud a pond. So, in addition to being attractive, they make your pond cleaner.

Submerged plants such as water-weed, *Elodea canadensis*—a fernlike plant with tiny white summer flowers—and Washington plant,

Water Gardens

Plant a water lily in a plastic tub of heavy garden soil so that its crown barely shows. Wet the soil and cover it with pea gravel, except around the crown.

Lower the pot into the pool, holding it up with bricks if necessary to keep the gravel surface about 10 inches underwater.

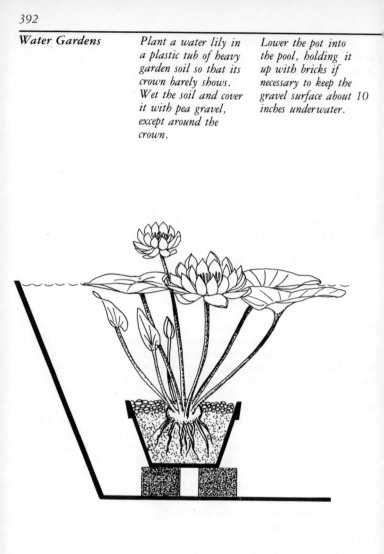

Cabomba caroliniana—whose lacy leaves whorl into fan shapes—are sold as cuttings in bunches of six. To plant them, simply press their stems into the soil in an earthen pond or into a bucket of soil topped with a veneer of gravel placed on the bottom of a lined pond. In a short time, roots will develop. Plant one bunch of these plants for every one to two square feet of surface area. If your pool is already green with algae, allow six to eight weeks after planting for the "cleaning" to take place.

Floating-leaved Plants
Water lilies and other plants that float on the surface provide a special elegance to the water garden. They are the perfect resting places for frogs and dragonflies, and most of them produce spectacular flowers, some of which are wonderfully fragrant. Water lilies, all of the genus *Nymphaea,* may be hardy or tropical. The hardy types are perennial—they can overwinter in a pond if their rootstocks are not allowed to freeze. They bloom during the day and close up at night, and their flowers usually rest right on the surface, in amongst the lily pads. Tropical water lilies may be day- or night-blooming, but they are not cold-tolerant. You must move them to a greenhouse pool in winter or allow them to die and replace them in spring. Tropical lilies hold their blossoms several inches—sometimes a foot—above their floating foliage, and they are generally larger than the hardy types.

Other floating-leaved plants include the yellow-flowered floating heart, *Nymphoides peltata,* whose green leaves are mottled with maroon, and the four-leaf water clover, *Marsilia mutica*, named for the shape of its leaves, which are marked with brown and yellow.

To plant water lilies, use plastic pans, tubs, or pails filled with heavy garden soil amended with aquatic plant fertilizer. Position the plant so that its crown just barely shows above the soil. Gently add soil around the roots and tamp it down. Saturate the soil and cover it with a half inch of pea gravel, keeping the plant's crown area free. Lower the pot into your pool so that the gravel surface is six to eight inches below the water's surface. Use bricks to support the pan, if necessary. In two to three weeks the plants will have adjusted to their new environment, and new leaves will grow to the surface. Gradually remove layers of bricks until the gravel surface is about ten inches under water.

Plant other floating-leaved plants in the same manner, adjusting depths according to the supplier's instructions for particular types.

Emergent Plants
Plants that root either beneath the water or at the very edges of a pond and reach skyward with foliage and flowers are called emergent plants, and sometimes bog plants, although the latter term can encompass floating plants as well. Because of their height, emergent plants can serve as backdrops to lower plants, or they can

stand alone to provide exciting vertical accents. Their rustling foliage and colorful blooms are assets to any water garden. Some examples are the tall, graceful water iris, which may be blue (*Iris versicolor*) or yellow (*I. pseudacorus*); pickerel rush, *Pontederia cordata*, with tall, arrowlike foliage and blue flowers; and the familiar graceful cat-tail. These are planted in the same way as water lilies, but correct depths vary with plant type.

Plants for Areas around Your Pool

The area outside your pool will remain dry, so it can become home to any number of nonaquatic plants. Simply choose those that will give the desired effect, complementing the aquatics you have chosen. These can range from ferns and ornamental grasses to flowers such as geraniums, marigolds, and petunias to shrubs and trees—especially those with spreading or weeping habits. Remember to plant trees only on the north side to avoid shading the pool.

Design Styles

There are probably as many styles of water gardens as there are designers, but most can be described as either formal or informal. Formal gardens are usually designed around a central water feature of symmetrical shape, and they often include paved areas that bring order and focus to the landscape. Although concrete is considered the traditional construction material for formal pools, formal-shaped fiberglass pools are generally available up to about six feet wide, and PVC-lined pools can reach virtually any size desired. Informal gardens reflect the free-flowing lines found in nature. They may be modeled after small ponds, streams, or bogs.

The following descriptions of sample gardens should start you thinking about ways to treat your own particular space. These are simple but elegant designs that require little maintenance once established.

A Formal Water Garden

The level backyard of a classically designed house can be a perfect setting for a formal pool. Designed in a square shape to reflect the straight lines of hedges, paths, and of the yard itself, such a garden can be either a large central feature in the landscape or a small accent for one calm, secluded area of a formal design. In either case, consider creating a sitting area near the pool so that its pleasures will be appreciated at close range.

One simple but elegant planting scheme for a large formal pool—about 12 feet square—might include just three types of floating-leaved plants. A hardy water lily, such as *Nymphaea* 'Pink Sensation,' could fill the center of the pond with handsome leaves six inches across and beautiful pink blossoms in summer. Surrounding this focal point on four sides might be groupings of aquatic ferns or four-leaf water clovers, *Marsilia mutica,* which create a surface carpet of attractive blue-green beautifully patterned with browns and yellows. Each of the four corners of the pool could be accented with delicate white snowflakes, which produce an abundance of white flowers—each almost an inch across—from spring through fall.

The purpose of this simple, symmetrical arrangement is to direct the eye toward the large water lily and at the same time complement it with attractive secondary plantings. Grouping the secondary plantings in fours reflects the four-sided shape of the pool itself. A bonus to this design are the subtle fragrances of the Pink Sensation lily and the white snowflake.

A Naturalistic Garden

In designing an informal, naturalistic pond, make it appear untouched by human hands—as if it had always been part of the landscape. The straight lines and perfect symmetry of the formal design are not found in nature, so they should not appear in a naturalistic water garden.

The diagram on page 396 shows a kidney-shaped pond, which could be prefabricated or created with a liner. It fits neatly into the location and provides two potential focus areas by virtue of its shape. In a sense, it is two ponds connected in the center, each of which can be designed in a slightly different way without sacrificing a unified effect. A rocky waterfall appears at the back of the pond to add the welcome sight and sound of cascading water. This is an optional feature that should be created by a professional.

The shore plantings that surround this water garden include an elegant dwarf Japanese maple, whose branches reach delicately over blue rug junipers and a corner of the pond itself. At one end of the pond is a collection of sun-tolerant plantain-lilies that extend to the beginnings of the rockery.

This portion of the pond is a spill-in for the waterfall. The opposite portion is a quieter area suited to an exciting collection of plants that cannot tolerate the moving water in the vicinity of the waterfall.

The edges of the pond are disguised with flat stones. This approach accomplishes two things: It adds to the overall natural appearance of the pond, and it helps blend the water garden into its setting. Plants placed in the area of the waterfall will tolerate moving water and complement the verticality of both the fall and the tall plantain-lilies on the shore. A water iris (*Iris* 'Her Highness') is the predominant plant, with beautiful straplike leaves that will grow nearly three feet tall and elegant, large white flowers held just above the foliage. Closer to shore there is a bit of spike rush, *Eleocharis montevidensis,* which grows lower than the iris. Almost directly in front of the waterfall is a clump of pickerel rush, *Pontederia cordata,* which also provides contrast to the irises. Its

Shore plantings	Japanese maple	1
	Acer palmatum	
	Blue rug juniper	2
	Juniperus horizontalis 'Wiltonii'	
	Plaintain-lily	3
	Hosta	
Pool plantings	Water lily	4
	Nymphaea 'Virginia'	
	Water lily	5
	Nymphaea 'Emily Grant Hutchings'	
	Spike rush	6
	Eleocharis montevidensis	
	Pickerel rush	7
	Pontederia cordata	
	Iris	8
	Iris 'Her Highness'	

This plan for a naturalistic water garden includes a waterfall that creates an area of turbulent water where rushes and iris thrive.

The calm area is reserved for delicate water lilies. Well-chosen shore plantings and an edge of flat stones help blend the garden into its setting.

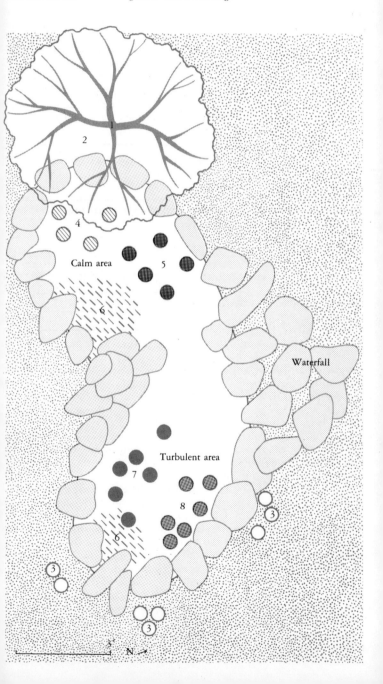

1
2
4
Calm area
5
6
Waterfall
Turbulent area
7
8
6
3
3
3
3
3" N →

foliage is arrowlike rather than straplike, and its flowers are blue.
In the portion of the pond where the water is calm and the delicate
foliage of the Japanese maple serves as backdrop, there are some
water lilies that require still water to thrive. The first is 'Virginia',
an excellent hardy water lily with large, white, nearly double
flowers that bloom during the day over quite a long season. The
second is a tropical night-blooming lily named 'Emily Grant
Hutchings'. This lily blooms from dusk to noon, so you can enjoy
it even after a long day at work. Its vivid cerise color seems to
radiate into the air. It is a profuse bloomer, often producing
clusters of flowers.

Finally, there is another planting of spike rush in front of the
'Emily Grant Hutchings' lilies. Here the airy, open spike rush sets
the stage for the water lily that rests behind it, and it balances the
other area of spike rush in the pond.

A Bog Garden

If water occurs naturally on your property in the form of a stream,
a pond, or a lake, take advantage of it by planting a bog garden.
Simply put, this is a garden of water plants that cannot tolerate
deep inundation. It is best created in the shallows at the edge of
the stream, lake, or pond. You can even construct a bog by using a
shallowly placed PVC liner, but do so only in naturally dry areas.
The bog garden is definitely low-maintenance, and it can be
attractive almost year-round.

Suppose you'd like to create a bog garden within a shallow incurve
of a natural lake or pond. To achieve a natural look, choose plants
that are natural species or varieties rather than more formal-looking
hybrids, and place them so that they do not give the appearance of
having been "designed." Many bog plants tend to spread easily, as
long as the water is shallow enough to meet their needs. If your
site consists of extensive shallow areas, use only clump-forming
types of bog plants, which do not spread rapidly, such as most
water lilies, golden club, or water arum.

Some excellent plants for a bog garden include the weeping willow,
which can provide an elegant background and gives the appearance
of water cascading from a fountain into the lawn or bog below, and
the graceful cat-tail, *Typha laxmannii,* which has beautiful four-foot-
tall foliage that arches into the air before bending downward. Its
flowing lines are perfect mimics of those of the willow.

A collection of arrowheads, *Sagittaria latifolia,* might be used for
subtle contrast to a willow and cat-tails because of their small
size—about 18 to 24 inches—and different foliage shape. This
genus of plants offers delicate white flowers in summer, but their
real beauty is in their arrow-shaped foliage. Both these and the cat-
tails are spreading plants that may have to be kept under control by
pulling up some from time to time.

Another attractive bog plant is the yellow snowflake, *Nymphoides geminata*, related to the white snowflake suggested for the formal garden. This plant has several attractive features: Its chocolate-brown foliage, intricately patterned with green veins, floats on the water's surface; and from spring through fall, there are delicate yellow flowers on stems that reach several inches above the contrasting foliage. This is another plant that spreads.

Water-tolerant irises are wonderful in bog gardens, serving as both backdrops and accents. The yellow flag, *Iris pseudacorus,* has three- to four-foot straplike foliage and masses of beautiful yellow blooms in spring. The Siberian iris, *Iris sibirica,* reaches approximately 36 inches and offers the same elegant foliage as the other water-tolerant irises. Its exquisite, showy purple flowers bloom from mid- to late spring and contrast with the blooms of yellow iris.

Golden club, *Orontium aquaticum,* is an excellent shallow-water plant for the front of a bog garden. It is a clump-forming plant that reaches up to 12 inches in height and has bunches of radiating, lance-shaped leaves and upward-arching white flower spikes tipped with brilliant yellow. Try placing this plant next to some yellow snowflakes and in front of several yellow water irises to complement them in both foliage shape and flower color.

These and many other bog plants can transform a wet, rather uninspiring site into one that is luxuriant, visually pleasing, and easy to care for.

Maintaining Your Water Garden

A water garden is easy to care for in summer, when the tasks are maintaining the water level by refilling it periodically, applying any fertilizers that plant suppliers suggest, removing spent flowers and leaves, and controlling spreading plants.

As the leaves begin to fall in autumn, stop fertilizing your hardy plants. After the first few frosts have damaged them, prune away the stems and dead leaves and lower the pots they are planted in to the bottom of the pool. If there is danger that their rootstocks may freeze—that is, that ice will form even at the bottom of your pool—remove the hardy plants and store them in their containers in a dark, cool area such as a cellar. Keep them moist and covered with a sheet of plastic until spring. Treat tender plants, such as tropical water lilies, as annuals; either discard them and replace them next year, or move them into a greenhouse pool.

Remember to leave the water in your pool all winter long. This keeps it from heaving as the surrounding earth freezes and thaws.

Drama in the Landscape

Whether you start simply, with a few choice aquatic plants in a small free-form pond, or more ambitiously, with a large formal pool or waterfall, your new water garden will reward your efforts soon after planting. It will add a unique sense of beauty, mystery, and romance to your landscape.

Water Gardens   *Listings in the Source column are page references to individual Taylor's Guides. A key to title abbreviations appears on page 11.*

	Source	*Zones*
Plant Choices		
Acer palmatum Japanese maple	S-293	5–8
Ajuga reptans Bugleweed	G-293	3–8
Asclepias tuberosa Butterfly weed	P-294	4–8
Cabomba caroliniana Washington plant	D-393	6–10
Eleocharis montevidensis Spike rush	D-395	6–9
Elodea canadensis Water-weed	D-391	3–10
Hosta spp. Plantain-lily	G-330	4–8
Iberis sempervirens Candytuft	P-352	4–8
Ilex crenata 'Helleri' Japanese holly	S-354	5–8
Iris pseudacorus Yellow flag	P-355	5–7
Iris sibirica Siberian iris	D-399	3–8
Juniperus horizontalis Creeping juniper	G-334	3–9
Liriope muscari Blue lily-turf	P-364	6–10
Marsilia mutica Four-leaf water clover	D-393	3–10
Miscanthus sinensis Japanese silver grass	G-433	5–9
Muscari armeniacum Grape-hyacinth	B-350	4–7
Nymphaea 'Emily Grant Hutchings' Water lily	D-398	3–10
Nymphaea 'Pink Sensation' Water lily	D-394	2–10
Nymphaea 'Virginia' Water lily	D-398	2–10
Nymphoides cristatum White snowflake	D-395	6–10
Orontium aquaticum Golden club	D-399	6–10
Pennisetum alopecuroides Fountain grass	G-435	5–9
Pontederia cordata Pickerel rush	D-394	3–9
Sagittaria latifolia Arrowhead	D-398	3–10
Sedum spp. Stonecrop	P-401	4–8
Typha laxmannii Graceful cat-tail	D-394	3–10

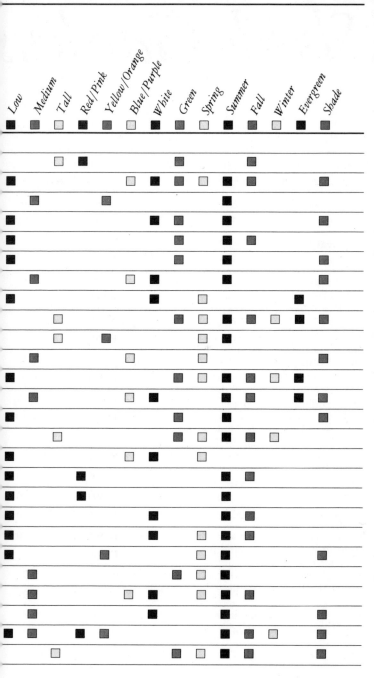

Shade Gardens

Panayoti and Gwen Kelaidis

Whether you are planning a shade garden because you already have a shady area in your yard or because you want to grow shade-loving plants, you have embarked on an intriguing type of gardening. Not only are shade plants very different from sun lovers, but the very mood of shade gardens is distinctive. Many of the standard border annuals and perennials require abundant sunlight to thrive, and so you must look to a new palette of plants.

Survival Strategies
Flowers, shrubs, and trees that grow well in the shade have different physiological strategies to survive out of direct sun. Some kinds gather light rays more efficiently, simply by having more chlorophyll per leaf surface, and thus are darker green. Others produce immense leaves with huge surface areas, allowing them to collect light for photosynthesis and thus make enough food even in low light. Still other shade plants, such as many forest flowers, are ephemerals. They pop into rapid growth in late winter, bloom, and then disappear entirely—both leaves and blossoms—as the leafy canopy overhead closes out the sun.

The sizes, habits, and needs of shade-tolerant plants are as varied and complicated as those of sun-lovers. By understanding the types of shade and soil you are faced with, you can match plants suited to the site and transform problem areas into beautiful landscapes. Bare corners sheltered by an overhanging roof become serene retreats, and scraggly lawns struggling for survival under tall trees turn into intriguing compositions when the right plants are introduced. The effects that can be achieved in a shade garden are just as colorful and pleasing as any sunny border of annuals, perennials, or shrubs.

Shade on the North Side
Do you have a shady area on the north side of your home? The cool light in such places is ideal for herbaceous perennials from cold climates that might succumb to heat damage in sunny spots. Ferns, in particular, respond to locations where their fronds can unravel out of the spring sun. Bordering a simple path with primroses and ferns can transform the north side of a building into a restful haven. Be sure to incorporate humus into the soil and mulch the whole bed with leaf mold or well-rotted compost.

Shade Under a Large Tree
Perhaps the classic area of frustration for many gardeners is the overgrown shade tree that casts such heavy shade that the lawn and flowers grow wispy and weak. The first step is to see whether tree limbs can be removed for 15 to 20 feet up the trunk without disfiguring it; such pruning will allow additional light to penetrate the canopy. Of course, the problem here may be not only the amount of shade, but also that moisture and nutrients are being sapped from the soil by the giant tree.

Before doing any additional planting in such a spot, it's a good idea
to incorporate generous amounts of manure, compost, peat moss,
and whatever soil-loosening amendments you can find. Under trees
as competitive as Norway maples or poplars, you must exclude the
tree roots from the soil in which you grow plants, either by
establishing the plants in containers, or by using a weed barrier
cloth that prevents tree roots from coming up into the surface layer
of soil. In lighter shade under such trees as oaks, it is the natural
replenishment of your soil with compost and leaves every fall that
will encourage vigorous growth of perennials at ground level.
In lighter shade areas, try combining lush plantings of shade-loving
bulbs such as snowdrops, winter aconite, and scillas with hardy
perennials such as hostas, lilies, veronicas, and phlox. The bulbs
will have safely become dormant by the time the perennials bloom.

Shade Cast by Hedges or Fences
Like giant trees, tall hedges and fences often cast extensive shade,
making these areas difficult garden spots. Moreover, hedges, like
trees, have tremendous root systems that can deprive smaller garden
plants of nutrition. But with a little care, additional water during
dry spells, and some extra fertilization, your hedge or fence will
provide an artistic background for a long-lived, dramatic shady
border. Most sunny-garden perennial border plants have
shade-loving counterparts. Leopard's bane is the sunflower for
shade, and astilbes will often perform better in part shade than in
full sun. Goatsbeard and bugbane, while barely noticeable in the
sunny garden, are practically fluorescent in the shade. Other
fine flowering choices for the shade of a hedge or fence are
cardinal-flower, bigroot cranesbill, and wall cress; the standby
pachysandra makes an excellent edge or filler.

Assessing the Degree of Shade
All forms of shade are not the same, and the type of shade in your
garden will affect your choice of plants and garden design. There
are six basic types of shade: dense, high, dry, situational, and
oblique, as well as the shade created by lath houses and arbors.

Dense Shade
Perhaps the most obvious shade is created by trees. All trees give
shade in summer. Evergreens also provide shade in the winter,
creating even cooler conditions. Deciduous tree shade varies a great
deal in density: Honey locusts and oaks give considerably less dense
shade than maples, so that a wider variety of plants may be grown
under the former. A maple's dense shade may limit plantings to
early spring wildflowers and annuals of tropical origin. Some trees
reduce understory growth by root competition. For example, the
silver maple has so many surface-feeding roots that very little
nutrition or water is left for other plants. Only a few very

aggressive plants, such as periwinkle or bishop's weed, can grow in its shade.

The soil itself may be altered by the type of tree. Pines and oaks, for example, create an acidic soil through the decomposition of their yearly fall of leaves and needles. Woodland plants such as trilliums and hepaticas thrive in their shade, as do azaleas, rhododendrons, and many members of the blueberry family. There are plants suited to grow beneath any kind of tree—except evergreens with branches sweeping down to the ground.

Ground covers are especially useful for filling dense shade beneath several large shade trees—replacing lawn, which needs greater sun. These low-growing plants have pleasing foliage much of the year and dramatic flowers throughout the spring. They tolerate a wide range of conditions, provided there is some humus incorporated in the soil and the site is never dry. Excellent choices include sweet woodruff, *Phlox stolonifera,* and foamflower.

High Shade

Cast by tall trees without low branches, high shade provides more light than dense shade. Light comes in from the sides. More air circulates under high trees, and the garden certainly conveys an expansive feeling. Many plants thrive in high shade, including small trees such as dogwood and redbud, woodland shrubs such as sassafras and witch hazel, rhododendrons, azaleas, and a tremendous range of wildflowers. Annuals like wax begonias, which flower best with a little sun, are the most successful here.

Dry Shade

This type of shade is often created by thirsty tree roots, or it can occur in dry climates where irrigation next to a building is impractical. Dry shade is one of the most challenging kinds of shade for the gardener. Only a handful of tough perennials thrive in these conditions: Sweet woodruff, pachysandra, English ivy, and bigroot cranesbill are ground covers that have successfully adapted to dry, shady conditions.

Situational Shade

Artificial boundaries—such as a house, fence, or hedge—separate and shade the outdoors through their placement, or situation. The shade on the north side of a building is very constant. Here ferns can be grown with great success, and the bright colors of tuberous begonias and impatiens may be added to the summer coolness. In sunny climates, situational shade is an ideal place to grow many broadleaf evergreens that would scorch in the winter sun beneath deciduous trees. It is also perfect for a cool rock garden.

Oblique Shade

The subtle shade given by a terrain that slopes to the north is called oblique shade. Since the sun's rays hit the ground at an oblique angle, total radiation and thus soil temperatures are much lower here than on a flat soil surface. The reduction in temperature makes for a longer, more constant snow cover in winter and less evaporation in summer. Many woodland plants, such as epimediums and primulas, will tolerate considerable sun if their roots are cool and never parched. Plants from northerly climes and from high elevations, such as the many variations of heather, may succeed in oblique shade better than in dense low shade or sunnier places.

Lath Houses and Arbors
Many types of artificial structures can create moving, speckled shade approximating the shade of woodlands without tree-root competition. In dry climates it is sometimes impractical to wait for tree cover, and you may want to create your own temporary or even permanent shade by building a lath house.

Laths are thin strips of wood. In building a lath house, align the strips from north to south so that shadows move across plants perpendicularly as the sun goes from east to west. In this way, no plants receive too much or too little sunlight over the course of the day. Arbors are excellent substitutes for trees if you wish to grow vines, such as clematis, that enjoy sun but need a cool root run.

Creating Multilevel Shade Gardens
Shade doesn't limit you to one size of plant. Just as you have a variety of plant options suitable for each type of shade, you can easily combine plants of different heights for a multilevel garden. Beneath your shade-casting tree, an understory of lower trees and shrubs and a third level of flowers and low ground covers can thrive. In layering plants, your composition will gain depth, texture, and personality.

Trees range in mature height from about 15 to more than 100 feet. If you have tall trees in your garden, consider adding an understory of shorter flowering trees, perhaps including shadbush, dogwood, or redbud. Large and small shrubs, useful for short periods of bloom and for fall color, form the next layer—viburnums, witch hazels, spicebush, sassafras, and many more.

Spring ephemerals, a unique class of plants that do all their growing in the brief spring period before the trees leaf out, are unique pleasures in the shade garden. Anemones, bloodroot, dutchman's-breeches, and a host of other woodland beauties can be combined in stunning array with spring bulbs. Daffodils in particular thrive in light shade, unlike tulips, which prefer more sun. Squills, anemones, and many ranunculus love the shade and coolness.

For summer color, there is quite a choice of flowers. Among good perennials are the many columbines, phlox, wood lilies, cardinal-

Shade Gardens

For a composition strong in depth and texture, layer plants beneath a tall shade tree. Start with an understory of flowering trees next to the trunk.

Then add small shrubs, perhaps chosen for spring bloom or fall foliage. Use shade-tolerant flowers or ground covers for the final transition to the lawn or patio.

flower, hostas, and astilbes. Impatiens and begonias represent the best of the summer annuals. Others that seem to prefer cool, shady spots include edging lobelias, garden balsam, and pansies. Annual plantings in shade are apt to weather the summer heat better than their sunny counterparts.

To cover a bare fence or a tree trunk, use vines of grape and woodbine. Try ground covers to create a stretch of unmown greenery: Corsican mint or periwinkle for quietude, spotted dead nettle or the variegated goutweed where a livelier effect is desired. For a lawn in light shade, there are many of the fine fescues, but the exact mixture that will perform best depends upon your conditions. Check with a local expert and plant a mixture of grasses designed for shade in your climate.

Using Foliage Plants

Flower colors need not be the main focus of the shade garden. Foliage is intrinsically artistic. The many shapes of leaves, the details of their design, the fine tracery of veins can be as showy as blossoms. Plants that originated in woodland settings often have leaves of special size, delicacy, and hue. Their textures vary from the papery thinness of columbines to the leathery toughness of rhododendrons. In planning your garden, think about the effects of the foliage in all seasons, particularly in midsummer when greens ripen to their lustrous best. Imagine the deep green of giant herbs gunnera or rodgersia alongside the fine laciness of maidenhair ferns and meadow rues. Or the splendid, glaucous, thick texture of a giant gray-leaved hosta contrasting with a purple-tinged ground cover such as ajuga. An artistic imagination can create a symphony of greens.

Variegated foliage is especially effective in a shady setting. Too many types in a small area may create a carnival atmosphere, but a properly sited plant with mottled foliage gives the impression of dappled sunbeams, almost surrealistic on a cloudy day. Golden-leaved plants can look ill or anemic in a sunny garden, but in the shade they seem to glow with an inner light, as if they had absorbed a portion of the sunset.

Fall colors of trees and shrubs are the special glories of a shade garden. What can be brighter than sugar maple leaves clinging to a mossy path after a rain? Many deciduous plants are even showier in the fall than in the spring. Take a little care in choosing plants with complementary fall colors to make the garden even more attractive as a place to work, relax, and entertain in the cool autumn temperatures.

Adding Shady Areas for Summer Comfort

Consider where shade is in relation to your house and kitchen. You may plan to add or expand a deck, patio, or walk where it is comfortable to stay outside in the hot weather. Shade gardens built around such features can be so beautiful and inviting that you will find yourself spending much of your leisure time outdoors. Here the garden can serve not only as a handsome backdrop but also as a screen to block an unpleasant view or improve a nice one. A few well-sited trees, such as honey locust and rain tree, can quickly transform a sterile, narrow backyard into an intimate, peaceful space. Avoid trees that will easily shed leaves, petals, or seeds— such as crabapples and hawthorns—and those with unpleasant-smelling fruits or flowers, like pear trees.

Creating a Year-round Garden
All gardens should strive to be attractive in all seasons, yet shade gardens are prone to a cycle of excesses in the course of the year. Plan to follow the explosion of ephemeral wildflowers in spring with the summer's glorious display of annuals. Choose a variety of plants with interesting bark or evergreen foliage to liven up the long winter season. A judicious selection of spring bulbs and wildflowers, annuals and perennials, and shrubs chosen for both flowers and fall color can fill the entire calendar year with garden pleasure. Why be satisfied with less? What year-round tenant would put up with a house that was furnished for only a few months?

Improving the Soil
Most shade-loving plants do well under conditions that are neither too dry nor too dark, as long as considerable humus is incorporated into the soil. The soils naturally formed under trees are very different in structure than soils of open country. They should be well-aerated as well as high in organic matter. A layer of leaves or compost on the surface will help replenish the humus, keep down weeds, maintain soil moisture, and provide continuing nourishment. Wood bark mulches give the shade garden a well-groomed appearance while serving many of the functions of leaf mulch. This is often used around trees and shrubs, but choose finer-textured leaf mold for wildflower or annual plantings. If you have a chipping machine, use the chips as topdressing.

Maintenance
Pruning is a crucial part of shade gardening. In plants more sun-loving in character, the nature of shade will encourage somewhat lankier growth. Remember—although excessive pruning will often encourage plants to send out even longer, weaker, and less attractive shoots—do prune feeble and low growth from trees to let as much light onto the planting areas as possible. In shade gardens, because there is usually less heat and wind to dry plants, watering is not as much of a problem, but be aware that trees and shrubs in intensively planted shade gardens will often steal much of the available moisture, so supplemental watering will be necessary.

Choosing Plants

As in any garden, the plants you choose depend on the effect you want to create as well as on the site itself. Once you have selected an area, determine what sort of shade you have, then try to assess what kind of planting scheme is appropriate. If you are situated in the country, a naturalistic woodland garden is a logical choice, using spring ephemerals, ferns, and bulbs. Bloodroot, wild ginger, and wild bleeding heart are other selections.

If you are in a highly structured urban setting, you may want to emphasize formal elements. For example, a balanced pair of dramatic rhododendrons—one plant on each side of the bed—not only give a formal look but provide long-season spring color and sumptuous evergreen leaves year-round. Miniature boxwoods, Japanese hollies, and the annuals impatiens and begonia are especially valuable for this style.

A Refreshing Oasis

Whatever plants you choose for your shade garden, the foliage and the many flowers will provide you with an oasis to refresh and delight. Whether secluded deep in shadow or dancing in dappled sun, the composition can give pleasure throughout the year.

Shade Gardens   Listings in the Source column are page references to individual Taylor's Guides. A key to title abbreviations appears on page 11.   Under Zones, W and C indicate warm- or cool-season annuals.

	Source	Zones
Plant Choices		
Adiantum pedatum Maidenhair fern	D-407	3–8
Ajuga spp. Bugleweed	G-293	3–8
Aquilegia canadensis Common columbine	P-288	4–8
Asarum canadense Wild ginger	P-294	4–7
Astilbe spp. Astilbe	P-296	5–7
Begonia grandis Hardy begonia	P-299	7–9
Calluna vulgaris Heather	G-306	4–6
Cercis canadensis Eastern redbud	T-317	4–8
Cimicifuga spp. Bugbane	P-312	3–8
Cornus florida Flowering dogwood	T-321	4–9
Dicentra cucullaria Dutchman's-breeches	P-320	4–8
Epimedium grandiflorum Longspur epimedium	P-328	4–7
Galanthus spp. Snowdrops	B-317	4–6
Gentiana spp. Gentian	P-338	5–7
Geranium macrorrhizum Bigroot cranesbill	P-340	4–7
Helleborus spp. Hellebore	P-346	4–8
Hosta spp. Plantain-lily	P-350	4–8
Impatiens wallerana Busy Lizzy	A-346	W
Iris spp. Iris	B-334	3–8
Ligularia spp. Ligularia	P-361	4–7
Lilium spp. Lily	B-340	4–7
Liriope spicata Creeping lily-turf	G-339	4–8
Mahonia aquifolium Oregon grape holly	S-369	4–8
Pachysandra terminalis Japanese spurge	G-348	3–8
Paxistima canbyi Canby paxistima	S-377	3–8
Quercus alba White oak	T-389	4–9
Rhododendron spp. Rhododendron/azalea	S-390	4–8
Sorbus aucuparia European mountain ash	T-397	4–7
Tricyrtis hirta Toad lily	P-411	5–8
Uvularia grandiflora Big merrybells	P-413	5–7

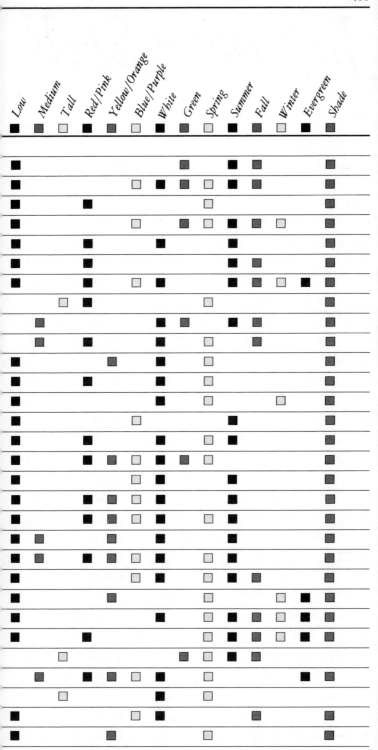

Japanese-Style

Elvin McDonald

A Japanese garden is a place of tranquility and harmony, an understated suggestion of natural beauty meant to encourage contemplation. While it may be inspired by the lush greenery, rocky waterfalls, or rolling hills of Japan, it does not simply re-create such natural scenes. It borrows ideas and elements, arranging relatively few plants, rocks, and structures to perfectly suit a particular site. Its spare lines and spaciousness are soothing in a way that busier Western designs are not. This, combined with the fact that they can be adapted to almost any space, makes Japanese-style gardens the perfect answer to the landscaping needs of many Western gardeners.

Aesthetic Principles
The traditional Japanese garden represents a perfect union of architecture and landscape. House and garden are intimately related, with every important interior space linked to the exterior by a window or other opening. The designer's goal is to effect a heightened awareness of all the elements that make up an arranged space. Sounds as well as sights are important, as is the way the composition will look in all seasons, all types of weather, and at any time of day. Structures such as shelters, paved pathways, and lanterns make the garden a place of welcome and comfort and control the observer's movement through the space.

Spacious Effects
A feeling of spaciousness comes from limiting the number of plants and manipulating scale. Japanese gardens are never designed as mere collections of plants. Each plant is deliberately chosen to play a role, sometimes small but nonetheless vital to the whole picture. The placement of these selected plants creates illusions of depth and space. Large or bright elements fill the foreground, and objects decrease in size and assertiveness the farther back they are placed. For example, the largest rocks, trees, or islands are set closest to the viewer, as are the showiest plants. Constructed features such as walks, bridges, and lanterns are kept small to make the surrounding areas look wider.

Open spaces and calm expanses are as crucial as arrangements of plants. Flat planes created by expanses of water, sand, moss, pebbles, or ground covers combine with low roof lines and other horizontal elements to give a placid feeling. Elements are balanced asymmetrically, with the main mass placed to one side of the scene; water is often added for its refreshing appearance, movement, and sound.

A Reverence for Age
Philosophical principles of age versus youth are expressed in the choice and even the pruning of some plants. The Japanese revere maturity, and their gardens emphasize the lasting over the

Gardens

ephemeral. Evergreens are preferable to deciduous plants, making the designs unaffected by seasonal change. Deciduous ginkgo, maple, and azalea foliage may add fall accents, but unchanging pines and hollies play the major roles. In the spring, azaleas, peonies, and perhaps a strategically placed clump of Japanese iris provide bloom, but these pass fleetingly, soon to be absorbed into tranquil surroundings of greens, blues, and muted earth colors. A wisteria—no matter how spectacular with its drooping, deliciously scented spring flowers and canopy of rustling leaves—is valued most for its old, gnarled, intertwining branches, all the more dramatic coated with ice or snow.

To simulate age, relatively young plants are often pruned or trained to look as if they've weathered many storms. Sometimes the rootball of a pine is planted at an angle so that its branches resemble the sails of a ship about to depart the shore. A young tree can be made to look windswept by pruning away branches and leaving only those aimed in one direction.

Essential Elements

Two elements common to most Japanese gardens are bamboo and rocks. Bamboo appears as both plant and structure. Living bamboos are used as screens, featured standing alone, or as a mostly evergreen backdrop for winter interest. The bamboos may act as trees, shrubs, or ground covers, or they may be clipped as hedges. Cut bamboo is crafted into posts, gates, and fences.

When steamed, bamboo can be bent into almost any shape. Bent split canes are often used as trip-rails to guide visitors. Another traditional bamboo construction is the *tsukubai,* or water basin, which is fed through a bamboo pipe so that water makes musical sounds as it drips. There is also a bamboo scoop made for drinking and washing, and a decorative item called a *shishi-odoshi,* or "deer-scarer," a sort of water scarecrow made of bamboo piping set on a pivot. Driven by running water, it produces a periodic booming sound that echoes through the garden.

It is quite possible to create a Japanese garden without plants, water, paths, or hills, but never without rocks. These may vary from boulders to pebbles, smooth or rough, bare or moss-covered. A tall and soaring rock creates excitement, while a flat and sprawling one adds to feelings of calmness and space. The Japanese consider each rock an individual having force, energy, and presence, and constantly changing with the weather and the movements of the sun. The art of placing rocks in the garden is said to be best learned by "listening to what they say."

Traditional Garden Types

The basic principles of spaciousness, manipulating space, and revering age have been applied in various settings throughout Japanese history. There are at least four traditional garden types:

the hill-and-pond garden, the dry landscape garden, the tea garden, and the stroll garden.

The Hill-and-Pond Garden

One of the oldest Japanese garden forms is the hill-and-pond garden, in which nature is imitated by man-made constructions. Hills and pond do not occur naturally but are built to represent mountains and ocean. The garden may rise from a piece of flat ground, making use of the earth excavated from the pond to form hills. (The famous Hill-and-Pond Garden at Brooklyn Botanic Garden was originally a flat city garbage dump.) Shrubs in such a garden are shaped by faithful, purposeful trimming to complement the undulating contours of mountains and clouds, as well as to maintain the appropriate scale. Trees are pruned and trained to look old and windswept. A major portion of a hill-and-pond garden can be seen from any point within it. The design is a fairly straightforward reproduction of familiar Japanese landscapes.

The Dry Landscape

Associated with Zen temples, the dry landscape garden fills a relatively small space and is meant to be an aid to meditation. It is designed for viewing from a veranda and is not to be entered except for maintenance. Nature is reduced to stones, raked gravel, and moss, creating what might be called a minimalist garden design. There are few, if any, plants, and the arrangement of rocks and raked patterns in the gravel suggests islands in a stream. A variety of raked patterns were used traditionally to evoke different movements of water—waves, ripples, or whirlpools, for example.

The Tea Garden

In the traditional *roji,* or tea garden, a stepping-stone path represents a mountain trail leading to and providing the setting for the teahouse. There is a stone lantern for light in the evening and a stone water basin in which guests rinse mouths and hands to purify themselves before the ritual tea ceremony. The plants in tea gardens are mostly evergreens, and the goal is to create a subdued atmosphere. A tea garden may be located some distance from the house, in the same way as a gazebo might be placed in a Western landscape.

The Stroll Garden

Stepping stones and stone lanterns also occur in a stroll garden, which sometimes includes a teahouse or a pavilion. An entire stroll garden cannot be viewed from any one point; experiencing it requires active participation. Movement through the garden is directed around a pond filled with islands and perhaps crossed by a footbridge. The path leads left, then right, to gradually reveal different vistas. The concept of *shakkei,* or borrowed scenery, may perceptually enlarge the garden. This involves leaving a space through which a distant vista can be seen—a mountain, perhaps, glimpsed through a row of trees.

Making Your Own Japanese-Style Garden
Traditional Japanese garden styles may at first seem unrelated to American gardens or yards, but in fact many of the principles at work in these designs are extremely effective and appealing here. Arrangements are simple and easy to care for, and they can be effective—especially in small areas—when they include only a few plants, or even none at all.

Designs for Entryways
To lend an elegant distinction to your entryway, consider combining elements from both the traditional tea garden—subtle dwarf evergreens and perhaps a small statue—and the dry landscape—decorative pebbles surrounding the plants. Or you can borrow the idea of stepping stones and pavilions from the stroll garden to highlight a side door. Lay a winding trail of flagstones leading to the door, and set a shingle-roofed wooden or bamboo arbor in front of it. Train a Japanese wisteria on the arbor for beautiful color and fragrance in spring and summer. Even the small, tea-garden touch of a stone lantern placed at the beginning of a walk or beside the garden steps will lend a special aura to any design.

Courtyards
A city courtyard is another site where a Japanese-style garden comprised of very few elements can be very useful. Based loosely on principles of the dry landscape, it could be as simple as a large boulder covered with moss, placed next to a Kousa dogwood tree and surrounded by water-polished stones. Such basic elements and forms afford an enticing view in all seasons, but the design would be especially effective in winter.

A Small Side Yard
If you have a narrow side yard that you reach through sliding glass doors, you may want to create a Japanese vista. Install a bamboo fence or screen opposite the sliding glass doors and set a Japanese statue, stone lantern, or water basin in front of it. Add stones, ferns, lily-turf, and mosses—but not too much at once. Give yourself time to become acquainted with the various elements. Add and take away, studying the effects at different times. Like the traditional dry landscape, this garden is designed with the view in mind, but unlike the model, it includes plants and is meant to be walked through. The goal is to develop a space that gives you visual pleasure and, in true Japanese tradition, allows you to escape from the pressures of life.

Japanese-Style Gardens

In traditional dry landscape gardens, rakes were used to create patterns in gravel. They symbolized movements of water, as shown below.

Calm water

Flowing water

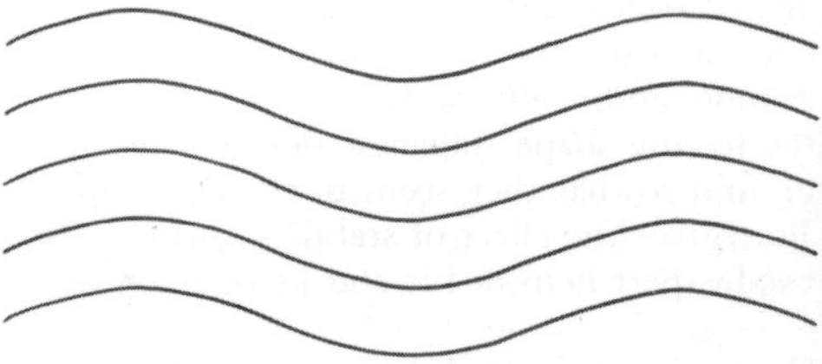

Waves

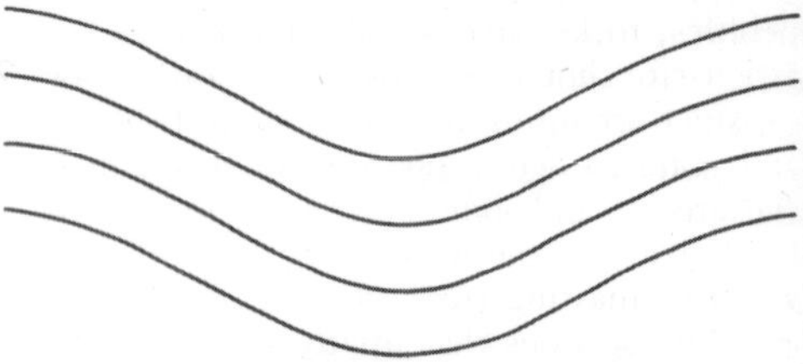

Floating fish net

Ripples

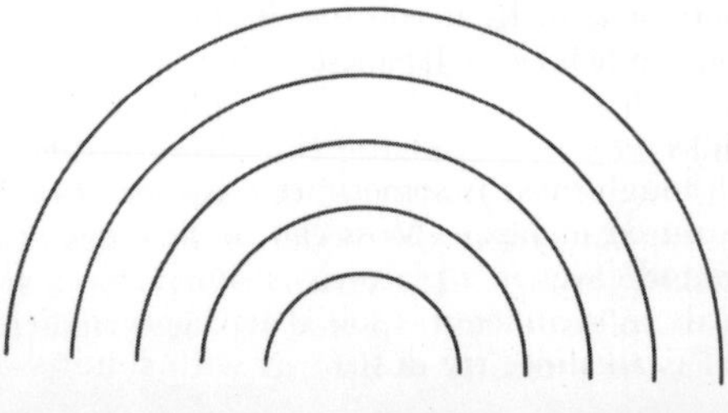

*Try these or other
abstract designs of
your own invention.*

Dry Landscapes for Many Sites

A simple dry landscape, using few or no plants, is easy to adapt
to a variety of sites. Although it can be enjoyed in any climate,
it is especially useful in arid regions. In a small, flat area create a
spare, refreshing design using only a two-inch layer of fine gray or
cream-colored gravel. An unlikely material that also works well as a
ground cover is turkey grit, available through livestock feed and
grain outlets. To keep weeds from pushing through the gravel, you
may want to lay down a sheet of plastic first, making holes in it
every few feet to allow water to drain through. Smooth the gravel
or grit over the plastic with the straight side of a metal garden
rake, and use the tined side to draw patterns.

A more ambitious garden could include one or several large rocks of
interesting shape. Japanese designers often set these deep in the
ground so that they seem to rise out of it from their widest point.
This gives the effect of stability and permanence. You will probably
need expert help to lift and place the rocks.

Designing Larger Areas

While it is best to limit a Japanese-style design for a small area to
pebbles, rocks, and perhaps a few well-chosen plants, a design for a
larger site should include more plants. If your yard has contours,
consider arranging it according to some of the principles of the hill-
and-pond garden—choosing rounded plants, dramatically shaped
evergreens, and some flowering plants for seasonal highlights. In a
level area, use the winding paths and screened views of the stroll
garden—massing trees, shrubs, and ground covers to divide the
area into sections that invite a visitor to walk through it. In
general, rely on plants for structure, letting Japanese aesthetic
principles guide your choice and arrangement.

Appropriate Plants

The best plants for a Japanese-style garden offer either unchanging
architectural forms or elegant, simple leaves or flowers that accent
without overpowering the scene. Fortunately, many of the most
popular Western garden plants originated in Japan, so it is easy to
find and grow the right types. Japan's climate is similar to that in
many areas of the U.S., with lows in the neighborhood of zero
degrees Fahrenheit, highs around 90 degrees, and 30 inches or
more of rainfall. If you live in a colder, drier, or warmer climate,
you can achieve a Japanese look by selecting locally adapted plants.

Moss

Although moss is sometimes considered a weed in the West, it is
treasured in Japan. Moss can be an attractive solution if you need a
ground cover in a place too shaded and moist for grass. Mosses need
shade in summer and soil that is acid and moist all year. If your
soil is alkaline, try dusting it with sulfur to make it more acidic.

Few nurseries carry mosses, so to start your own planting you'll have to transplant pieces of moss sod from the wild or from other parts of your own landscape. Always avoid collecting more than you need.

The cool days of spring and fall are the best times to transplant moss. Lift sections up carefully with a knife or trowel. Keep the moss moist and replant it quickly by pressing it down into loosened soil. To plant it on a rock, first cover the rock surface with a mixture of soil and water. Help the moss become established by watering it well, keeping the weeds out, and promptly removing any leaves that may fall and compact on its surface in winter.

Ground Covers and Ferns

One ground cover seen very often in Japanese landscapes is the lily-turf (*Liriope* species). Originally from Japan and China, it adapts easily to American gardens and comes in a variety of colors from green to nearly black, sometimes striped with white or cream. Whether dwarf—1 to 6 inches—or tall—12 to 18 inches—its effect is the same: a dense fountain of grasslike leaves that are essentially evergreen in all but the coldest climates.

Another popular Japanese landscape plant is the hosta, or plantain-lily. Some miniatures are only six inches tall, while others form massive clumps two feet tall or more. Some have plain green leaves, others are chartreuse to yellow-green, and still others are nearly blue. There are also variegated cultivars.

Southern wild ginger makes an elegant ground cover in partial shade and moist, humusy soil. It has perfectly heart-shaped leaves that are appealing en masse.

Any fern that grows well locally may be used in a Japanese-style garden. One favorite that is widely distributed in the temperate northern hemisphere is the lady fern, *Athyrium filix-femina.* Other likely choices include the maidenhair, *Adiantum pedatum;* rock polypody, *Polypodium virginianum;* and Christmas fern, *Polystichum acrostichoides.*

Of all suitable ground covers for a Japanese garden, the Japanese spurge, *Pachysandra terminalis,* is perhaps familiar to the most Americans. It looks best covering large areas, uninterrupted except possibly by an important shrub, tree, or fountain of tall grass.

Perennial Flowers and Vines

The flowers in your Japanese-style garden should have simple, elegant shapes. Several familiar wildflowers are appropriate, including jack-in-the-pulpit, *Arisaema triphyllum;* dog-tooth violet, *Erythronium* species; Solomon's-seal, *Polygonatum biflorum* and *P. odoratum;* and purple trillium, *Trillium erectum.* Irises, with their tall, straplike leaves and delicate flowers, are often used in or around ponds. The crested iris; Japanese iris, *Iris kaempferi;* and yellow flag are some of the best.

Use water lilies to add exotic touches to pools or ponds. The hardy types grow best in most areas of the U.S., but if you live in a warm climate, try the dramatic tropical types. If you have space, include the sacred lotus, *Nelumbo nucifera*, with its sweet-scented pink flowers that grow up to ten inches across. (See the essay on Water Gardens for instructions on planting water lilies.)

Shrubs and Trees

Because of their size and permanence, shrubs and trees are used in Japanese gardens to create perceptual illusions or dramatic effects. They are also valued for their long lives. Among the best evergreens to try in American gardens are littleleaf box, various hollies and junipers, and dwarf forms of Norway spruce, white pine, and *Cryptomeria japonica*—especially the cultivar 'Elegans Nana'. *Leucothoe* species, leatherleaf mahonia, Japanese photinia, and the weeping forms of English yew and Canada hemlock are also attractive, as are the Hinoki false cypress, lace-bark pine, Scotch pine, and "Japanese" forms of cedar, black pine, and umbrella pine. Use flowering evergreens for seasonal accents. Evergreen azaleas and rhododendrons, Japanese skimmia, *Camellia japonica*, mountain laurel, and the glossy abelia are some of the best.

Deciduous trees and shrubs offer delicate flowers or unusual foliage. For flowers at midlevel on the horizon use shrubs such as the Japanese beautyberry, buttercup winter hazel, smokebush, and tree peony. Some of the best showy flowering trees include serviceberry, Kousa dogwood, star and Loebner magnolias, Japanese stewartia, and Siebold viburnum. Cherry trees are famous in Japanese gardens for their clouds of spring blossoms, and among the best to try are the Japanese flowering cherry, the weeping Higan cherry, and the Yoshino cherry.

The Japanese maple is a familiar sight in traditional Japanese gardens, with its spreading branches and rich red fall foliage. Include other deciduous trees for their beautiful leaves: paperbark maple, corkscrew willow, dawn redwood, Katsura tree, maidenhair tree (*Ginkgo biloba*), and sour gum or tupelo (*Nyssa sylvatica*).

A Calm Beauty

A Japanese-style garden can take many forms, from a courtyard decorated with raked pebbles to a rolling landscape filled with carefully arranged plants. Whatever its scope, it should be planned organically, with the site as starting point, rather than conceived and then forced to fit the available space. Understanding the Japanese philosophy of garden design—the unusual but practical ways of arranging space, structures, and plants—will help you imagine new ways to give your garden a special distinction.

Japanese-Style Gardens	*Listings in the Source column are page references to individual Taylor's Guides. A key to title abbreviations appears on page 11.*

	Source	Zones
Plant Choices		
Abies homolepis Nikko fir	T-291	5–6
Acer griseum Paperbark maple	T-294	5–8
Acer palmatum Japanese maple	S-293	5–8
Adiantum pedatum Maidenhair fern	D-418	3–8
Anemone × *hybrida* Japanese anemone	P-285	5–8
Asarum shuttleworthii Southern wild ginger	G-301	6–8
Berberis thunbergii 'Crimson Pygmy' Barberry	S-301	4–8
Buxus microphylla Littleleaf box	S-304	5–9
Cornus mas Cornelian cherry	T-322	5–7
Cotoneaster horizontalis Rockspray cotoneaster	S-326	5–8
Ginkgo biloba Maidenhair tree	T-341	5–9
Hosta lancifolia Narrow plantain-lily	G-330	4–8
Hydrangea anomala petiolaris Hydrangea	G-394	4–8
Ilex crenata Japanese holly	S-354	6–8
Iris cristata Crested iris	P-354	4–8
Iris pseudacorus Yellow flag	P-355	5–7
Kalmia latifolia Mountain laurel	S-358	5–9
Liriope spp. Lily-turf	G-339	6–10
Magnolia stellata Star magnolia	S-368	3–8
Miscanthus sinensis 'Gracillimus' Maiden grass	G-433	5–9
Nandina domestica Heavenly bamboo	S-373	7–9
Pinus parviflora Japanese white pine	T-376	5–7
Prunus yedoensis Yoshino cherry	T-384	6–8
Rhododendron kaempferi Torch azalea	S-392	5–8
Sasa veitchii Kuma bamboo	G-438	6–9
Wisteria floribunda Japanese wisteria	G-411	4–9

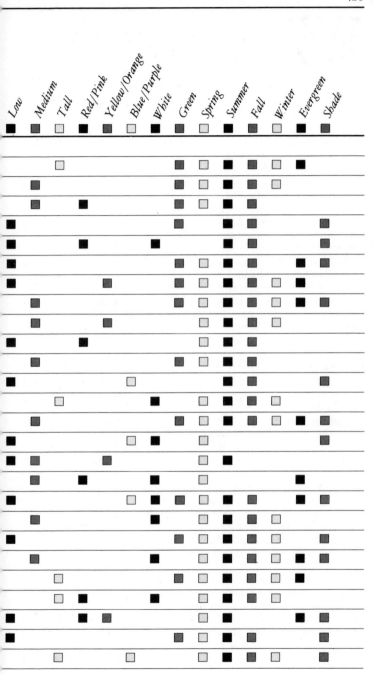

| Low | Medium | Tall | Red/Pink | Yellow/Orange | Blue/Purple | White | Green | Spring | Summer | Fall | Winter | Evergreen | Shade |

Winterscapes

William Mulligan

For most gardeners in northern and temperate climes, winter is a
time of suspended animation, a holding pattern when only the
imagination is active. Practicality dictates preparing the garden for
the seasonal onslaughts of cold, wind, and snow. But nature's allure
is not dispelled by the first frost.

The natural winter terrain has a haunting beauty all its own. With
their muted gray bark, leafless trees create mauve-tinted hillsides,
and when their branches are transformed into a lacy filigree of frost,
the winter canopy seems almost too storybook to be real.

Rather than dismiss winter as a season to be endured, why not plan
an eye-catching landscape? You can enrich your winter garden by
highlighting bark textures, branches, colorful berries, or seductive
fragrances and hues. Numerous hybrids and cultivars offer color,
texture, and unusual form not found in the wild. Grouping your
choices to their best advantage will give your garden impact in all
seasons.

Evaluating Your Garden

First take advantage of existing plantings, formal or naturalistic.
Carefully assess your property in its present state—you may discover
any number of plants with valuable winter appeal.

In looking over your yard, remember that in winter exposed areas
are at the mercy of the elements, creating an environment few
plants can survive. Notice the hills and valleys of your garden—
what areas are open to the harsh climate and which offer seclusion?
Those that are exposed will need especially hardy plants, but by
providing some shelter against the wind and cold, you may well be
able to grow plants not regarded as hardy enough for your locale.
Within your own small landscape or garden such protected areas
may exist naturally. Or you can create them with stands of shrubs
or trees, walls, fences, or other barriers. Bodies of water also
moderate temperature extremes.

Planning a Garden

If you are planning a whole new garden, start small, with either a
pocket garden, a planting limited to just outside a window or a
door, or a diminutive formal garden. Later you can apply what you
have learned, especially about the kinds of plants you value most,
to larger spaces. Whatever the size, make a simple design sketch
before you begin, noting all existing plants as well as suggested
new ones.

Staging is all, and contrasts of every kind attract and delight the
eye. Placing a plant of divergent color, shape, texture, or growth
habit—prostrate or upright, climbing or rounded—alongside an
existing plant emphasizes the outstanding features of both. Don't
overlook the value of mulches for creating color and textural
contrast. Fine- or coarse-ground pine bark, pine needles, buckwheat
hulls, and pebbles provide backdrops to set off and highlight

plantings of every kind. Use the same type of mulch in various areas to help unify your design.

In a winter garden, strong lines—horizontals, verticals, and angles—are starkly delineated. No one kind should dominate; all should be harmoniously combined into an intriguing, pleasing design. You can diminish the impact of the dominating vertical lines of tree trunks or tall ornamental grasses with a horizontal row of small yews, low-growing shrubs, or ground covers such as English ivy or prostrate evergreens. Straight lines may be softened by rounded or open spreading plants, both bare-branched and evergreen.

Color and Texture

Among the vast array of trees and shrubs appropriate for your site, seek those strong in color and texture of bark, or in displays of foliage, berries, flowers, or overall form in winter. When making your selections in spring or fall, keep in mind their often hidden winter characteristics.

Trees

Winter may rob trees of leaves, but in turn, it reveals the beauty of limb surfaces. Birches, with their elegant silvery-white markings, are the deciduous stars of the winterscape. The European white birch has weeping branches that deserve a place of prominence, perhaps installed alone on a broad expanse of lawn or snow. For greater interest in texture and color try the large canoe birch, which unfurls its outer bark in thin, parchmentlike layers. The river birch's brown papery bark peels in strips to uncover new pink wood beneath. As its name indicates, it prefers moist soil and would be well placed alongside a stream or a pond.

The paperbark maple is a fine small tree that looks handsome without leaves. Its orange- to pale brown outer bark peels away in patches, exposing a red-brown inner surface. The valued Oriental cherry presents a graceful form, and some cultivars offer striking satiny red bark. Two species of dogwood have glossy, brightly colored bare stems that slash the winterscape with vertical streaks: *Cornus alba* 'Sibirica' has salmon red stems; *Cornus sericea* 'Flaviramea' light yellow-green.

Trees that retain their leaves are the mainstays of the winter landscape. Many have variegated foliage, and one of the most impressive is thorny eleagnus 'Maculata', with densely packed light green leaves splashed by deep yellow. Variegated Japanese euonymus has white leaf borders on 'Albomarginata' and gold on 'Aureo-marginata'.

Shrubs

The winter garden's most valuable resources, shrubs are cornerstones of appearance and protection. Conifers are essential to the beauty of

Winterscapes

the winterscape, whether for color—such as the soft blue-green of certain spruces—or shape—from majestic natural silhouettes to whimsical topiaries made from yews. For overall design and to accentuate color and texture contrasts, use conifers next to or alternated with broadleaf evergreens.

For a single specimen shrub that you want to stand alone, proudly displaying its green leaves, nothing quite surpasses leatherleaf mahonia, which also has clusters of yellow blooms in early winter. Witch hazel's tiny yellow petals offer delicious fragrance in the depths of winter. Bright, vigorous cultivars are 'Chinese' and 'Hybrid'.

For generous displays of intensely colored fruits and berries, try rockspray cotoneaster, with its clusters of red berries and low, ground-covering form; or common winterberry, with gray bark and orange-red berries. Winged euonymus has orange berries and interestingly mottled bark; scarlet fire thorn 'Lalandei', a good hedge candidate, produces large clusters of bright orange-red berries. Japanese barberry, with red berries on heavily thorned stems, forms the perfect natural barrier against animal and human intruders. Finally, try snowberry for pure white berries.

Silhouetting

Call attention to interesting or intricate plant shapes by using contrasting backgrounds—such as a line of evergreens, a hedge, a wall, or a fence—to set off their silhouettes. This design technique is especially effective in winter. If you are lucky, a blanket of snow will give dramatic contrast to dark branches.

For bizarre bare-branch configuration, nothing exceeds the contortions of Harry Lauder's walking stick, *Corylus avellana* 'Contorta'. Named for the Scottish singer who carried a cane fashioned from one of its crooked stems, this shrub bears large green leaves in summer. But in winter all its branches are revealed to be as twisted as corkscrews, tracing uniquely interesting line patterns on the winterscape and catching the attention of every eye. Another attractively intricate silhouette is the royal azalea.

Flowers in Winter

By concentrating on bulb plants, perennials, and shrubs that bloom well into the beginning and end of the cold season, you can have continuous flowers practically throughout the winter months. Bloom times vary from zone to zone.

Bulbs

Crocus, the welcome harbinger of spring, punctuates the snow with patches of white, purple, and yellow. For early-winter to midwinter bloom, choose *Crocus imperati,* with enchanting, cup-shaped flowers, off-white on the outside and lavender inside. *C. chrysanthus* offers golden yellow bloom from midwinter through early spring. Hybrids of this species are various combinations of cream, yellow, and purple-blue. Pale lilac flowers with yellow centers are provided from mid- to late winter by *C. sieberi*. For similar pale purple color in late winter, try *C. tomasinianus*.

Glory-of-the-snow is the common name for a collection of Mediterranean bulbs featuring short clusters of delicate, star-shaped flowers. As with crocuses, they are excellent choices for brightening lawns, borders, beds, and rock gardens from midwinter on. The blooms of *Chionodoxa luciliae* are bright blue, and the hue of the cultivar 'Pink Giant' is indicated by its name. *C. gigantea* has larger pale blue petals with white centers.

Snowdrop, *Galanthus,* a long-cherished winter staple among northern gardeners, grows best in the shade and shelter of trees and shrubs. Varieties of this bulb differ slightly in shape, color, and markings. Plant several mixed kinds and enjoy a steady bloom from the beginning of winter to mid-spring.

Like the snowdrop, winter aconite needs the protection of a shaded bed or a shrub canopy. This delightful bloomer will carpet the ground with elegant yellow flowers in early winter.

Spring snowflake is a bulbous plant that heartily weathers the worst winter conditions, providing the more exposed areas of your garden with bloom. Its pendulous, bell-shaped white flowers, appearing from mid- to late winter, are delicately tipped with green. In contrast, squill needs as little wind and cold exposure as possible to produce its pale blue, star-shaped flowers in midwinter. Plant them among white snowdrops and yellow winter aconites.

Although most familiar to gardeners as spring bloomers, three species of the daffodil, genus *Narcissus,* are notable for their mid- to late-winter flowering—*N. asturiensis, N. bulbocodium,* and *N. cyclamineus,* whose variety 'February Silver' has orange-yellow trumpets with cream-color petals. All are compact with small, delicate, yellow-trumpet blooms.

Hardy Perennials

Among the self-renewing ornamentals used as border plantings, hellebores and bergenias may be singled out for their significant winter displays. Hellebores are highly susceptible to frosty winter winds and need some sort of protection. Some species maintain glossy, deep green leaves throughout the year, in addition to blooming from midwinter to mid-spring. For example, *Helleborus foetidus* grows to 18 inches and presents clusters of yellowish-green flowers tipped with purple. The evergreen Christmas rose reaches a height of one foot, and its white, saucer-shaped blooms appear in midwinter. The leaves of the Lenten rose drop in winter, giving way to flowers that range in color from white to pink to purple for about two months, after which the foliage returns.

English primrose grows as high as six inches and displays bright yellow flowers in late winter and early spring. The many varieties provide showy displays of off-white, yellow, pink, red, or purple flowers up to two inches across and 12 inches high. The wandering shoots of *Primula juliae* form a three-inch-thick mat of light green leaves, making it an excellent choice for a rocky area. Its tiny reddish-purple blooms abound from late winter to late spring. The 'Wanda' hybrid has one of the most striking and enduring displays of any winter bloomer, with many vivid purple flowers.

Bergenias, dependable favorites for winter beds and borders, are trouble-free. Their large round leaves turn gold or coppery just before flowering and drop as the blooms appear. *Bergenia crassifolia*, the best-known form, grows to 12 inches, with pale pink blooms asserting themselves in midwinter.

Heaths and Heathers

If you especially want pronounced splashes of color throughout the gray days of winter, plant some of the many varieties of heaths, *Erica*, and heathers, *Calluna*. Shrublike in habit—with tiny, needlelike evergreen leaves—most heaths and heathers form low-growing mounds up to 18 inches tall. These tufts bear small, bell-shaped flowers ranging from red through pink to cream and white. Use them in rockeries, along a slope, or in beds with mulch to outline the rounded clumps and complement their color.

Most heaths and heathers require acidic soil, but the two heaths that are the most vigorous against winter conditions tolerate slightly alkaline to neutral soils. Spring heath, which grows to a foot high and has a spread of two feet, bears its flowers from late autumn to mid-spring. Depending on the cultivar, flower color ranges from red to white, and leaf color from dark green to yellow. *E. × darleyensis* blooms from the middle of fall to the end of spring in shades of pink and white. It grows to a height of two feet and has a spread of four feet. Best heathers for the winterscape are hybrids of *Calluna vulgaris*: 'H. E. Beale' flowers pink in early winter; the golden yellow mounds of 'Golden-Carpet' and 'Blazeaway' bloom in the fall, showing reddish-orange foliage throughout winter.

Winter Climbers

Numerous climbers and vines can cover walls, fences, trellises, and ground with foliage color and texture throughout the winter. English ivy 'Gold Heart'—with green, gold-centered leaves—and 'Buttercup'—with yellow leaves—are favorites. Algerian ivy carries yellow-bronze leaves, and Persian ivy 'Dentato-variegata' is marked with pale green and white. American and Oriental bittersweet—shrubby twiners ideal for arbors and pergolas—display brilliant red berries, each framed by an opened seed pod of bright yellow. The Japanese honeysuckle cultivar 'Halliana' has handsome green foliage that will remain all winter where temperatures stay above zero degrees Fahrenheit.

Ornamental Grasses

The larger relatives of lawn grasses brave temperatures as low as − 30 degrees F. and offer shades of wheat and straw, sometimes tipped with tall, silver-gray seed plumes. Growing in sprays from noninvasive, compact clumps that increase in size every year, these perennials turn the winterscape into a gallery of living sculpture. Plant them in a row at the back of a border, standing alone in the middle of the lawn, or in groupings of several kinds in island beds. Their softly rustling reeds will delight the ear as well as the eye. Especially attractive are the Japanese silver grasses 'Gracillimus', 'Zebrinus', and 'Variegatus'; fountain-grass; variegated purple moor grass; feather reed grass; and Scottish tufted hair grass.

Finally there is the yucca. Not a grass but grasslike in its sculptural configuration, this popular clump-former is, ironically, a desert dweller that survives bitter cold as far north as zone 4. Its three-foot spray of sword-shaped, dark green leaves makes a strong statement on the winterscape, remaining unchanged except for tall flower spikes in summer. The variegated leaves of 'Bright Edge' are particularly arresting against a bank of snow.

A Winter Sanctuary

The plan on page 428 shows you an example of a winterscape, with a bench and pathways for enjoying plantings close up and from a distance. The bench, sheltered against prevailing northerly winds by a red-berried pyracantha hedge, is positioned to catch the rays of the low-lying winter sun. White-blooming Christmas rose and fragrant-flowered witch hazel are also within the enclave.

'Sibirica' and 'Flaviramea' dogwood define the garden's southern boundary. Alternating to accentuate their contrasting red and yellow-green stem canes, they silhouette the sculptural Japanese silver grasses planted directly in front of them. Paperbark maple, Harry Lauder's walking stick, and a single azalea also exhibit bare-branch silhouettes and bark textures and colors. The all-green mahonia contrasts with the stark leafless trees and shrubs.

All of the flowering plants shown bloom from early winter to midwinter in a variety of colors. The rock garden is blanketed in white heaths, pink heathers, yellow crocus, and pale blue glory-of-the-snow. Yellow is present in the 'Gold Heart' ivy at the foot of the maple and in the mahonia's blooms. Leafy bergenias present pink blooms in midwinter, in beds hugging the paths.

Whether you follow all or part of this plan or create one on your own, a design strong in form, line, texture, and winter color will extend your gardening pleasure throughout the year. Carefully examine existing plants on your site, adding choice new ones to contrast and highlight their "off-season" appearance. A garden in winter can be as vital as at other times of the year—with a different, more reflective mood.

Trees and shrubs	Siberian dogwood	1
	Cornus alba 'Sibirica'	
	Golden-twig dogwood	2
	Cornus sericea 'Flaviramea'	
	Royal azalea	3
	Rhododendron schlippenbachii	
	Harry Lauder's walking stick	4
	Corylus avellana 'Contorta'	
	Paperbark maple	5
	Acer griseum	
	• Leatherleaf mahonia	6
	Mahonia bealei	
	Scarlet fire thorn	7
	Pyracantha coccinea	
	• Chinese witch hazel	8
	Hamamelis mollis	
Rock garden plants	Creeping juniper	9
	Juniperus horizontalis	
	• Heather	10
	Calluna vulgaris 'H. E. Beale'	
	• Spring heath	11
	Erica carnea	
	• Crocus	12
	Crocus chrysanthus	
	• Glory-of-the-snow	13
	Chionodoxa gigantea	
Ground covers and grasses	Japanese silver grass	14
	Miscanthus sinensis 'Zebrinus'	
	English ivy	15
	Hedera helix 'Gold Heart'	
Winter-blooming perennials	• Siberian tea	16
	Bergenia crassifolia	
	• Christmas rose	17
	Helleborus niger	

In this plan, winter-blooming shrubs and flowers, denoted by bullets, are combined with plants whose colorful stems or bark, evergreen foliage, or interesting silhouettes provide special interest in winter. There is a sitting area sheltered by a fire-thorn hedge, and a rock garden of heaths, heathers, and flowers flanks the path.

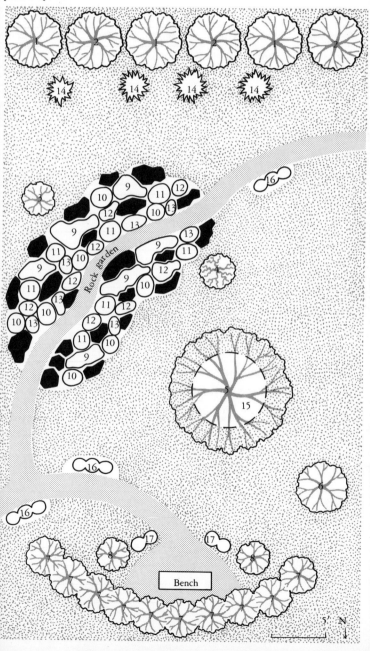

Winterscapes

Listings in the Source column are page references to individual Taylor's Guides. A key to title abbreviations appears on page 11.

Plant Choices

Abeliophylum distichum Korean abelialeaf	S-291	5–8
Acer griseum Paperbark maple	T-294	5–8
Betula nigra River birch	T-307	5–10
Betula papyrifera Canoe birch	T-307	3–7
Calamagrostis acutiflora stricta Feather reed grass	G-419	5–9
Calluna vulgaris Heather	G-306	5–7
Cornus sericea 'Flaviramea' Dogwood	S-322	3–8
Crocus imperati Early crocus	B-301	4–7
Elaeagnus pungens 'Maculata' Thorny eleagnus	S-333	7–9
Eranthis hyemalis Winter aconite	B-310	4–6
Erica carnea Spring heath	G-318	5–7
Galanthus spp. Snowdrop	B-317	4–6
Helleborus niger Christmas rose	P-347	4–8
Ilex verticillata Common winterberry	S-355	4–9
Lonicera fragrantissima Winter honeysuckle	S-366	5–8
Mahonia bealei Leatherleaf mahonia	S-369	7–9
Miscanthus sinensis 'Gracillimus' Maiden grass	G-433	5–9
Primula vulgaris English primrose	P-389	5–6
Rhododendron schlippenbachii Royal azalea	S-393	5–7
Yucca filamentosa Adam's needle	P-418	5–8

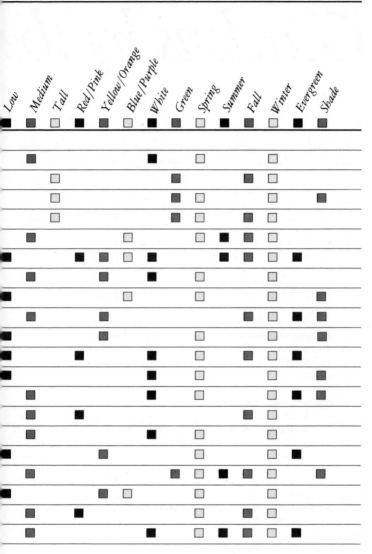

Low | Medium | Tall | Red/Pink | Yellow/Orange | Blue/Purple | White | Green | Spring | Summer | Fall | Winter | Evergreen | Shade

Gardens by the

George Taloumis

The beauty of a garden by the sea cannot be matched. There are plants that dance—and even sing—to the rhythms of the constant winds. Violent storms transform trees and shrubs into fascinating forms. The smell of salty air mingles with the fragrances of the garden: The pungent scent of pine is overwhelmed by the perfume of roses and stock in the North, gardenias and passion-flowers in the South. Fogs roll in from the sea, enveloping the garden and creating mystery and romance.

Whether you wish to create a garden by the sea that is large or small, to be enjoyed in summer or all year round, you should make the most of what the site already has to offer. Emphasis should be on the view, be it a tiny vista or a large expanse. A vital part of the scene might be a bay, inlet, creek, or marsh with teeming bird life. Low-growing plants will help keep the panoramas visible. If you are lucky enough to have sand dunes, preserve them, using their soothing shapes as part of your design. Pay particular attention to trees that have been twisted and tortured by the wind. Properly pruned and fed, they will come back to be highlights of your retreat.

Working with the Elements

The haunting and impelling beauty of the seaside is deceptive; the elements can also be cruel and destructive. There are plants that are equipped by nature to survive by the sea. Pitch pine, red cedar, and Scotch pine all have long root systems that probe deep into the ground for anchorage and moisture. Many plants, such as willows and tamarisks, have long, narrow leaves that stand up to the wind. Some have flexible branches that can whip about in the wind without breaking. Some species of Australian pine, or beefwood, have been naturalized in southern Florida, where they form dependable windbreaks. Horsetail tree tolerates brackish soils and salt spray and even withstands clipping and shearing into hedges to serve as a background for flowering shrubs, perennials, and annuals. In choosing your plants, take advantage of those proven to be hardy in your area.

Supplementing the Soil

Except where you use plants native to the water's edge, such as beach plum and bayberry, most of your garden will need to be fortified with organic matter and fertilizer to thrive. Peat moss, compost, shredded leaves and bark, leaf mold, old and dried manures, and refined wood chips are various kinds of humus that can make soil more nutritious. Use dark mulches to absorb rather than reflect heat and sunlight, to hold in moisture, and to help keep weeds under control.

Choosing Trees

Trees add height and interest to any garden—moving in the wind,

Sea

providing shade, and serving as backdrops to smaller plants. Best
known needle-leaf evergreens for colder regions include red cedar
and Japanese black, pitch, and Scotch pines. American arborvitae is
excellent for hedges. American and English hollies are superb
seaside plants—broadleaf evergreens that are tolerant of being
submerged by saltwater during hurricanes. Among evergreen trees
for warmer regions of the country are Australian pine, Norfolk
Island pine (*Araucaria heterophylla*), Monterey cypress, gray-leaved
olive (*Olea europaea*), and the slender Japanese cedar (*Cryptomeria
japonica*), often grown in hedges as a windbreak.
Deciduous trees for colder areas include English, pin, red, and
willow oaks. Slender-leaved trees, like willows and Russian olive
(*Elaeagnus angustifolia*), are useful by the sea because they expose less
leaf surface to the shredding wind.
Sargent crabapple, Washington and Arnold hawthorns (*Crataegus
phaenopyrum* and *C. arnoldiana*), and shadblow serviceberry
(*Amelanchier canadensis*) are among small trees whose foliage, flower,
fruit, form, and adaptability to seaside conditions make them
choice candidates. Others include flowering and Kousa dogwoods,
Scotch laburnum, sassafras, gray birch, and Japanese tree lilac.

Selecting Shrubs
Shrubs are even more varied and flexible than trees in their
usefulness by the sea. Use them in foundation plantings, along
walks and paths, around and under small and large trees, as formal
or informal hedges,and even as specimen plants in lawns. Bayberry,
beach plum, and rugosa roses top the list of shrubs for seaside
gardens. These grow in nature at the water's edge, constantly
defying the elements and winning out.
Other accommodating shrubs are red osier and yellow-twig
dogwoods. Scotch and warminster brooms offer yellow pea blossoms
in early summer. Speckled alder is good for wet places; arrowwood
and some viburnums are excellent in shade. Common buckthorn
makes a healthy hedge, and high- and lowbush blueberries are
popular for their fruits. Choose pfitzer, sargent, and andorra
junipers among evergreens to cover slopes. Lilacs and tatarian and
winter honeysuckles are popular for their blossoms. The deciduous
common winterberry is known for its bright red berries, perfect for
use in Christmas decorations along with white pine, arborvitae, and
other greens.

Hardy Vines
Do not overlook the merits of vines in a seaside garden. Give their
stems and aerial roots the protection and support of an arbor, trellis,
fence, or wall and watch them thrive.
The native American bittersweet and the Oriental bittersweet are
known for their adaptability to seaside abodes, and their brightly-
colored berries are a boon for Halloween and Thanksgiving

decorations. Virginia creeper, or woodbine, and deciduous Boston
and evergreen English ivies will cling to brick, stone, and other
rough surfaces.
Japanese honeysuckle will survive where few other vines will,
but remember that, like bittersweet, it can become a pest if not
restrained. Climbing roses, on the other hand, will thrive but not
take over. The vigorous 'American Pillar' and the vivid red 'Blaze'
will adorn arbors, picket fences, trellises, and lamp posts. Try
combining hybrid clematis with climbing roses. Purple 'Jackman',
white 'Henryi', and lavender 'Ramona' are some old standbys.

Ground Covers

In an area where a lawn is difficult, if not impossible, to maintain,
it is sensible to rely on other ground covers. Low evergreens such as
the andorra juniper or a low deciduous shrub such as the beach
plum can blanket an area with interesting texture. The often-used
low, suckering pachysandra thrives by the sea, as does the colorful
creeping phlox. The annuals sweet alyssum and portulaca are other
flowering options. Sweet-smelling thymes, spotted dead nettle, and
hardy candytuft are all worth your attention.
In shade, try foamflower (*Tiarella cordifolia*) and lily-of-the-valley.
Creeping Jennie (*Lysimachia nummularia*) is a fast grower with
yellow flowers. Paxistima is especially good in sandy soil.
Dichondra, trailing rosemary, and mesembryanthemum are
recommended for the warmer parts of the seacoast garden. The
evergreen bearberry (*Arctostaphylos uva-ursi*) forms a dense, spreading
carpet on sandy soils.

Perennials

There is a long list of perennials for the seaside garden. They
provide color from spring to fall in the North, year round in
warmer regions. Peonies and daylilies are familiar examples, as are
the herbs chives, artemisias, lemon balm, mints, and lamb's-ears.
Given some degree of protection against wind and salt spray, they
will perform admirably. Rosemary is a favorite in California and
other warm areas.
Some flowers of unusual shape to include in your design are
astilbes, which have fluffy pink, red, or white plumes; Carolina
thermopsis (*Thermopsis caroliniana*), displaying spiked yellow
blossoms; and the veronicas, with dense, narrow spikes of tiny blue,
purple, or pink flowers. Try gold-dust, or basket-of-gold (*Aurinia
saxatilis*), as an early spring bloomer whose masses of golden yellow
flowers contrast well with hyacinths, grape hyacinths, and early
tulips.
Red bee balm and loosestrife, including such varieties as 'Morden's
Pink' and the shorter 'Rose Queen' are other dependable favorites.
Coreopsis makes a good cut flower, with daisy-shaped yellow
blossoms atop slim stems; and blanketflower is admired for its red,

yellow, or bronze blooms. False sunflower, also called sneezeweed (*Helenium autumnale*), grows four to six feet high with autumnal daisy blooms in red, orange, or mahogany.

More perennial flowers to consider are globe thistle, especially the variety 'Taplow Blue'; gas plant, including its pink form; and any number of sedums, with emphasis on showy stonecrop, including the peerless 'Autumn Joy'. Shasta daisy blooms in early summer; yarrows disperse their ferny leaves with flat clusters of tiny pink or yellow blossoms all summer long. Silver king artemisia is a gray-leaved medicinal herb that can be dried for winter bouquets. Lamb's-ears has soft, velvety, gray leaves; and spearmint is a fast-spreading herb that must be contained but is desirable for its fragrant leaves, which can be used in soups and salads.

Annuals

Most annuals are fast growing, especially when set out as well-developed seedlings, providing abundant color and cut flowers in a matter of months. This applies to sun-loving zinnias, marigolds, petunias, asters, calendulas, garden balsam, heliotropes, sunflowers, scabiosas, salpiglossis, sweet alyssum, geraniums (where treated as annuals), and ageratum. Reserve flowering tobacco, impatiens, wax begonia, coleus, fuchsia (where not hardy), browallia, and torenia for shade. Ageratum, portulaca, sweet alyssum, lobelias, and dwarf marigolds form tapestries out of gardens along the Atlantic and Pacific. Orange-and-yellow lantana bloom without stopping in the hottest places, as do gazania and lampranthus—popular on the West Coast.

Bulbs

Use bulbs freely for flowers by the sea. In fall, plant the hardy favorite snowdrops, crocus, eranthis, hyacinths, daffodils, tulips, scillas, and grape hyacinths. In the North, tender bulbs such as dahlias, tuberous begonia, gladiolus, fancy-leaved caladiums, tigridias, tuberoses, and calla lilies must be dug up in fall and stored for the winter. Of course, in the warmer parts of the country these are year-round plants, able to stay in the ground without being lifted.

Gray-leaved Plants

Trees, shrubs, perennials, annuals, and fragrant herbs with gray or silver-toned foliage play especially important roles in the seaside garden. Their color acts as foil and background for bright flowers, but it has a practical origin. The tint comes from tiny hairs on one or both leaf surfaces that catch salt crystals and protect the plant. These hairs also cut down on moisture evaporation. Some of the best gray-toned plants are the common dusty miller (*Senecio cineraria*); lavender cotton, or santolina; and various yarrows, including the tall and showy 'Coronation Gold'.

Gardens by the Sea

Designing Your Seaside Retreat
The physical layout of your garden is your first design
consideration. Plots of irregular size, intrusive structures, and large
rocks, trees, and shrubs require special planning. Then consider
what effect you desire—formal, informal, or naturalistic.
The formal garden demands careful, thoughtful planning. It has
carefully laid out beds and often a single central feature. This may
be a small flowering Kousa dogwood, a golden chain tree, a statue,
or perhaps a fountain circled by potted plants. Paths of brick,
gravel, and turf encourage strolling. A distinctive, easy-to-maintain
alternative to a lawn is a walking area comprised of a two-inch layer
of white or gray rocks or crushed pebbles. Stepping stones or slabs
can be worked in for easier footing.
The informal garden is less structured, but its various parts must fit
together harmoniously. Try grouping trees and shrubs. Place masses
of colorful perennials in borders along fences or along the side of
the house. Set off this color with an open area of lawn or flagstones.
Bring the garden indoors by designing a cutting garden of free-
flowering plants such as zinnias, dahlias, marigolds, petunias,
coreopsis, gaillardias, and strawflowers.
To imitate nature, examine your site to see what already exists
topographically—rock outcrops, slopes, marshlands, bogs, dunes—
and organically, in the way of native and introduced plants. It is
possible to grow a wide variety of low-growing rock plants such as
gold-dust, edelweiss, and hardy candytuft in pockets of soil on or
around stones.

Working with Slopes
Banks and slopes falling gently or abruptly to the water's edge are
often problematic. Clothe them with hardy plants to improve their
appearance and also to keep soil from eroding. In the North,
junipers, rugosa roses, beach plum, and the glossy-leaved ground
cover bearberry are ideal. Use native beach grasses, and do not
scorn the seaside goldenrod (*Solidago sempervirens*), which will bring
gold blossoms in September and October and can be dried for
winter arrangements. In the warm South, rely on lantana,
lampranthus, and mesembryanthemum.

One-color Schemes
Another approach to an evocative seaside design is the one-color
garden. Try one in which only white flowers are featured: Flowering
or Kousa dogwoods, Sargent crabapple, white peonies, iris,
petunias, snapdragons, dahlias, shasta daisies, and patience plants
will do well in the North. Combined with variegated plants, such
as hostas and red osier dogwood, they impart a distinctively elegant
and appealing effect. For warmer areas, try oleander and gardenia as
the background for a variety of smaller-flowering petunias, sweet
alyssum, and lantana.

The all-blue garden is a particularly appealing meeting of sea and sky. Here, utilize Colorado blue spruce, jacaranda in the warm South, rose-of-Sharon 'Bluebird', and such blue-flowering annuals as blue laceflower, love-in-a-mist, ageratum, lobelia, and the South African blue lily-of-the-Nile (*Agapanthus africanus*), which is grown as a pot plant in the North.

Container Plants
Growing plants in containers lets you have choice vegetation where there is no open ground. Doorways, driveways, porches, balconies, rooftops, sun decks, and the rims of swimming pools are prime locations. In containers, you can prepare any kind of soil mixture to cater to an individual plant's needs.

Containers also impart an architectural quality. Yews in handsome and elegant pots look vastly different from the same plants in open ground. And they can be shifted anywhere for immediate effect. A pot of pink petunias instantly alters the tone of a party table. Do not let size be a deterrent. Large boxes, tubs, and planters can accommodate such evergreens as arborvitae, upright yews, hemlocks, and rhododendrons. Forsythias, azaleas, and viburnums make excellent container shrubs for their spring blooms.

In summer, work houseplants into the overall scheme. Sheltering them on the terrace or under a lath will keep out excessive sun and rain. Grouped together, they will brace each other against the wind. You may want to plunge the pots up to their rims into the ground, but remember that they will most likely pick up sow bugs, black vine weevils, and other insects and slugs that will come back into the house with them. To control pests, clean the pots thoroughly before bringing them indoors. Wash the leaves and blossoms gently and spray with an all-purpose insecticide.

Achieving Your Dream Garden
With careful planning and a long-range point of view, you can create a beautiful garden by the sea. The idea is to do as much as you can within the range of your energy, age, knowledge, and pocketbook. Take on a little at a time and consider how much help you will need with the mundane chores of weeding and mowing. Bear in mind that moisture and humidity at the shore encourage certain garden pests and diseases. You will need to remember to spray for aphids, Japanese beetles, red spider mites, mildew, and black spot on roses.

Your seaside retreat may take a bit more effort than inland gardening, but once it is accomplished, the refractions of light on the water, the movement of the waves, the smell of brine—the ever-changing spectacle of sea, sun, and sand—will make it all worthwhile. Everything by the sea has a way of sparkling. A way of scintillating. A diaphanous quality equaled nowhere else on earth.

Gardens by the Sea	Listings in the Source column are page references to individual Taylor's Guides. A key to title abbreviations appears on page 11.	Under Zones, W and C indicate warm- or cool-season annuals.	

	Source	Zones
Plant Choices		
Achillea spp. Yarrow	P-274	3–9
Arctostaphylos uva-ursi Bearberry	S-297	2–6
Celastrus scandens American bittersweet	G-384	3–8
Cornus kousa Kousa dogwood	T-321	5–8
Cupressus macrocarpa Monterey cypress	T-327	8–10
Cytisus × praecox Warminster broom	S-328	6–8
Gardenia jasminoides Gardenia	S-342	8–10
Hedera helix English ivy	G-392	5–9
Hibiscus moscheutos Rose mallow	A-341	5–8
Lampranthus spp. Ice plant	G-336	9–10
Myrica pensylvanica Northern bayberry	S-371	3–6
Narcissus pseudonarcissus Common daffodil	B-354	5–6
Nyssa sylvatica Sour gum	T-366	4–9
Petunia spp. Petunia	A-386	W
Pinus sylvestris Scotch pine	T-377	3–8
Pinus thunbergiana Japanese black pine	T-378	5–9
Rhododendron spp. Rhododendron/azalea	S-391	5–8
Rosa rugosa Rugosa rose	S-398	3–7
Rosa setigera 'American Pillar' Climbing rose	R-305	5–8
Santolina chamaecyparissus Lavender cotton	G-359	6–9
Sedum spectabile Showy stonecrop	P-401	4–8
Senecio cineraria Dusty miller	A-303	W
Skimmia reevesiana Reeves skimmia	G-363	7–9
Tagetes tenuifolia Dwarf marigold	A-408	W
Thuja occidentalis American arborvitae	T-399	3–7

	Low	Medium	Tall	Red/Pink	Yellow/Orange	Blue/Purple	White	Green	Spring	Summer	Fall	Winter	Evergreen	Shade
(key)	■	▨	□	■	▨	□	■	▨	□	■	▨	□	■	▨
	■			■	▨		■			■				
	■			■			■		□				■	
		▨			▨				□	■				▨
		▨					■		□					
			□					▨	□	■	■	□	■	
		▨			▨				□					
	■	▨					■		□	■	■		■	▨
	■							▨	□	■	■	□	■	▨
	■	▨		■	▨		■			■				
	■			■	▨	□			□			□		
	■	▨						▨	□	■	▨			
	■				▨				□					
			□					▨	□	■	▨			
	■			■	▨	□	■			■				
			□					▨	□	■	■	□	■	
			□					▨	□	■	■	□	■	
	■	▨		■	▨	□	■		□				■	▨
		▨		■			■			■				
		▨		■						■				
	■				▨					■			■	
	■			■						■				▨
	■						■		□	■	▨			
	■						■		□				■	▨
	■				▨					■				
			□					▨	□	■	▨	□	■	

Gardening in

Allan R. Taylor

Natural steppe landscapes—the sagebrush plains of Wyoming, the vast deserts of the American Southwest—are expanses of serene beauty. The great variety of plants that survive here have a uniquely attractive appearance, a direct response to their dry, inhospitable habitat.

Cacti have succulent leaves, stems, and roots; and the whites, grays, and blues of salvias, santolinas, artemisias, and thymes are a result of their waxy or woolly leaf coverings, designed to thwart evaporation. The thorns and spines of a cactus are thought to shade the plant. Blackbrush and others twist their branches to present as little surface as possible to sun and wind. In another survival battle, some desert plants have large, brilliant blooms to attract the pollinators so elusive in the desert.

It is not only the plants themselves but their arrangement that makes the natural dry landscape distinctive. The desert floor is either largely bare or covered with clumps of ground-hugging plants. Up to 50 percent of a site may be, or appear to be, barren of growth. Groups of plants cluster where moisture is available at least seasonally, such as along a streambed that is dry most of the year. Away from such depressions, plants arrange themselves in regular intervals according to the amount of space each root system needs in its search for moisture. The soil surface between plants is usually cloaked with small, tightly interlocking stones left behind by scouring wind and rain.

Dry Areas in Any Climate

You can take cues from such dramatic terrain and plants to create a garden of rare and unusual beauty anywhere there are dry conditions. If you live in or near desert regions, you have a wealth of natural landscapes to emulate and plant material to draw on, but sun, rain, air currents, and soil composition interact to form relatively dry areas in all regions and climatic zones. Thus it is possible to use drought-tolerant plants even in areas with very cold winters and much snow, provided you choose hardy varieties, such as sagebrush and winter-fat, and control moisture.

Create a dry landscape, or xeriscape, composed entirely of plants adapted for dry growing conditions, in an area you know is drier than others on the property. You can identify such a site by noticing that nonnative plants growing there show signs of drought stress—stunted growth; dry, brown-edged leaves; the whole plant frequently drooping and sickly-looking when compared with similar plants growing nearby under better conditions.

Dry areas are frequently found near the house, especially where exposures, drainage, and ground water systems have been changed. The foundation area of a house, for example, is usually dry, as are the narrow strips of ground between sidewalk and street. In general, any area that receives or retains little water is a potential dry site for an arid garden.

Dry Sites

Creating the Right Conditions

You can create dry areas deliberately, even in areas of high rainfall or low temperatures, where you would not expect to find desert plants. The direction the garden faces is important. In general, northern exposures are relatively cool in all seasons and should be avoided. Southern and western exposures are best in all but the very hottest climates. Of course, some very hot exposures can be cooled by shading, and even some northern exposures can be made successful.

Perhaps you have an area on the south side of your house or garage with a wide roof overhang. In many ways this is ideal for growing dryland plants. The overhang guarantees that very little unplanned moisture will reach the area, and heat and light reflected from the wall will create a proper habitat for desert plants, such as cacti, that might otherwise have a difficult time. You might also consider building a special bed for dryland plants—a berm, or a low, continuous mound of soil decorated with mulch and rocks around the plants.

A word of caution: For most gardeners, using native or exotic drought-tolerant plants will require investing considerable time and money, the more so if the garden is not in a naturally dry area. Expect to spend a great deal of time merely waiting—for replies to inquiries, for seedlings to grow, and for slow-growing plants to mature. Remember that superior gardens are works of art, taking time to achieve, and are not for the impatient or hasty. The rewards, on the other hand, are great.

Planning a Harmonious Garden

The compatibility of the dry landscape with its surroundings is important. Avoid jarring juxtapositions and abrupt transitions. For example, an informal desert garden should not be placed near a formal rose garden. But an herb garden, though quite formal in design, would not be an uncomfortable neighbor to the dry landscape. Many traditional herbs such as the salvias, the thymes, rosemary, oregano, and basil are from the arid Mediterranean regions and thus exhibit the same characteristics.

Try to harmonize your arid garden with permanent structures such as houses, sidewalks, and fences. Raised beds or terraces built of rough timbers make easy and natural transitions from building to garden. Screen a low wood fence with taller plants, such as green-leaf manzanita, sumac, and joint-fir for cold areas. In a warm climate, use the evergreen barberries and English lavender. Blend the fence into the garden with St. Johnswort or rockroses. Do not try to conceal sidewalks and paths—they frame the picture, boldly defining the garden's boundaries.

In choosing a site, keep in mind how the garden will be viewed. If you are planning a large garden to be entered or observed from only one place, make this vantage point the lowest or the highest in the garden, with the land rising or falling gently away. On the other hand, if the planting is to be viewed from several angles, or even all around, place the highest and lowest points toward the center of the plot. The slopes need not be excessive; indeed, steep grades are very atypical of natural landscapes. But remember, an absolutely level surface is to be avoided.

A good first step in designing your garden is to build a scale model sandbox in the shape of your site. Use slightly moist sand, small stones of varying sizes and shapes, and twigs representing shrubs and trees to experiment with various contours and arrangements. Remember to create several different levels, unless the planting is very small. Do not expect your model to be perfect; many good possibilities will occur to you as you stand on the ground itself.

Preparing the Site

Site preparation is often simply a matter of redistributing existing soil, adding the necessary sand and fine gravel for good drainage. If a great deal of contouring must be done, you should probably hire a professional who can supply, or at least deliver, additional soil and rocks.

Large rocks are visual anchors and points of interest in a planting. Field boulders that have lain for centuries in an exposed position are ideal. If you want to create a ledge or outcrop, choose stones that can be put together in a natural way. Sedimentary, or stratified, rocks are best; fit them together as closely as possible and plant the crevices between them with stonecrops, aubrietias, or arabis, which grow there in nature. (Read the chapter on Rock Gardens for specifics on choosing and placing rocks.)

Creating the Proper Soil

To determine how well your soil drains, put some into a container with drainage holes—a wooden box or a large plastic pail will do fine. Pour in a known quantity of water and measure what comes out. The amounts should be nearly the same. You may need to change the structure and chemistry of the soil, making it nonacidic and loose enough for rapid and complete drainage. To determine the acidity of your soil, buy a soil test from a garden center or consult with your county agent.

If your soil fails the drainage test, amend it to create a proper mix for dryland plants. To topsoil, which is essentially loam, add some coarse sand like that used for commercial concrete. If your soil contains a great deal of clay, mix in massive amounts of sand and humus until it neither retains too much moisture nor becomes bricklike when dry. Experiment in raised beds or terraces to find the right kinds and amounts of ingredients for soil of the right texture. Expect amendments to make up more than half of the prepared soil. If you have acidic soil, add ground or chipped limestone until the soil tests at least neutral.

To prepare any soil for drought-tolerant plants, work it to a depth of about 18 inches. An alternative for growing arid plants from the West in high-rainfall areas of the eastern United States is to spread pure sand at least a foot deep on the surface of the existing soil.

Where to Buy Plants

Some ingenuity and patience will help you find sources for almost any plant you desire, no matter where you live. Check first with local suppliers, then look for advertisements in gardening magazines and publications of special societies. Botanic gardens and research stations in arid regions are also excellent sources of advice and information. State native plant societies can make very valuable recommendations. If you would like to try growing plants from seed, check with botanic gardens and arboretums as well as commercial wild-seed collectors.

Place plants purchased by mail into pots, rather than directly into the garden, and shelter them until they have clearly recovered and are growing. Be sure to "harden" the plant before setting it into the soil. That is, if the plant has been away from hot sun and wind, expose it to these progressively for about a week. You may want to keep all of the plants for a particular season in pots, to be planted at the same time, so you can try a number of different arrangements before actually planting.

Choosing Plants

There are abundant North American native and exotic plants to choose from for a garden on a dry site, and they fall into three slightly different categories. First are those that tolerate heat and dry air but have normal moisture requirements, such as sagebrush, saltbush, greasewood, and creosote bush. These plants survive in arid regions by growing in or along watercourses or by tapping water deep underground with their extensive root systems.

Next are plants highly adapted for heat, dry air, and dry soil—the cacti are an example. Their water-conserving structure results in a variety of attractive shapes—accordionlike ribs that expand as the plant absorbs water, for example.

Third are the annuals that take advantage of brief wet spells to do all of their work—germinate, grow, blossom, and seed. Many of these plants, such as the corn and California poppies, Texas bluebonnet, and moss rose, are extremely colorful and should be included in any dry landscape.

Select deciduous trees and shrubs for their appearance both in and out of leaf. Some forms of the native Western American scrub oak, *Quercus gambellii,* are good examples; the leaves are pink to auburn in early spring, turning a rich, glossy green in summer, and in fall to a brilliant orange or dark red. After the leaves have fallen, the tight, twiggy branches are equally attractive. Evergreens are best for winter color—use pines, evergreen barberries, manzanitas, mountain mahoganies, and the cliff rose. Evergreen dwarf oaks, such as *Quercus turbinella,* are also very attractive.

Creating a Composition
In choosing plants, keep in mind their many different growth habits. You may wish to emphasize a particular characteristic—perhaps succulence or thorniness, using cacti, yuccas, or stonecrops. Or feature junipers, manzanitas, or heaths for their evergreen foliage. You might concentrate on horizontal lines with plants of low, compact habit, such as thymes. Or try planting in themes, featuring only cacti or only gray-foliaged plants, such as the different sages.

If you have a mixture of "body types"—some sparse and thorny, such as the shrubby chollas, and some of unusual color, such as the blue algerita, red Japanese barberry, or silverberry—shift them around according to size and shape. For example, a mound-forming prickly pear cactus should look fine with any other plant of similar shape, whereas an upright, open cactus might not.

Scale is the real key to harmony. Avoid placing tiny plants next to giant ones, whatever their shapes. Create focal points by careful placement of "architectural plants"—those special in some way: very tall, wide, or unusual in appearance. For the most part these will be trees or large shrubs: aleppo or pinyon pines, an Italian cypress, a strawberry tree, a Seville orange, or perhaps a large manzanita or a palo verde. After placing them, set the remaining smaller shrubs or herbaceous plants as complements. Fill the foreground with lower plants—creeping phloxes, rock roses, poppies, or wild zinnia, for example—and the background with the taller barberries and penstemons.

Final Touches
After planting containerized or bare-root plants, cover the entire garden with about an inch of pea gravel. If there is no rain, water the garden occasionally until new growth begins on the plants. Then apply water only if there is evidence of drought stress. In theory, an established garden of drought-tolerant plants should have no water needs as long as you have provided for drainage if rainfall is excessive. Do not use fertilizer after planting. Too much might cause the plants to grow unnaturally or even kill them.

Continuing Care of the Garden
If you have planned carefully, your after-care should be minimal. Those plants not adapted to your garden conditions will die, leaving a planting in balance with nature. Watch nonnative plants closely the first few seasons for troublesome local insects or diseases. You may need to remove the affected plants.

The only necessary ongoing care should be routine removal of self-seeded weeds and windblown trash. If you live in an area with relatively high rainfall, apply a balanced commercial fertilizer once a year to replace nutrients lost through leaching.

Designing with Dryland Plants

To help you compose your garden using dryland plants, two sample plans are shown, on pages 446 and 450. The first is for a warm-climate garden of about 1,000 square feet, filled with plants from the Mediterranean region. The second is a small bed of five by eight feet, displaying plants from the cold arid regions of the American West. While the plans show specific choices, there are many other trees, shrubs, ground covers, and flowers to substitute on the basis of personal preference or availability. Some of the best of these are discussed below.

It should be stressed that there is no horticultural or design reason why plants for each of these sample gardens should not be grouped differently, provided they meet the conditions of the site and your own specifications. By choosing hardy varieties, you can even create either garden in areas with winter lows to −20 degrees Fahrenheit. The recommended trees are small, 20 to 35 feet high. Tall shrubs are from 4 to 12 feet high, short shrubs from 1 to 4 feet tall.

Mediterranean-Style Gardens

Gardens have flourished in the Mediterranean area since the Renaissance, with some elements going back to Roman times. They boast two extremely attractive features: They are evergreen, and they are highly aromatic. For a Mediterranean-style garden, select about three trees, five large shrubs, and from 12 to 20 miscellaneous smaller plants that will form clumps.

Additional plants may be added to any of the categories in the same proportion, but an arid garden should not be overloaded. There are large numbers of choice selections for each plant type mentioned below—explore and experiment until you find the most pleasing combination.

Trees and Shrubs

Good trees for such a garden are the hardy silk tree and the Judas tree, both of which have pink flowers. Recommended evergreens are Seville orange, Italian cypress, laurel, and aleppo pine. There are many beautiful Mediterranean shrub varieties readily available in the U.S. The deciduous smoke tree is widely planted in North America for both its foliage and its lacy, "smokelike" flowers. The evergreen strawberry tree is symbolic of the Mediterranean region; tree heath, myrtle, oleander, and Spanish broom all have attractive flowers, some fragrant.

Good shorter shrubs are the attractively flowering rockroses (*Cistus*), and lavender. Poterium, a Mediterranean native not commonly grown in gardens, belongs to the rose family and is notable for its extremely tangled growth habit. The twisty, zig-zag twigs and

Gardening in Dry Sites

Plants from the Mediterranean region fill this garden. Bullets denote aromatic kinds, and dark shading indicates low ground. The area crossed by a dashed line is shown at right in elevation.

Trees and shrubs grown for foliage	Aleppo pine	1
	Pinus halepensis	
	Cretan barberry	2
	Berberis cretica	
	• Rosemary	3
	Rosmarinus officinalis	
	Dwarf juniper	4
	Juniperis communis var. *hemisphaerica*	
Spring-flowering trees and shrubs	Judas tree	5
	Cercis siliquastrum	
	Spanish broom	6
	Spartium junceum	
Spring-flowering with interesting fruit	Strawberry tree	7
	Arbutus unedo	
	• Seville orange	8
	Citrus aurantium	
Summer-flowering trees and shrubs	• Crimson-spot rockrose	9
	Cistus ladanifer	
	Hidcote goldencup St. Johnswort	10
	Hypericum patulum 'Hidcote'	
	• Lavender	11
	Lavandula angustifolia	
Small plants set around sitting area	• Thyme	
	Thymus serpyllum	
	Rockroses	
	Cistus spp.	
	False rockcress	
	Aubrieta deltoidea	
	Broom	
	Genista sagittalis	
	Pinks	
	Dianthus spp.	
	Tulips	
	Tulipa spp.	

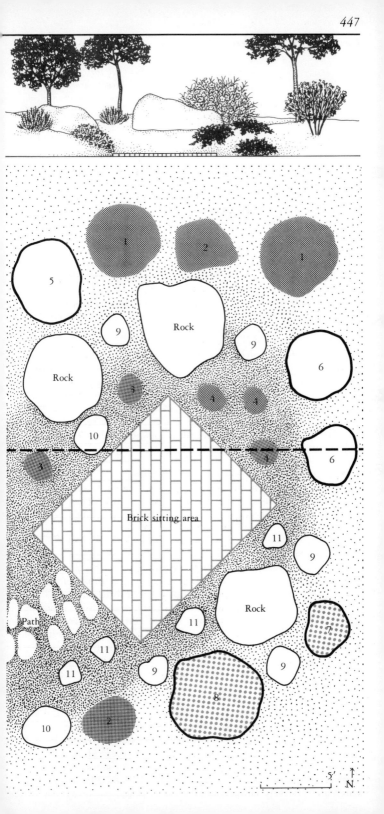

branches are so tight that peasants use the plant to filter water of leaves and large particles. Other desirable low shrubs are *Cytisus scoparius* and *Genista hispanica*—both commonly called broom—Cretan barberry, some daphnes, Hidcote goldencup St. Johnswort, rosemary, santolina, and several dwarf junipers.

Ground Covers and Bulbs
Flowering ground covers with attractive foliage common to rock gardens do well in Mediterranean gardens. These include alyssum, rock cress, common thrift, species geranium, candytuft, rock soapwort, and thyme. A number of well-known herbaceous perennial plants that have choice flowers are the dark red corn poppy, iris, pinks, sage, and mullein.

The Mediterranean region is the source of most of the spring-flowering bulbs in cultivation. For a natural effect, avoid the many hybrids that have exaggeratedly large flowers; choose instead from the rich array of desirable species forms in the genera *Allium, Anemone, Crocus, Cyclamen,* and *Tulipa.* Two plants of exceptional beauty are king's spear, *Asphodeline lutea,* a perennial herb with tall spikes of stunning yellow, lilylike flowers; and the sea daffodil, *Pancratium maritimum,* with evergreen foliage and heavily fragrant, large white flowers.

A Western American Garden
There are many handsome plants native to the cold desert of the Colorado Plateau, but few gardeners know and use them in cultivation. A garden designed with the plants described below will be truly unique.

Trees and Shrubs
Several western native trees would be suitable for this garden. The desert willow (*Chilopsis linearis*) has showy white, pink, or purple flowers; and some forms of the scrub oak have brilliant red fall foliage. Scrub juniper, mountain mahogany, and pinyon pine are other attractive evergreen options. For tall shrubs, the round-leaf buffalo berry has permanent silver foliage, whereas algerita has blue. Fendlera and cliff roses have spectacular flowers and intricately branched forms. Joint-firs are beautiful for both their whiplike, leafless branches and the striking yellow flowers in late spring on the female plants.

No less handsome are the short shrubs. Manzanita is one of the finest in the world, with tough, leathery evergreen leaves and very showy pink flowers. Silverberry has iridescent silver foliage during the growing season, and female plants bear shiny silver fruits. Chief among water conservers are the agaves and yuccas. Hardiest are forms of *Agave utahensis* and *A. parryi.* Favorites among yuccas are soapweed, banana yucca, *Yucca elata,* and *Y. angustissima,* all of which are relatively large.

Cacti and Ground Huggers

Most evocative of desert regions, the best cacti for cold areas are either prickly pears or dwarf barrel types. Some of the most beautiful prickly pears are beavertail and grizzly bear cacti, and the chollas *Opuntia imbricata* and *Opuntia leptocaulis*. Hardiest among the barrel types are the colony-forming echinocerei, notably the king's crown cactus (*Echinocereus triglochidiatus*), whose flowers are of a striking scarlet color.

Although there are many ground huggers in the West, not many can rightly be called ground covers. An exception is pussytoes, which has hairy gray foliage. Creeping juniper is exceedingly drought- and cold-tolerant in its northwestern form, but one plant will eventually expand to cover a very large area—up to 25 or 30 square feet. Probably the finest ground huggers are the native dwarf atriplexes and the wild zinnia.

Annuals and Perennials

You can create stunning compositions with flowering annuals and perennials. The Rocky Mountain bee plant and the butterfly weed are familiar favorites on the Colorado Plateau. Purple-flowered blazing star, tall, thistlelike mentzelias with large satiny-yellow flowers, and the many Indian paintbrushes all deserve to be grown.

A choice flower favored worldwide is the California poppy. Lupines are another very large group, the favorite being the Texas bluebonnet. Probably the best all-around western plant is the penstemon. Include at least one in your garden: *P. barbatus, P. utahensis,* and *P. eatonii* are red; *P. strictus* a deep blue; *P. palmeri* a tall, pink biennial; and *P. caespitosus* a blue-flowered creeper. Unknown to most gardeners outside the West, the orange-red hummingbird's-trumpets, *Zauschneria,* are distant relatives of the fuchsia. The biennial scarlet gilia, also called skyrocket, produces an astounding array of red trumpet flowers its second year. Wild zinnia forms a low clump of rich yellow flowers with an equally rich orange center. It is rather late in awakening in the spring, so do not assume it has died and pull it out. Actinellas are elegant yellow daisies, forming tidy clumps anywhere from four to ten inches in height.

Enjoying Your Garden

Once it is planned and established, you can begin to collect the dividends of your garden: ownership of a unique collection, admiration of friends, and an ever-increasing intimate knowledge of the life cycles of a fascinating group of plants—those adapted for life in the harsh steppes and deserts.

Gardening in Dry Sites	*This plan uses plants native to the cold arid regions of the American West. Dark shading indicates low ground, and the area crossed by a dashed line is shown at right in elevation.*	Key □ *White flowers* □ *Yellow flowers* ▦ *Pink to magenta flowers* � *Red to orange flowers* ■ *Blue to purple flowers*

Perennials and biennials	Pussytoes	1
	Antennaria spp.	
	Creeping penstemon	2
	Penstemon caespitosus	
	Blazing star	3
	Liatris punctata	
	Indian paintbrush	4
	Castilleja spp.	
	Penstemon	5, 6, 7
	Penstemon palmeri	5
	Penstemon barbatus or *P. eatonii*	6
	Penstemon strictus	7
	Actinella	8
	Actinella spp.	
	Wild zinnia	9
	Zinnia grandiflora	
Cacti	King's crown cactus	10
	Echinocereus triglochidiatus	
	Beavertail cactus	11
	Opuntia basilaris	
	Tree cholla	12
	Opuntia imbricata	
	Grizzly bear cactus	13
	Opuntia erinacea	
Evergreens	Banana yucca	14
	Yucca baccata	
	Algerita	15
	Berberis hematocarpa	
	Soapweed	16
	Yucca glauca	
	Manzanita	17
	Arctostaphylos patula	
	Century plant	18
	Agave parryi or *A. utahensis*	

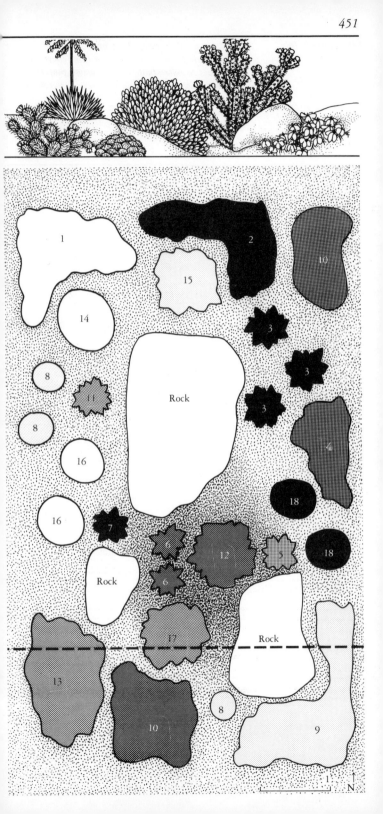

| Gardening in Dry Sites | Listings in the Source column are page references to individual Taylor's Guides. A key to title abbreviations appears on page 11. | Under Zones, W and C indicate warm- or cool-season annuals. |

	Source	Zones
Plant Choices		
Arabis procurrens Rock cress	G-296	5–7
Arbutus unedo Strawberry tree	T-302	6–9
Arctostaphylos patula Manzanita	D-448	5–6
Artemisia tridentata Sagebrush	D-440	3–7
Berberis hematocarpa Algerita	D-444	5–7
Ceratoides lanata Winter-fat	D-440	4–5
Cercocarpus intricatus Mountain mahogany	D-448	5–6
Cistus spp. Rockrose	S-318	7–10
Cotinus coggygria Common smoke tree	S-325	5–8
Cowania mexicana Cliff rose	D-448	6–7
Cyclamen spp. Cyclamen	B-303	7–10
Dianthus spp. Pinks	P-319	4–8
Elaeagnus commutata Silverberry	D-448	3–5
Ephedra viridis Joint-fir	D-448	5–7
Eschscholzia californica California poppy	A-328	W
Genista pilosa Broom	G-323	6–8
Helianthemum nummularium Rock rose	G-327	6–8
Iris danfordiae Iris	B-334	5–7
Lavandula dentata French lavender	S-361	9–10
Myrtus communis True myrtle	S-372	9–10
Opuntia humifusa Prickly pear	P-375	4–10
Papaver rhoeas Corn poppy	A-383	C
Penstemon spp. Beardtongue	P-378	4–9
Pinus halepensis Aleppo pine	T-376	8–10
Salvia spp. Sage	P-395	4–10
Zinnia grandiflora Wild zinnia	D-449	5–7

Low	Medium	Tall	Red/Pink	Yellow/Orange	Blue/Purple	White	Green	Spring	Summer	Fall	Winter	Evergreen	Shade
■	▨	□	■	▨	□	■	▨	□	■	▨	□	■	▨
■						■		□	■				
		□	■							▨		■	
	▨		■			■		□				■	
	▨						▨	□	■	▨	□	■	
	▨						▨	□	■			■	
■							▨	□	■	▨	□	■	
		□					▨	□	■	▨	□	■	
	▨		■			■		□	■				
		□		▨	□	■	▨		■				
	▨			▨		■		□				■	
■			■			■		□	■	▨			▨
■			■			■		□	■				
	▨						▨		■				
	▨			▨				□				■	
■				▨					■				
■				▨				□	■	▨	□	■	
■			■	▨		■		□	■			■	
■				▨				□					
■	▨				□				■				
	▨	□				■			■			■	
■	▨			▨					■			■	
	▨		■		□	■		□	■	▨			
■	▨		■		□	■		□	■				▨
		□					▨	□	■	▨	□	■	
	▨			▨	□	■	▨		■				▨
■				▨					■				

A Naturalistic

Judy Glattstein

The appeal of the natural landscape comes from its inherent
harmony. Plants in a woodland, meadow, or bog suit their sites
perfectly, having adapted over the centuries to conditions of shade,
sun, or moisture. They have spread into places where their needs
are best answered, coexisting in an ecological balance.

In designing your own landscape, you can take a cue from nature
and let the character of a particular site direct your choice and
arrangement of plants. All areas of your yard have counterparts in
nature. You could turn an open space into a meadow-in-miniature
or a shady spot into a woodland garden. Transform a poorly drained
area from an eyesore into a lush bog garden, or take advantage of a
dry foundation area to experiment with dramatic desert plants. This
concept, using garden plants to landscape a site so that it resembles
a wild setting, is called naturalistic gardening.

Matching Design to Site

To achieve a natural look, choose plants that originated in a climate
similar to your own and that occur in nature under the same kind
of conditions you have in your yard. The specific type of plant will
depend on what kind of landscape you are creating—woodland,
meadow, bog, or dry landscape. For example, hostas and
epimediums, which are native to the woodlands of Japan, are
perfect candidates for woodland gardens in the eastern and
northwestern U.S. Succulents and herbs from the Mediterranean
region are suited to desert gardens in other areas with mild winters
and dry summers, such as parts of California. (The essay Gardening
in Dry Sites gives specific information about naturalistic gardening
in dry areas.)

Placing Plants for a Natural Look

Straight lines and regular spacing rarely occur in nature. Some
plants of a given species may grow together, while others are more
spread out. Tall plants do not always grow behind shorter ones.
Also, a wild landscape grows in layers. In a woodland there are tall
trees, understory trees, shrubs, and herbaceous plants. In meadows
there are tall and short grasses and flowers. Think how different
these arrangements are from the traditional perennial flower bed, in
which the tallest plants are placed in the back, the midsize ones
next, and the low plants in front.

Ironically, it takes careful orchestration of plant selection and
arrangement to duplicate the seeming lack of order in a natural
landscape. A "random" planting is deceptively difficult to achieve.
Some gardening guides suggest that you arrange bulbs by throwing
them into the air and planting them where they fall. While this
method does give you a random arrangement, it is not based on
how bulbs occur and spread naturally. Try this instead: Cast an
imaginary coarse net over the ground. It will crumple in the
hollows, with its meshes closer together than in the flat areas. Here

Effect

plants would grow more thickly because there is extra moisture. This is a good way to visualize the placement of a large number of a given species. If the number is smaller—say a dozen or so—first plant a colony of seven or eight fairly close together. A little distance away—the space will vary with the scale and size of the plant—place one plant. At another point, plant a group of two or three. This arrangement gives the impression of self-sowing and natural increase.

Mixing Sizes
In addition to avoiding uniform spacing, you will want to avoid uniform size. All the plants of a particular species in a wild grouping are not of the same age or size. There are mature plants, some just reaching flowering size, and some juvenile plants and seedlings. So instead of relegating your seedlings to a separate propagating area, set them directly into the garden. And allow those plants that are thriving in their surroundings to reproduce naturally. Given the proper conditions for growth, even trees and shrubs will propagate themselves without human help.

Choosing the Right Plants
The ideal naturalistic garden draws on many plant groups. Trees, shrubs, perennials, bulbs, herbs, ground covers, and even annuals can all be part of the design. The general rule is to avoid hybrid plants with exceptionally large, fancy flowers or leaves, such as hybrid tea roses, peonies, or gladiolus. Aside from their formal looks, such plants make extra work because they require spraying, pruning, staking, and winter protection. If you do use hybrids in a naturalistic design, remember that when they reproduce from seed the new plants will be different from the parents in height, color, or other characteristics. Self-sown seedlings from non-hybrid plants will closely resemble their parents.
A word of caution: Don't try to collect native, or wild, plants and transplant them into your garden. Obviously, if more than a few people did this, they would endanger the very environment they are trying to duplicate. Fortunately, there are many cultivated varieties of all types of plants that look very similar to their wild relatives. And there are some nurseries that specialize in cultivating wildflowers for sale. Be wary of suppliers who try to offer collected flowers as cultivated ones. You don't want to encourage such destructive practices.

Using Existing Plants
Perhaps the plants already growing in your garden can be used in your new design. Examine existing trees and shrubs to determine whether they would fit into the scheme. Some judicious pruning and feeding may improve their appearance and they will be effective immediately, unlike a new plant that may take years to mature.

Consider rearranging some of the herbaceous plants, loosening straight lines or formal groupings to achieve a more pleasing design. Watch the plants grow throughout the year before pulling any out. A plant that looks dowdy at one time of year may reveal unexpected assets of flower, fruit, foliage color, or branching pattern at a different time.

Starting on a Small Scale

A good way to try your hand at naturalistic landscaping is to redesign a small area of your yard that may suffer from an overly formal or clichéd design. Suppose there is a large pin oak in your lawn, surrounded by a ring of pachysandra like a ballerina in a tight tutu. If the tree is tall enough that the lower branches let dappled sunshine through, there are many naturalistic design possibilities. You could introduce one of the native American shrubs that will grow in moderate shade, such as *Azalea nudiflora*, with its lovely pink flowers. Or plant a leucothoe, native to the Blue Ridge Mountains, to provide an evergreen winter accent. Still a third choice is oakleaf hydrangea, which has large trusses of flowers late in the summer and handsome leaves. You could even retain the planting of pachysandra, enlarging it to give an irregular outline and adding a mix of perennials and wildflowers to break the uniformity of height and texture. Or consider an arrangement as simple as a weathered gray log or boulder behind one of the larger ferns, such as *Osmunda cinnamomea*.

A Miniature Meadow

Naturalistic plantings can be used to liven up small sunny sites as well. There may be a dry, grassy strip beside your driveway in which weeds are thriving. Let the lawn grow. Lawn grasses will reach a surprising height if they are not cut ritually every weekend. Add butterfly weed, stiff-leaved aster, goldenrod, or yarrow for a mix of colors in late summer. Many of the daisies are very good in this sort of planting because they reseed prolifically and thus increase their numbers. Coreopsis, the prairie coneflower, gaillardia, goldenrods, and black-eyed susans are also valuable for this reason.

A Bog Garden

Any wet area in your yard, such as a pond bank in full sun, may be a good place for a naturalistic bog garden. Start with some shrubs that thrive in wet soils—such as button bush, with its fuzzy balls of white flowers in summer—and red twig dogwood—especially noted for the brilliant color of the young wood in winter. Both have very strong root systems and will help hold a pond bank from erosion. Another candidate is common winterberry, a deciduous holly with red berries in winter. Because the plant drops its leaves in fall, the remaining berries are especially showy.

A good tree for wet locations is the sour gum. In time it will make an imposing specimen, but even young trees will provide striking, colorful displays in the fall. The river birch has an attractive exfoliating bark, which peels back in strips to reveal yellow-pink inner bark.

Several irises will actually grow in shallow standing water, especially the blue flag and the yellow flag. Cardinal-flower, with its tall spikes of small, brilliant red flowers in late summer, will also tolerate water. Bee balm, a member of the mint family with red or pink flowers, likes a moist soil, but keep water away from its roots. The pink turtlehead will grow near, or occasionally in, shallow water. Its flowers really do look like turtle heads! One primrose that enjoys wet soil is the handsome Japanese primrose. Its multiple tiers of flowers on a single stem, in white or strong pink, look lovely when reflected in the still water of a pond. The cinnamon fern and the interrupted fern will reach heights of four feet and more when grown in wet places. Even plants that are often used in the shade, such as astilbes, will grow well in sunny, wet locations. Turn to the Water Gardens essay for more suggestions for a bog garden.

Woodland Gardens

Look at the plants in the traditional shade garden. There are the readily available annuals—coleus, begonias, and impatiens. The perennials include hostas and astilbes, ground covers are ivy, myrtle, or pachysandra. These are all nice plants, but they are so overused that you may think no other plants will grow in the shade. They are also too often arranged in the same manner: some hostas around a tree, with a band of pachysandra, and an edging of impatiens. A naturalistic woodland garden is a refreshing break from this pattern, and it is not difficult to accomplish.

In nature woodlands grow in layers, from large trees to understory trees down to shrubs, then perennials, wildflowers, and bulbs to provide the finishing touches. Choose plants that will grow well under conditions of broken deciduous shade, in moist, mildly acid soil rich in humus. Such conditions will exist under a specimen dogwood tree, for example, or an oak tree, or in a foundation planting of azaleas and rhododendrons. Those trees and shrubs provide the dappled sunlight that the smaller plants require.

Before beginning a woodland garden, notice what type of tree is providing the shade. Some maples, such as the Norway maple, and beeches, such as the American, have very shallow root systems that take moisture and fertility from the surface soil, making it difficult to grow other plants beneath them. Tall, deep-rooted trees such as white oaks do allow smaller understory trees, such as flowering dogwood and Japanese maple, and shade-tolerant shrubs to thrive beneath them.

The basics of planting are the same for the woodland garden as for most other gardens. Remove all weedy plants. If there are desirable

A Naturalistic Effect To place bulbs for a natural look, group a dozen or so densely in a hollow. Place several smaller groups a short distance away, and one or two single bulbs beyond, on higher ground.

This method also applies to arranging herbaceous or woody plants, on sloping or level ground. It simulates the wild growth of a parent colony and seedlings or immature plants.

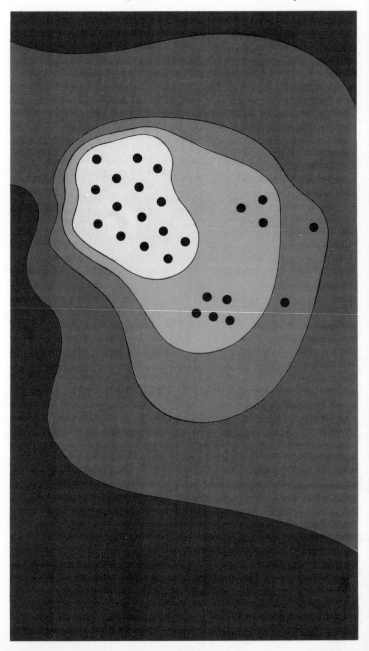

plants in the area, dig them out, set them in a large pot or box with soil around their roots, and keep them in the shade. Water them periodically and replant them as soon as possible. Some native plants you might expect to find in a shady woodland area include ferns, trillium, bloodroot, violets, and jack-in-the-pulpit.

Once the area is clear, work the soil well. Since woodland plants grow best in soils high in organic matter, add leaf mold, compost, or peat moss, using a four-inch layer well mixed with the soil. Dig a moderate amount of 5-10-5 fertilizer into the soil as you prepare it, following the instructions on the bag. The best time to do this work is in early spring or early fall.

Select and arrange plants according to the principles of suitability, random spacing, and mixed heights already discussed. Most woodland wildflowers blossom in early and mid-spring, before the trees are completely leafed out, to take advantage of the extra sunlight for their growth and flower. You will want to re-create this pattern of bloom, but because you want interest in the summer and fall as well, choose some plants for their attractive leaf form and texture or fall to winter color.

Flowers for the Woodland Garden

Suitable perennials for a woodland garden might include foxglove, with its tall spikes of flowers; the Christmas and the Lenten roses, *Helleborus niger* and *H. orientalis;* various primroses; epimedium of all sorts; astilbes, with their plumy flower spikes in white, pink, or red; spotted lungwort, or Bethlehem sage, which has an attractive silver-spotted leaf and pink buds that turn blue as they open; Siberian bugloss, with blue flowers like those of forget-me-not; and hosta, with small to midsize leaves.

Some native wildflowers that can be obtained as cultivated plants are also popular for the shady naturalistic garden. Green-and-gold, *Chrysogonum virginianum,* has dainty small golden daisies; *Disporum flavum* and big merrybells have arching stems and yellow bell-like flowers in the spring. The barren strawberry has a leaf like that of the fruiting strawberry and a pale yellow flower; it makes a good ground cover. The native eastern columbine has nodding, spurred, bell-like flowers of red and yellow. Short-lived, it usually reseeds and provides new plants for continued bloom. The hardy wild geranium, *Geranium maculatum,* has rosy pink flowers and will cover large areas in moist sites. *Iris cristata,* a spreading dwarf plant with blue flowers, is valuable as a transition plant between sunny and shady areas.

Phlox are native plants, so it is especially appropriate to use them in a naturalistic garden. There are several excellent species for the shade: Wild sweet william has narrow green leaves and 12-inch stalks topped with clusters of blue flowers. Creeping phlox is a lower, evergreen carpeting plant with blue, pink, or white flowers carried above the foliage.

Red baneberry bears attractive glossy red fruit in July on plants with a ferny foliage. Later in the season, doll's-eyes, *Actaea pachypoda,* has white berries, each with a black dot. Both of these are poisonous and should be avoided in gardens where there are small children. A bug bane, *Cimicifuga racemosa* has long white wands of flowers that may reach six or more feet in height. Since the flowers appear in July, they provide interest when not much else is in bloom in the shade.

Ferns are excellent for shady gardens because of their delicate, lacy fronds, which provide such good textural contrast to other, bolder foliage. Select ferns that grow in clumps rather than rapidly spreading varieties, which might prove too invasive in a small garden. The Christmas fern, *Polystichum acrostichoides,* is evergreen, while the maidenhair fern, *Adiantum pedatum,* is deciduous. Both of these are medium in size and grow best in soils high in organic matter, moist but well drained.

Bulbs can also add to the appeal of a woodland garden. Avoid large hybrid tulips and daffodils, which will look out of place. Instead, use the so-called minor bulbs, which really have a lot of impact when used in a mass. Since they are inexpensive, use them on a lavish scale. Plant a minimum of 25 of one variety. Snowdrop is an excellent choice, as it will multiply and increase freely. *Anemone blanda,* the windflower, is another good choice, as are the winter aconite, any of the erythroniums, and the guinea-hen flower. A caution: If you suspect mice, voles, or chipmunks, do not use crocus. The varmints seem to prefer this bulb.

Blue is a lovely color, and there are several possibilities in that shade. Both glory-of-the-snow and the Siberian squill provide this coveted color. Low-growing varieties of daffodils, such as the hybrids 'February Gold', 'Jack Snipe', 'Tête-à-tête', or species such as *Narcissus obvallaris* can be used in the same manner. Remember to use these little bulbs in groups, placing a couple of smaller groups of three to five a distance away to mimic natural propagation.

Meadow Gardens

Anyone who has ever tired of mowing a lawn can understand the appeal of a meadow garden: A meadow is mown only once a year. Creating one is not quite as simple as some seed suppliers' advertisements would have you believe, but the reward of looking out on a colorful field of blossoms and soft grasses is well worth some extra effort.

A natural meadow is a mixture of grasses and flowering perennials. A meadow garden may also include some annuals, but most have trouble competing with the thick roots of grasses and perennials. The best grasses to use in a meadow garden are the bunch grasses, such as andropogons, which are fine-textured and grow to about three feet. They turn to shades of gold and beige in late summer.

For flowers in a meadow, choose vigorous species that seed or spread easily. This includes many composites or daisies—such as the fall asters, oxeye daisy, prairie coneflower, liatris, black-eyed susan, and the goldenrods. Try some plants that are especially attractive to butterflies, such as butterfly weed, bee balms, and legumes like wild indigo and lupines.

Plant your meadow garden in a relatively flat, sunny site. Many suppliers offer special meadow seed mixes to be sown in well-prepared soil. It is best to combine seeds with started plants to give some instant color while the seedlings become established. But even so, creating a meadow takes time. Most professionals agree that it takes several years to achieve the full effect. Seed mixes that include a high percentage of annuals give a brilliant display in the first year, but the flowers usually do not drop enough seed for a repeat performance. Some seedling perennials may be choked out by weeds such as ragweed or lambs quarters. Patience and some experimentation are required, but once you've created an ecological balance, your meadow will be virtually self-sustaining.

Although it's done only once a year, mowing is the most important aspect of meadow maintenance. It serves to keep down the growth of brush and allows the wildflowers to flourish. Mow in early spring before the plants begin their new growth. Cut first at six to eight inches or higher using a scythe or electric mower. Then cut again immediately, down to three to four inches, breaking up the resulting litter so that it will decompose more rapidly. Do not cut lower or you may damage the crowns of the perennial plants.

Allow the meadow to grow naturally through summer and fall, leaving the plants standing through the winter. They will provide food for birds as well as visual interest. The plants will sow seeds, increasing naturally. You may want to add more seed or seedlings yourself in spring, at least in the first few seasons, which may be rather sparse. You'll also need to keep an eye on invasive plants, such as Queen Anne's lace, and weeds like ragweed and lambs quarters, pulling out any that threaten to choke out other plants.

While meadow gardening is gaining in popularity in most areas, it is still frowned on in a few communities where manicured lawns are sacrosanct. There have even been court cases brought against meadow gardeners, but most have been dismissed or overturned on appeal. It is a good idea to check with your local government to be sure there are no restrictions in your area.

Harmonious Vistas

Whether you create a woodland, meadow, bog or dryland garden, designing your landscape naturalistically gives you not only beautiful vistas but an understanding and appreciation of nature's subtle beauty. With the busy pace of daily living, it is pleasant to have a harmonious reminder of the natural world at your doorstep.

A Naturalistic Effect *Listings in the Source
column are page
references to individual
Taylor's Guides. A key
to title abbreviations
appears on page 11.*

	Source	Zones
Plant Choices		
Aquilegia canadensis Common columbine	P-288	4–8
Arisaema triphyllum Jack-in-the-pulpit	P-290	4–7
Astilbe spp. Astilbe	P-296	5–7
Betula nigra River birch	T-307	5–10
Brunnera macrophylla Siberian bugloss	P-301	4–7
Cephalanthus occidentalis Button bush	S-314	5–10
Chelone lyonii Pink turtlehead	P-309	5–7
Chrysanthemum leucanthemum Oxeye daisy	P-310	3–8
Cornus florida Flowering dogwood	T-321	5–9
Cornus sericea Red osier	S-322	3–8
Digitalis grandiflora Yellow foxglove	P-322	4–7
Echinacea purpurea Purple coneflower	P-326	4–9
Epimedium spp. Epimedium	P-327	4–7
Gaillardia aristata Blanket-flower	P-335	4–8
Hydrangea quercifolia Oakleaf hydrangea	S-351	5–9
Ilex verticillata Common winterberry	S-355	4–9
Iris cristata Crested iris	P-354	4–8
Iris versicolor Blue flag	D-457	5–7
Kalmia latifolia Mountain laurel	S-358	5–9
Leucothoe catesbaei Fetter-bush	S-362	5–7
Lupinus spp. Lupine	A-361	4–6
Phlox stolonifera Creeping phlox	G-350	4–8
Primula spp. Primrose	P-388	5–8
Pulmonaria saccharata Bethlehem sage	P-391	4–7
Quercus palustris Pin oak	T-390	5–9
Rudbeckia hirta Black-eyed susan	A-397	4–8
Solidago spp. Goldenrod	P-405	4–8
Trillium grandiflorum Snow trillium	P-412	5–8
Uvularia grandiflora Big merrybells	P-413	5–7
Viola spp. Violet	G-374	5–8
Waldsteinia fragaroides Barren strawberry	G-375	5–8

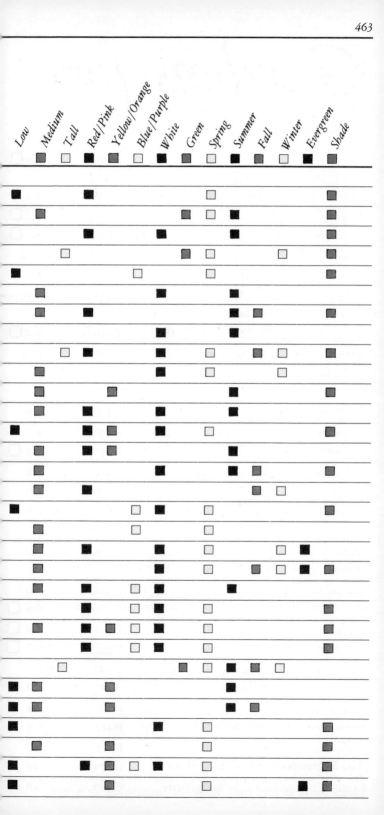

Gardens for

Barbara McEwan

The arrival of birds, butterflies, chipmunks, and other wildlife to your garden is a compliment, a sign that nature approves and accepts your involvement in its plan. Songbirds call from shade trees or pluck bright berries from a shrub; iridescent hummingbirds rival your showiest flowers; butterflies sail and flutter through the air like floating blossoms; and squirrels and chipmunks perform comic antics on the lawn.

Although all gardens naturally attract some wildlife, you can entice more or particular kinds to your yard by planting the trees, shrubs, and flowers they prefer. In return for the pleasure of watching these creatures you will be serving their needs, especially in winter when berries, fruits, and seeds can literally save lives.

You don't need a large site to create a wildlife garden. A small number of well-chosen plants will appeal to quite a few species of birds, butterflies, and small mammals. Even people who live in cities can create quite successful wildlife gardens on carefully planned plots the size of ordinary vegetable gardens.

Know the Wildlife in Your Area

Before you begin planning a wildlife garden, find out which animals live in your immediate area. If neighbors feed birds or other wildlife, ask them for a list of the species they've seen. Contact a local nature center, bird club, or natural history museum to ask for information on animals often sighted. Use regional field guides to discover which species live where, how to identify them, and how they behave. Learning the habits of the animals you're likely to attract can help you establish a more effective plan.

Choosing a Site

Since the purpose of planning a wildlife garden is to observe the animals it attracts, try to place it near a window or sitting area. A warning about windows, however: Any expanse of glass that reflects vegetation is likely to fool birds, who will crash into it and be injured or killed. To prevent such accidents, add a mesh screen or hang wind chimes or other decorative elements in front of the window.

Nature will not always play on a set stage. Butterflies will oblige by coming very close to a window, and a nice variety of birds can also be tempted within several feet of the house. A house wren, robin, or cardinal will even nest there. But most birds and animals prefer to keep their distance. You can achieve the best effects by considering your entire yard in your wildlife garden plan and by being willing to stroll through it to glimpse these more timid species.

The Importance of Grouping Plants

No matter which animals you want to attract or what types of plants thrive in your area, the key to landscaping for wildlife is the

Wildlife

same: Group your plants in clusters. A single deciduous tree or
shrub is rarely of sufficient bulk to be adequate cover for wildlife
except during the summer, and a few widely scattered flowers may
not be noticed by butterflies or hummingbirds.

Most animals prefer a gradual transition in height of vegetation.
The best planting will consist of a large tree with one or more
smaller trees or tall shrubs next to it, and shorter shrubs or a flower
bed tying them all into the lawn. Use only two or three different
species in a cluster. A widely varied grouping will produce a
cluttered appearance and will not necessarily attract more animals.
If you don't have space for a large tree, substitute tall shrubs.

If possible, provide a strip of cover several feet wide between plant
groupings. This might consist of a flower bed, a hedge, brush
piles, or an unmowed area. Some of the birds and mammals
you wish to attract may in time become very bold in your
presence, but even they need a dense hiding place.

Hedges are useful for practical purposes of screening or fencing, and
they are valuable to wildlife because they provide food, nest sites,
and protection from predators. If they consist of needle-leaf
evergreens, or shrubs with arching branches such as forsythia and
spirea, hedges may be just one shrub in depth. Plant more upright
shrubs two or three deep and stagger them.

Just as you will appreciate color in the garden from early spring to
winter, the wildlife in your area will benefit from plants that serve
their needs year-round. Choose flowers that will provide nectar-
feeders with food in summer and fall as well as spring. Plant shrubs
that will blossom at different times, and remember to choose some
for berries that persist in winter.

Plants to Attract Birds

Birds travel widely, often in astounding numbers. Small birds
usually migrate at night. Under a cloud cover associated with a low
pressure system, literally thousands of birds may pass low overhead,
their journey marked only by the soft chirps they make as they fly.
When they reach the proper latitude, they drop down to search for
the best areas in which to find food and shelter.

Providing Food

Land birds fall into two categories, insect eaters and seed eaters,
although most birds will eat both, depending on availability. Many
species may supplement these basics with fruits and berries when
their preferred food is not readily available.

Whether you are aware of it or not, your yard is already producing
quantities of seeds and hosting numerous insects. Even a single
crabgrass plant disperses thousands of seeds, and insects abound in
any garden setting. What will make your garden more attractive to
birds than others around it are fruit-bearing plants.

Some trees and shrubs that are favored sources of food for birds are flowering crabapples such as Radiant, Snowdrift, Van Eseltine, and White Angel; Oregon grape holly; pyracantha; chokeberry; and American cranberry bush. Check field guides for clues to the best choices to attract your favorite birds. To provide seeds, try growing a patch of sunflowers in a small sunny area.

Plants for Shelter

In addition to food, birds need nest sites and shelter from the elements and from predators. Tree cavities are natural nest sites for many species. Perhaps a large tree in your yard is already home to a family of flickers or titmice. Other birds, such as the catbirds and mockingbirds, prefer dense or thorny trees and shrubs in which to build their nests. If you want to harbor particular birds, check a bird guide that includes information on nesting. The preferred height of nesting sites also varies with the species. This is another reason to group plants of staggered heights. As your plants mature, they may "outgrow" some animals and attract others.

In deciding how to offer extra shelter, balance the birds' needs with the style of your garden. While birds would prefer naturalistic surroundings that include brush piles and weed patches, you probably want a more manicured look. If there is room in your yard to hide a brush pile, consider using it to dispose of Christmas trees and pruned branches, providing an extra fortress for the birds. If not, meet the wildlife halfway by planting stands of thick evergreens or dense deciduous plants.

Some examples of trees and shrubs that many birds favor for nesting and cover include Japanese hollies, cotoneaster, Austrian pine, junipers, spruce, mountain ash, hackberry, Japanese barberry, Washington hawthorn, pyracantha, honeysuckle, and other hedge plants. Some of these also offer berries.

Luring Hummingbirds

In a category all their own, hummingbirds are a special treat to watch, with their bright colors and whirring wings, flitting from blossom to blossom like large, exotic bees. Most of the over 300 species of hummingbird live in South America, but several nest in the U.S. If you live in the East, the hummingbird that you will see is the ruby-throated. West of the Mississippi, you may also be visited by the Anna's, Costa's, Allen's, black-chinned, or rufous hummingbirds.

Like other birds, hummingbirds eat insects—small spiders and aphids are favorites—but they also need large amounts of nectar to meet their high energy requirements. They respond best to red, orange, and pink blossoms that are tubular in shape, either large and solitary or in loose clusters of small blossoms. In the Southwest they may also respond to green, a color that is easily seen against the region's dominant browns. A hummingbird's long tongue is adapted to penetrate and pollinate blossoms like those of the trumpet vine or fuchsia. Adding such flowers, as well as certain flowering trees and shrubs, to your garden should bring these jewellike animals within view.

Hummingbirds can be very belligerent and territorial, so it is best to grow flowers for them in several places on your property. Since their favorite blossoms include both sun- and shade-lovers, this is not difficult to do. Include as many plants as you can, and do your best to have their bloom periods overlap. Make your plantings large enough so they are not overlooked.

In areas of full sun, try two popular annuals, salvia and zinnias, which bloom from early summer until frost. These come in sizes ranging from dwarfs to 36 inches tall. Other choice annuals for sunny sites include flowering tobacco and four-o'clocks, which are easy to seed right in the garden; snapdragons, which do best in cool weather; bright-flowered impatiens; hyssop, a pretty herb; and sweet william in both annual and biennial forms.

Among perennials for sunny sites, choose red-flowered bee balm, a native American herb; penstemon, which ranges in size from 18 to 36 inches and flowers profusely during the summer; butterfly weed, which will also attract its namesake; *Kniphofia uvaria,* or red-hot poker, a spectacular plant with orange-tipped, yellow flower clusters.

In partial shade include several favorite American wildflowers: columbine, bleeding-heart, or coral bells. All three are spring-blooming perennials. Try several colors of moss pink together, in a mixed planting. Or use it or carpet bugle as a ground cover.

Planting for Butterflies

With their delicate, colorful wings and graceful movements, butterflies are welcome visitors to any garden. These "flying flowers" gather nectar from many plants, pollinating them as they feed. In the wild, butterflies seek precisely the "weeds" that humans usually try to eradicate. They have been the victims of widespread habitat destruction and have been harmed by insecticides, so creating a haven for butterflies is good conservation as well as a visual treat.

The key to attracting butterflies is to choose their favorite flowers and place them together for easy visibility. A shallow pool of water will also lure them. Butterfly weed, a native perennial herb bearing small orange flowers, can be placed by itself, and flowering shrubs give you a grouping of blossoms in one planting. Include one or several shrubs as specimens, depending on your space. Butterfly bush is a particularly good choice because it blooms in summer, when many flowers have finished their show. Some cultivars extend the season into fall. This shrub, with its profusion of flower spikes in purple, pink, white, or yellow, is exceptionally dramatic. It is a favorite of swallowtails and American painted ladies. Compact cultivars of mock orange and lilac are stunning choices for spring color, and weigelas, which bloom later in spring, do double duty by attracting hummingbirds. Tatarian honeysuckle, a ten-foot shrub, needs a lot of room, but it grows well everywhere and is a special favorite of butterflies. Use button bush in wet conditions and New Jersey tea in dry habitats.

Some of the best perennial flowers for a butterfly garden include phlox, coreopsis, and rudbeckia. Coreopsis is short-lived but self-sows freely, so be sure to provide enough space. Rudbeckias, which include black-eyed susans, are stouter and more compact than coreopsis, and there are some very spectacular types with red and orange coloring. Catnip is an under-used perennial herb that butterflies favor. Be sure to buy *Nepeta mussinii*, ornamental mauve catnip, rather than *N. cataria*, the delight of cats.

Alyssum, a common annual, is a particularly good choice for a butterfly garden because it blooms from late spring until frost. Other annuals to try include asters and sunflowers, both American natives. Asters bloom from late summer to frost, and they also come in perennial forms. The annual sunflowers range in size from two to twelve feet high. Verbenas, which also may be annual or perennial, bloom from midsummer to frost. Cosmos are easy annuals to grow from seed right in the garden. Lantana is small enough to plant in a window box or patio planter, thereby extending feeding areas and bringing butterflies closer.

Attracting Mammals

Luring squirrels, chipmunks, raccoons, rabbits, deer, and other animals to your property can cause both pleasure and trouble. While interesting to watch, they may be destructive. An irresistible furry raccoon, for example, can wear out its welcome by raiding your trash cans night after night. But, especially if you have children who would enjoy watching animals, you may want to take precautions—such as using locking trash-can lids—and make your garden inviting to some of the small mammals in your area.

Squirrels are found in many yards, even in urban areas. They require rather large trees in which to build their nests, and they travel from these in search of the 100 pounds of food each one eats in a year. Much of their time is spent searching for acorns and other nuts to see them through the winter. Conifer seeds, corn, summer and fall fruits, mushrooms, buds, twigs, and flowers of various trees will also attract squirrels.

Like squirrels, chipmunks are dependent on large quantities of acorns and nuts, with sizable portions of seeds and fruits supplementing their diet. Raccoons may wander into suburban neighborhoods, upland forests, and farm lands, although they seem to prefer wetter sites. They eat a wide variety of plant and animal matter and live in hollow trees or burrows. Rabbits are vegetarians, eating leaves, twigs, and tree bark. They nest by creating depressions in the ground, and they need fairly dense brush—a hedge or branch pile—for cover. Deer require the cover of larger wooded areas with fairly young trees, interspersed with or adjacent to areas of crop land, meadows, or lawns. They are fond of fruit trees, grapevines, corn, and soybeans. A block of salt will also entice them out of the woods.

Shelters and Feeders

You may want to supplement your plantings for wildlife with structures such as shelters or feeders. Many birds will accept man-made houses, and you can make your own from scratch or a kit. First do some research about the best type for the birds you want to attract. Each species prefers a house of a certain size and height above the ground. Leave the birdhouse natural, or stain it—never paint it. Provide holes for drainage in the bottom and for ventilation toward the top. Make sure the house opens from the front, top, or bottom for easy yearly cleaning. Expect to wait a year or so for the house to weather and be accepted.

Special feeders designed to attract hummingbirds consist of red bases below clear plastic bulbs containing a mixture of one part sugar and four parts water. Boil and cool the "nectar," and never substitute honey for sugar, since it is easily contaminated.

Place any type of feeder where you can most easily enjoy watching the birds it attracts and where there are shrubs or trees nearby to provide cover. Do not start any feeding program unless you intend to continue it through the winter.

Sources of Water

All the animals you might want to attract will appreciate a source of clean water. The easiest way to provide it is in a shallow birdbath or trough. The ideal container has sloping sides, a wide rim, and a rough bottom. Some birds like a raised bath, while others prefer one at ground level. Dripping water is an extra enticement, so consider a bath with a small fountain. Locate the water container near a shrub where birds can perch and dry off after bathing. Check the water daily, and replenish it as necessary. Clean the container often, and never allow chemicals or fertilizer to run into it.

Enjoying Your Garden

In the world of wildlife, good news travels fast. With proper planning and planting, your wildlife garden will be full of birds, butterflies, and small mammals within a few seasons. It will be a true sanctuary—a reliable source of food and shelter—very important in this age of widespread habitat destruction. In return for your consideration the wildlife will provide many happy hours of watching and learning.

Gardens for Wildlife   *Listings in the Source column are page references to individual Taylor's Guides. A key to title abbreviations appears on page 11.*   *Under Zones, W and C indicate warm- or cool-season annuals.*

	Source	Zones
Plant Choices		
Aronia spp. Chokeberry	S-298	5–9
Asclepias tuberosa Butterfly weed	P-294	4–8
Buddleia spp. Butterfly bush	S-303	6–9
Celtis occidentalis Common hackberry	T-314	4–8
Coreopsis spp. Coreopsis	P-314	4–9
Cornus mas Cornelian cherry	T-322	5–7
Cotoneaster spp. Cotoneaster	S-325	5–8
Crataegus spp. Hawthorn	T-322	4–8
Hibiscus syriacus Rose-of-Sharon	S-348	5–8
Juniperus spp. Juniper	T-347	3–9
Liquidambar styraciflua Sweet gum	T-353	5–9
Liriodendron tulipifera Tulip tree	T-354	5–9
Lonicera spp. Honeysuckle	S-365	3–8
Malus spp. Crabapple	T-356	4–10
Melia azedarach Chinaberry	T-363	7–10
Mirabilis jalapa Four-o'clock	A-370	7–10
Monarda didyma Bee balm	P-371	5–8
Morus spp. Mulberry	T-365	5–8
Nicotiana alata Flowering tobacco	A-375	W
Nyssa sylvatica Sour gum	T-366	4–9
Picea spp. Spruce	T-371	3–7
Pyracantha spp. Fire thorn	S-388	5–9
Salvia splendens Scarlet sage	A-400	W
Sambucus canadensis American elderberry	S-401	3–9
Sorbus aucuparia European mountain ash	T-397	4–7
Viburnum trilobum American cranberry bush	S-419	3–7
Weigela florida Weigela	S-421	4–8

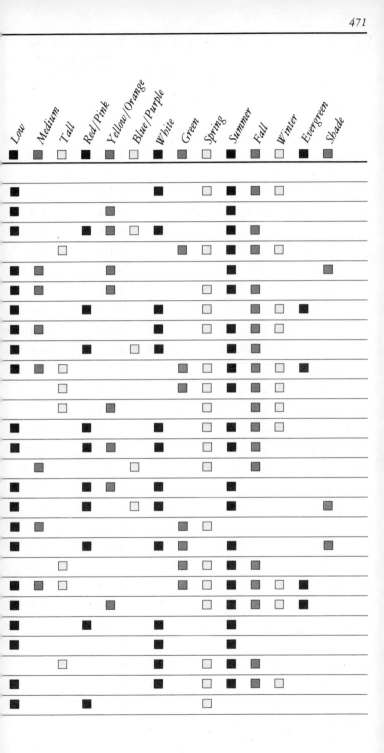

Glossary

Alpine
A plant from mountainous, high-altitude regions.

Annual
A plant whose entire life span, from sprouting to flowering and producing seeds, is encompassed in a single growing season.

Berm
A mound, small hill, or ridge of earth created for plant display or to direct water runoff.

Biennial
A plant whose life span extends to two growing seasons, sprouting in the first growing season and then flowering, producing seed, and dying in the second. See also Annual and Perennial.

Broadleaf evergreen
An evergreen plant that has broad leaves and is not a conifer.

Bulb
A short underground stem, the swollen portion consisting mostly of fleshy, food-storing scale leaves.

Conifer
A cone-bearing tree or shrub, often evergreen, usually with needle-like leaves.

Cultivar
An unvarying plant variety, maintained by vegetative propagation or by inbred seed.

Deciduous
Dropping its leaves in fall; not evergreen.

Dripline
The circular area under a tree from the trunk to the outside tips of the branches.

Dwarf
A plant that, due to an inherited characteristic, is shorter and/or slower-growing than the normal forms.

Evergreen
Retaining leaves for most or all of an annual cycle.

Hardiness
The ability of a plant to withstand winter cold; often expressed in terms of geographic zones.

Herbaceous perennial
An herb that dies back each fall but sends out new shoots and flowers each year.

Humus
Partly or wholly decomposed vegetative matter; an important constituent of garden soil.

Hybrid
A plant resulting from a cross between two parent plants belonging to different species, subspecies, or genera.

Microclimate
The climatic conditions of a particular garden or site, taking into account degree of shade, wind, humidity, and rainfall.

Naturalized
Established as a part of the flora in an area other than the place of origin.

Needle-leaf evergreen
An evergreen plant that has needle-like foliage; usually a conifer.

Perennial
A long-lived plant that regrows each year from a persistent rootstock.

pH
A symbol for the hydrogen ion content of the soil, and thus a means of expressing the acidity or alkalinity of the soil.

Semi-evergreen
Retaining at least some green foliage well into the winter, or shedding leaves only in cold climates.

Standard
A tree or shrub that, by grafting or training, is restricted to a single, tree-like stem, usually shorter than normal, and in which all growth is concentrated in a terminal crown of foliage.

Succulent
A plant with thick, fleshy leaves or stems that contain abundant water-storage tissue. Cacti and stonecrops are examples.

Woody
Producing hard rather than fleshy stems and having buds that survive above ground in winter.

Photo Credits

Gillian Beckett
Contributor Gillian Beckett is a well-known English horticultural photographer.
71H, 97, 283

Sonja Bullaty and Angelo Lomeo
A celebrated husband-and-wife team, Sonja Bullaty and Angelo Lomeo have contributed to many leading publications, including the Time-Life gardening series.
67F, 71D, 113, 125, 243, 257, 259, 277

Karen Bussolini
Contributor Karen Bussolini is a garden and architectural photographer in Greenwich, Connecticut.
191

Rosalind Creasy
Contributor of the essay on landscapes to harvest, Rosalind Creasy is an expert in "edible landscaping" and author of *The Complete Book of Edible Landscaping* and *Earthly Delights*.
67A, 75, 77, 83, 89

Barbara Damrosch
General consultant and author of the essays on designing your property and landscaping with flowers, Barbara Damrosch is a landscape designer and author of *Theme Gardens*.
241

Ken Druse
A garden photographer and writer living in New York City, Ken Druse is a contributing editor for *House Beautiful* and former editor of *Garden Design*.
69D, 177, 183

Derek Fell
A widely published garden writer, Derek Fell has also photographed thousands of plants. His publications include *Annuals,* an HP Book; his photographic work appears in numerous illustrated articles on gardening.
67B, 67C, 67D, 67E, 67G, 67I, 69H, 71A, 71B, 71J, 79, 81, 87, 95, 105, 107, 115, 117, 119, 121, 123, 129, 131, 135, 143, 151, 153, 163, 169, 199, 201, 207, 211, 213, 215, 217, 225, 235, 237, 239, 249, 269, 281, 287, cover

Charles Marden Fitch
Photographer Charles Marden Fitch is a media specialist and horticulturist. Many of his photos are taken in his own garden.
69A, 93, 159, 161

*Where letters appear,
they refer to the Visual
Key and read left to
right, top to bottom,
A–J.*

Pamela J. Harper
A well-known horticultural writer and lecturer, Pamela Harper has also taken more than 80,000 photographs of plants and gardens.
71c, 111, 133, 247, 279

Margaret Hensel
Landscape designer Margaret Hensel lives in the Berkshires and·has traveled throughout England photographing gardens for *Horticulture* and *American Horticulturist*.
71f, 85, 197, 271

Saxon Holt
A San Francisco-based commercial photographer, Saxon Holt specializes in plants—agricultural, ornamental, and native. His photographic work appears in Ortho Books and publications of The Nature Conservancy.
71e, 181, 265, 267

Richard W. Lighty
Director of the Mount Cuba Center for the Study of Piedmont Flora in Greenville, Delaware, Richard W. Lighty has a photo collection of more than 13,000 slides.
71i, 145, 285

Elvin McDonald
Contributor of the article on Japanese-style gardens, Elvin McDonald is Director of Special Projects at the Brooklyn Botanic Garden and a widely published garden writer/photographer.
69j, 185, 227, 229

Lynne M. Meyer
A landscape designer and contractor in the Washington, D.C., area, Lynne Meyer has contributed several essays and photographs to *Horticulture* magazine and has an extensive photographic library.
67j, 139, 155

Gary Mottau
A respected horticultural photographer, Gary Mottau is a frequent contributor to *Horticulture* magazine.
103, 171, 203

Muriel and Arthur Orans, Horticultural Photography
A nutritionist/landscape designer and architect/engineer, respectively, Muriel and Arthur Orans operate a major horticultural stock photography library in Corvallis, Oregon.
69i, 101, 221, 263

Photo Credits

Robert Perron
A respected photographer for over 25 years, Robert Perron specializes in aerial photographs of seacoasts. His work has appeared in over 80 magazines and 30 books.
255

Harry Smith Collection
The Harry Smith Collection is one of the largest libraries of horticultural photographs in the United Kingdom.
67H, 99, 137, 165, 193, 233

Steven Still
Consultant on the plant charts and a contributing photographer, Steven Still is a professor at Ohio State University in Columbus and author of *Herbaceous Ornamental Plants*.
69B, 69E, 69G, 71G, 147, 149, 167, 189, 209, 275

George Taloumis
Author of the essay on gardens by the sea, George Taloumis is a gardening columnist for the *Boston Globe* and *Flower and Garden* and is also a widely published garden photographer.
223, 251, 253

Charles Thomas
Author of the water gardens essay, Charles Thomas is a garden writer and president of Lilypons Water Gardens in Maryland.
69F, 195

Linda Yang
Author of *The Terrace Gardener's Handbook*, Linda Yang is the city garden writer and sometime photographer for The Home Section of *The New York Times*. Her work has appeared in numerous horticultural publications.
69C, 175, 179

Index

Chanticleer Staff

Publisher: Paul Steiner
Editor-in-Chief: Gudrun Buettner
Executive Editor: Susan Costello
Managing Editor: Jane Opper
Project Editor: Carol McKeown
Text Editor: Mary Luders
Associate Editor: Lisa Leventer
Production Manager: Helga Lose
Production Assistants: Gina Stead-Thomas,
Christian Adams
Art Director: Carol Nehring
Art Associates: Ayn Svoboda, Cheryl Miller
Picture Library: Edward Douglas
Drawings: Dolores R. Santoliquido,
Alan D. Singer, Edward Lam
Zone Map: Paul Singer

Design: Massimo Vignelli